THE NEW MIDDLE AGES

BONNIE WHEELER, *Series Editor*

The New Middle Ages presents transdisciplinary studies of medieval cultures. It includes both scholarly monographs and essay collections.

PUBLISHED BY PALGRAVE:

Women in the Medieval Islamic World: Power, Patronage, and Piety
  edited by Gavin R. G. Hambly

The Ethics of Nature in the Middle Ages: On Boccaccio's Poetaphysics
  by Gregory B. Stone

Presence and Presentation: Women in the Chinese Literati Tradition
  by Sherry J. Mou

The Lost Love Letters of Heloise and Abelard: Perceptions of Dialogue in Twelfth-Century France
  by Constant J. Mews

Understanding Scholastic Thought with Foucault
  by Philipp W. Rosemann

For Her Good Estate: The Life of Elizabeth de Burgh
  by Frances A. Underhill

Constructions of Widowhood and Virginity in the Middle Ages
  edited by Cindy L. Carlson and Angela Jane Weisl

Motherhood and Mothering in Anglo-Saxon England
  by Mary Dockray-Miller

Listening to Heloise: The Voice of a Twelfth-Century Woman
  edited by Bonnie Wheeler

The Postcolonial Middle Ages
  edited by Jeffrey Jerome Cohen

Chaucer's Pardoner and Gender Theory
  by Robert S. Sturges

Crossing the Bridge: Comparative Essays on Medieval European and Heian Japanese Women Writers
  edited by Barbara Stevenson and Cynthia Ho

Engaging Words: The Culture of Reading in the Later Middle Ages
  by Laurel Amtower

Robes and Honor: The Medieval World of Investiture
  edited by Stewart Gordon

Representing Rape in Medieval and Early Modern Literature
  edited by Elizabeth Robertson and Christine M. Rose

Same Sex Love and Desire Among Women in the Middle Ages
  edited by Francesca Canadé Sautman and Pamela Sheingorn

Listen Daughter: The Speculum virginum and the Formation of Religious Women in the Middle Ages
  edited by Constant J. Mews

Science, the Singular, and the Question of Theology
  by Richard A. Lee, Jr.

Gender in Debate from the Early Middle Ages to the Renaissance
  edited by Thelma S. Fenster and Clare A. Lees

Malory's Morte Darthur: *Remaking Arthurian Tradition*
  by Catherine Batt

ELOQUENT VIRGINS FROM THECLA TO JOAN OF ARC

Maud Burnett McInerney

ELOQUENT VIRGINS FROM THECLA TO JOAN OF ARC
© Maud Burnett McInerney, 2003

First published 2003 by
PALGRAVE MACMILLAN™
175 Fifth Avenue, New York, N.Y. 10010 and
Houndmills, Basingstoke, Hampshire, England RG21 6XS.
Companies and representatives throughout the world.

PALGRAVE MACMILLAN is the global academic imprint of the Palgrave Macmillan division of St. Martin's Press, LLC and of Palgrave Macmillan Ltd. Macmillan® is a registered trademark in the United States, United Kingdom and other countries. Palgrave is a registered trademark in the European Union and other countries.

ISBN 0–312–22350–1 hardback

Library of Congress Cataloging-in-Publication Data
McInerney, Maud Burnett.
   Eloquent virgins from Thecla to Joan of Arc/Maud Burnett McInerney.
      p. cm.—(New Middle Ages)
   Includes bibliographical references and index.
   ISBN 0–312–22350–1
      1. Virginity in literature. 2. Literature, Medieval—History and criticism. 3. Classical literature—History and criticism. I. Title. II. Series.

PN682.V56M38 2003
809'.93353—dc21   2002032203

A catalogue record for this book is available from the British Library.

Design by Newgen Imaging Systems (P) Ltd., Chennai, India.

First edition: September, 2003
10 9 8 7 6 5 4 3 2 1

Printed in the United States of America.

Matri, sorori, filiae:
Anne, Melissa, Lucy

CONTENTS

LIST OF ILLUSTRATIONS

Illustrations placed at the end of chapter 3

1. *Le Mystère de Sainte-Reine* 1999 performance.
   By permission of the Amicale du *Mystère
   de Sainte-Reine*, 21150 Alise-Sainte-Reine, France.

2. Martyrdom of Thecla, from Mélanie van Viervliet de la
   Sainte Famille, *Vierges Martyres de la Primitive Église*
   (Paris: Casterman, 1887).

3. Wolfgang Traut, illustration from *Opera Hrosvite,
   illustris virginis et monialis germane, gente saxonico orte,
   nuper a Conrado Celte inventa* [Impressum Norumbergae,
   1501]. By permission of Special Collections, University
   of Missouri-Columbia Libraries.

4. The Virtues, from Hildegard of Bingen's *Scivias*,
   ed. Adelgundis Führkotter and A. Carlevaris,
   Corpus christianorum: continuatio medievalis 43, 2 vols.
   (Turnhout: Brepols, 1978). Made from a hand-colored
   photo reproduction (1927–33) of the lost original.
   Courtesy of Brepols Publishing, Turnhout, Belgium.

5. Detail from the Saint Barbara Tryptich, attributed to
   the Master of the Saint Barbara Legend, ca. 1465–75.
   Philadelphia Museum of Art: purchased with the
   W. P. Wilstach Fund, the George W. Elkins Fund, and
   funds from the proceeds of the sale of deaccessioned
   works of art.

6. Joan of Arc, by André Allar, Domrémy, France.
   Author's photo.

ACKNOWLEDGMENTS

The friends and colleagues who have contributed to this book are legion. I would like to thank Howard Bloch, who encouraged me to begin thinking about virgin martyrs longer ago than I care to admit, and Bonnie Wheeler, who convinced me to finish the book; Carolyn Dinshaw, Carol Clover; Philip Damon, Anne Burnett, Kathleen Kelly, Kate Henry, Amy King, Ria Davidis, Theresa Tensuan, Anne Dalke, Graciela Michelotti, and Virgil Burnett, who all read bits and pieces over the years; Ross Kraemer, Ann Matter, Joseph Farrell, Nicholas Watson, Brent Shaw, Chris Forbes, and Michael Cobb who were willing to talk about topics from Tertullian to odd Latin idioms to queer theory; my colleagues in the English Department at Haverford College; the many students who have suffered my interest in hagiography with patience and sometimes even enthusiasm, especially Bridgit Gillich, Mimi Helm, and Christian DuComb. Haverford supplied a summer research grant that permitted me to look at paintings and stained glass in France, and the members of the Department of Ancient History at Macquarie University in Sydney very kindly allowed me to masquerade as one of them while I wrote the first two chapters. I am deeply indebted to Bruce Barber, Sharon Strauss, Carol Henry, and Christin Choi for performing many important but tedious tasks. Finally, none of this would have been possible without the patience and support of Jeremy McInerney, and the encouragement of James and Lucy in the writing of what they call my "great big book."

Parts of chapter 4 appeared in *Hildegard of Bingen: A Book of Essays* (Garland, 1998), which I edited; they are reproduced by permission of Routledge Inc., part of The Taylor and Francis Group. Some of the argument of chapter 2 appeared in an earlier form in an essay entitled "Rhetoric, Power and Integrity in the Passion of the Virgin Martyr" in *Menacing Virgins: Representing Virginity in the Middle Ages and Renaissance*, edited by Kathleen Coyne Kelly and Marina Leslie (Newark: University of Delaware Press, 1999); reprinted by permission.

INTRODUCTION

GENUINE DEVOTION, IMAGINARY BODIES

On the first weekend in September, the small Burgundian village of Alise-Ste-Reine venerates its patron saint by presenting the *Martyrdom of Saint Reine*. You can, if you like, attend Mass on the Saturday evening, and then follow a torch-lit procession of costumed figures to the outdoor Théâtre des Roches to see the first performance of the *Martyrdom*, but the real celebration begins on Sunday morning at a place in the valley known as the Three Elm Trees, even though the three trees that presently grow there are chestnuts. From this point, a colorful procession begins to wind up the hillside to the theater. The Roman soldiers, red-cloaked and glittering with armor, take the lead on horseback. They are followed by virtually the entire population of the town, costumed as Gallo-Romans, and grouped around a series of *tableaux vivants*. There are four dumbshow Reines in addition to the one who will act in the *Martyrdom*, each accompanied by a crowd of other girls of the same age, all wearing appropriately symbolic colors. The four-year-old Reine comes first, dressed in white and walking between her parents at the head of a crowd of other tiny children, boys as well as girls, whose parents sometimes have to carry them up the steep road. Next comes Reine the shepherdess, also dressed in white and carrying distaff and spindle, with a following of other twelve-year olds. The fifteen-year-old Reine is cloaked in blue, and known as Reine *méditante*; she paces along with her eyes lifted to heaven. Then there is a little gap in the procession before the appearance of Reine the martyr, her pink dress marked with stylized blood-stains, walking between the pair of executioners who hold the ends of the chains that bind her arms. An electrical murmur from the crowd lining the road always follows her as she walks; she is the star of the show. Last of all comes Reine triumphant, mounted on a chariot, all in white and gold, and carrying the martyr's palm. Once she has passed, the audience falls into step behind the procession and hurries to the top of the hill, to take up places in the Théâtre des Roches.

Meanwhile, another procession has been approaching from the neighboring town of Flavigny, which took the relics of the saint into the safekeeping of its fortified walls in 866 and has refused to return them ever since. While the girl who will reenact the martyrdom of Reine walks up one side of the Mont Auxois, the gilded *chasse* containing the relics of the real Reine is carried up the other, returning for one day out of the year to the site of her passion and death. When the relics reach the theater, Mass is celebrated again. Many of the groups of pilgrims who attend annually will spend the entire time on their knees on the hard and rocky ground, rising only at the end to touch the sacred relics. When this ritual is over, the *chasse* departs again, jealously guarded by inhabitants of Flavigny; once it is gone, the stone platform where Mass was celebrated is a stage again, and it belongs to the girl in pink. The cruel and lecherous Olibrius falls in love with her, she makes melodramatic speeches professing her virginity and her love of Christ in galloping alexandrines, her father betrays her and tries to kill her, she is tortured and eventually beheaded—the play, written by a nineteenth-century cleric, is long and its poetic and dramatic merits are dubious, but that is really not the point. In some sense, the performance of the *Martyrdom* is not supposed to be acting; when the girl in pink steps onto the stage where the saint's relics have so recently rested, she *is* Reine, virgin and martyr, for the space of an hour or two.

I first saw the *Martyrdom* performed when I was eleven or twelve, and for a short period in a generally agnostic adolescence I believed totally, not in Christianity, but in the passion of that girl in pink. A few years later, a classmate of mine was chosen to play Reine—not Reine *martyre*, as it turned out, although she certainly let us think so for a time, but one of the dumbshow Reines. All the girls of Alise would be involved in the pageant in one way or another, and those of us from other villages were terribly envious. Although we tried to pretend disinterest or even scorn nearly all of us went to the play that year. It was chilly and the sky continually threatened rain, but we stood through the long Mass and sat on the rough ground through the much longer play. We watched Reine defy her parents and the Roman governor, we watched her suffer dreadful torments (conducted offstage and conveyed by ever bloodier costumes) and betray nothing but scorn for those who abused her. She was brave, she was confident, she was entirely in charge of her own destiny, and she had great lines:

> Shed my blood, it is pure, it's the blood of our heroes
> Those old Gaulish warriors who gave it in floods
> For the sake of our nation in one final combat. . .[1]

I doubt that I was the only girl in the crowd wishing with all my heart that it could be me up there on the stage, fighting those battles and speaking those lines.

The *Martyrdom* is described in all the posters and leaflets advertising it as an "unique mystery," as though it were a medieval mystery play. The phrase is misleading; unique it may be, but it is not a mystery play. The earliest performance of a "tragedy" of Saint Reine was in 1661, while the version performed to this day was written in 1878 by a Dominican seminarian.[2] The lines that so stirred my fourteen-year-old heart reflect nineteenth-century ideologies by identifying Reine with another local hero, Vercingetorix, whose last stand against Julius Caesar on the plateau above the village marked the end of Gaulish resistance to Roman power. In the humiliating aftermath of the Franco-Prussian war, the French made figures from the pre-Roman past into the focus of national fervor, and an enormous statue of Vercingetorix, looking surprisingly like Napoleon III, looms on the hillside above the Théâtre des Roches.

Saint Reine herself is the kind of saint who is the despair of historically minded hagiographers. She is traditionally supposed to have been martyred under Decius in 253, but it seems somewhat unlikely that even if Alise did have a Christian community so early any persecutions would have taken place in such a small provincial town; attested martyrdoms in the Roman period occur almost exclusively in major urban centers like Lyons, Caesarea, or Carthage, where they could be witnessed by the greatest number of people and thus serve the most efficient monitory purpose, and where the full apparatus of the Roman judiciary was in place. Nor is there any mention of a cult devoted to Reine until the beginning of the eighth century; neither Gregory of Tours nor Venantius Fortunatus, both of whom wrote in praise of the martyrs and with special attention to Gallo-Roman saints, mentions her. While archaeological evidence demonstrates a Christian presence in Alise as early as the late fourth century, the indications suggesting a cult to Saint Reine at that period are tenuous at best.[3] The first textual mention of such a cult occurs in the early eighth century in the cartulary of Flavigny. The *passio* of Saint Reine is preserved in a manuscript from the end of the same century, but it is the sort of document that the great hagiographer Delehaye qualified as pure plagiarism. The legend it recounts is identical to that of Saint Margaret, which predates it by at least two centuries, down to the names of the Roman persecutor (Olibrius) and the authenticating witness (Theophilus).[4] In the seventeenth century, the authenticity of the relics preserved at Flavigny since Carolingian times was challenged by the importation of another "authentic" relic from Osnabruck in Westphalia, an arm bone. Since the Flavigny relics included two complete arms, Protestant pamphleteers had a field day with the notion of a three-armed saint.[5] None of this has affected popular devotion to the saint in the least; this year, her feast day will once again draw crowds of pilgrims from all over France, for whom

Reine is an icon of purity in a fallen world, an intercessor, a promise of spiritual liberation, an example of the workings of divine justice.

Saint Reine is fortunate among virgin martyrs in that her cult has survived with so much vigor into the twenty-first century.[6] Others were not so lucky. Reine's twin, Margaret of Antioch, enormously popular during the later Middle Ages, was suppressed by the Holy See in 1969, when the Roman Calendar was reorganized and purged. The application of strict historical criteria to the lives of the saints affected virgin martyrs perhaps more seriously than any other category of saints. Thecla, Justina, and Catherine of Alexandria were all omitted from the Revised Calendar on the grounds of non-historicity, while other virgin martyrs like Ursula were downgraded, permitted only local cults. One of the reasons for such decisions was the extraordinary similarity of the legends attached to virgin martyrs; not only was the *vita* of one saint often applied wholesale to another, as is the case of Reine and Margaret, but even presumably independent legends betray overwhelming similarities. The virgin is always beautiful, always of good family, her chastity always somehow threatened. She undergoes a series of tortures and confrontations, and inevitably dies, usually decapitated. The narrative has the stability of folklore, and this has contributed to make it seem suspect, or simply tedious, to many hagiographers of the nineteenth and twentieth centuries.

As a genre, in other words, the narrative of the virgin martyr becomes purely literary earlier than almost any other form of hagiography; at the same time, however, these stories have until very recently been overlooked by literary critics as well as historians of religion, precisely because of their similarity.[7] They have become part of what Lee Patterson calls the "not-literature of history," perennially overlooked and under-read. The extraordinary longevity of cults like that of Reine or Margaret, whose legend was declared apocryphal by Pope Gelasius as early as 464 but who went on to become one of the most popular saints in the West during the Middle Ages, depends not on veracity but on necessity. The virgin martyr survives not because she was real, but because she fulfilled essential functions in the lives of those who were devoted to her. It is precisely the imaginary nature of the virgin martyr that proves her indispensability; she did not exist, and it was necessary therefore to invent her. Indeed, the history of the genre suggests that the virgin martyr was of special importance to two groups of people who only rarely overlap, to women and to theologians. To women, generally excluded by the construction of late antique and medieval society from the exercise of power, she could promise independence and a very particular kind of authority. For theologians, on the other hand, it became increasingly essential during the early centuries of Christianity to recuperate the image of the virgin martyr precisely in order to limit and control that potential for independence. This is, of course, a generalization, and there were exceptions to the rule, or at any rate complications of it, on both sides. Nonetheless, a long look at the history of the virgin martyr allows us to observe what is a remarkably extended battle, one without any final resolution, to determine the meaning and implications of the virgin body.

From the beginning, the issue of virginity always implicates both sex and gender. This is a fact that has often been resisted, either implicitly or explicitly, by historians. John Bugge, for instance, insists in *Virginitas: The History of an Ideal* that the original meaning of virginity is both asexual and ungendered: "The early history of the question permits no simple distinction between male celibacy and female virginity."[8] He argues that only in the twelfth century does virginity become a specifically feminized quality, and he sees this feminization as a distinct falling away from what he perceives as the more universal claim of "Christian gnosis." Of the thirteenth-century English texts known as the Katharine Group he writes, ". . .however feminist in tone was the devotional literature produced for women, these works do retain many of the commonplace features of the more authentic understanding of virginity as asexuality."[9] This formulation equates, perhaps unwittingly, feminism (of the thirteenth-century variety) with inauthenticity. Similarly, Peter Brown, in his magisterial history of sociosexual relations in the early church, *The Body and Society*, tends to overlook or at any rate to diminish the very different values that sexual renunciation could have for men and for women, and to use chastity and virginity as if they were synonyms, even though many of the writers whom he discusses keep the terms quite distinct. Both of these scholars have allowed themselves to be seduced by the antisexist rhetoric (often confused with but never identical to profeminist rhetoric) of the great patristic writers like Paul and Augustine; explicit statements in the writings of the fathers in which sexual equality appears to be promised in the next world if not in this one permit them to overlook if not to excuse the powerful misogyny that informs much of early Christian writing. They thus fail to recognize that to imagine virginity as an asexual ideal in a world in which sexuality itself is gendered feminine, as was the body itself, is to make the asexual functionally masculine.

R. Howard Bloch's *Medieval Misogyny* provided an important corrective to such oversights by acknowledging the degree to which the rhetoric of virginity, which the Middle Ages inherited from the patristic period, operated not in the service of sexual equality but as a deeply repressive, antifeminist ideology.[10] "If," Bloch asks, "according to the early Christian articulation of gender, woman is imagined to represent the flesh, or a flaw of the flesh insofar as she embodies embodiment as opposed to mind, how is it possible to imagine her virginity?"[11] Bloch maps the aestheticization and disembodiment of virginity and its transformation into a radically overdetermined state, definitively inaccessible to women, in the work of writers like Tertullian, Augustine, and Jerome. From the moment of its earliest appearance in print, Bloch's argument was controversial; some feminist readers of his work suspected him of being fundamentally a medieval misogynist himself, and argued that his critique of the essentializing misogyny of patristic writers merely reinscribed the ideology it professed to deconstruct.[12] Such responses seem to me to betray a somewhat unsubtle reading of Bloch's admittedly super-subtle argument; nonetheless, Bloch does in one significant respect reproduce the effect of the rhetoric which is the subject of his critique. Like the patristic writers whose self-implication in their own discourse he demonstrates, Bloch makes women themselves disappear as material, historical subjects. His insistence that the "affective element of antifeminism" is "unknowable" seems to me disingenuous;[13] the affective element may be difficult to recuperate, but it is clearly visible in the writing of women themselves, if we only take the time to look, in Hrotsvitha's prologues proposing a defense of women from their misrepresentation by the Roman dramatist Terence, for example.

Bloch is in good company when he makes women disappear from his discussion. The kind of paradoxical and therefore impossible virginity Bloch identifies in these patristic writers reaches its pinnacle in Derrida's *Double Session*, in which the hymen is constructed as purest impossibility and thus becomes the perfect and perfectly empty signifier, irremediably separated from any body, let alone the particular and obstreperous female body. The critical impulse to figure virginity in purely negative terms, however, as the rejection or denial of femininity or the female or sex or meaning, can be traced back at least as far as Freud and Levi-Strauss. In "The Taboo of Virginity," Freud both represents virginity as a condition peculiar to women when he defines it as "the state in a woman of being untouched,"[14] and makes it into a condition entirely without positive value. He is interested, in fact, exclusively in the loss of virginity, since he sees defloration as one of the preconditions of the necessary subjection of female to male in human society. Defloration initiates the woman into a sort of sexual bondage, and "some such measure of bondage is. . . indispensable to the maintenance of civilized marriage and to holding at bay the polygamous tendencies which threaten it" (193–94). Freud's "taboo of virginity" is actually a taboo on defloration, since it is not the virgin who is taboo, but the act of rupturing her hymen; Freud multiplies examples from primitive cultures in which this action is accomplished by someone other than her husband, in order to conclude that "defloration has not only the one, civilized consequence of binding the woman lastingly to the man; it also unleashes an archaic hostility against him" (208). Nowhere is the possibility of virginity maintained, preserved, valued for its own sake even raised; it is always something to be lost. In Levi-Strauss, as Simon Gaunt has noted,[15] virginity violates the "principle of reciprocity," which demands the exchange of women; indeed, the virgin's consciousness of just how efficiently her decision to withhold her body from the traffic in women can disrupt social systems is a prominent feature particularly of late antique stories about virgin martyrs like Thecla. In a much-discussed passage,[16] Levi-Strauss insists that "women themselves are treated as signs, which are misused when not put to the use reserved to signs, which is to be communicated."[17] The woman who chooses virginity refuses to be communicated; she may be choosing instead to communicate, but this is an avenue Levi-Strauss does not pursue. For both Freud and Levi-Strauss, virginity is explicitly and exclusively a female phenomenon; neither one, however, considers the question of what virginity might mean, not just *for* but *to* women. This book poses that unasked question, and even hopes to answer it, although the answer may prove both fragmentary and contradictory. Evidence for what women thought and felt, for how they understood the roles prescribed for them by male-dominated society, is heartbreakingly rare, especially for late antiquity. Nonetheless, by reading through misogynist writings on virginity and by establishing the evolution of the virgin martyr as icon in a specific historical and cultural context, it is possible to recover a vision of virginity not as an always empty negative, but as a real, livable choice, which shaped the experience of women as material, historical subjects over a very long time—for good and for ill.

Alongside the tradition of asexual, bodiless, negated, and silent virginity runs one in which the virgin is, on the contrary, possessed of both sex and gender, of body and of voice. The various words for virgin in learned and vernacular languages, *parthenos*, *virgo*, *vierge*, *pucelle*, *meiden*, all have as their primary meaning the sexually intact body of the female of the human species. When the impulse to aestheticize, intellectualize, or spiritualize the quality of virginity runs up against this quirk of common usage, strange fissures and stresses begin to appear in the theological rhetoric that wants to render virginity asexual. It proves to be difficult if not impossible for most writers to imagine a male virgin, and perhaps even more difficult to imagine a body without the constitutive signifiers of sex and gender. The female virgin body, on the contrary, is not only eminently imaginable but profoundly appealing. To women, it could offer an imitable model, one that permitted the expression of a peculiarly feminine form of sanctity.

The value of the virgin martyr as role model is quite obviously problematic. The strict link created by the genre between virginity and death is potentially profoundly antifeminist, and has certainly been experienced that way in the twentieth century, as the example of Maria Goretti so clearly demonstrates. In premodern societies, however, sexual renunciation was the very opposite of life-denying, especially for women. The single greatest threat to a woman's life before the twentieth century was child-birth; the choice of a celibate life was thus eminently logical and eminently healthy, a point that many late antique and medieval treatises on continence make graphically. A thirteenth-century treatise on virginity memorably describes the "cruel distressing anguish, that fierce and stabbing pain, that incessant misery, that torment upon torment, that wailing outcry. . .that fear of death"[18] and the accompanying humiliations that characterize labor. Since women bore the greatest burdens of sexual life, they appeared to have far more to gain through sexual renunciation than men. Freed of the bio-logical consequences of sexual behavior, why should they not participate as fully as men in social and intellectual life? Over and over again, through-out the history of Christianity, the lives of celibate and especially virgin women implicitly pose this question. The concept of virginity could even be seen as giving women a faint edge in the battle for chastity, because it is a concept that is primarily imagined both as feminine and as characteristic of the female body. Sexual renunciation thus seems to hold out two extra-ordinary promises to women: that it may allow them to function as the equals of men in the world of ideas, and even that it may provide them with an avenue to sanctity particularly their own, from which men are excluded. Both of these possibilities aroused outrage in the Fathers of the Church and in many of the medieval churchmen who followed them. The rhetoric of virginity thus comes to be deployed in two opposing directions: to claim freedoms of various sorts for women in the name of virginity, and to deny women such freedoms in the name of virginity. Each of these intents generates a series of different arguments, which tend to be based upon particular ways of imagining and reimagining the virgin body. These cor-poreal fantasies then evolve along several interesting trajectories, accumu-lating around the highly charged figure of the virgin martyr and forming what E. Jane Burns has called a "doubled discourse," which is both a reaction to and an embodiment of an apparently misogynistic stereotype.[19] In this book, I elaborate a sort of he says/she says method, pairing pro- and antifeminist writings on the subject of virginity in an attempt to reveal the complex ideological uses to which the narrative of the virgin martyr was put.

The lines of identification and imitation established by a given retelling of the story of the virgin martyr may be inflected along a variety of tra-jectories, as the example of Reine suggests: to this day, the young woman chosen to enact her must be "pretty, intelligent, able to sing, and most importantly of all absolutely above suspicion in her private life."[20] If she acquires a boyfriend between one September and the next, she will not be asked to resume the role. Playing Reine thus makes a girl an instant local celebrity, giving her a kind of visibility and opportunity she might otherwise never achieve in a rural community, and simultaneously binds her to a strict and anachronistic code of sexual conduct. Reine was a vehicle for nostalgic nationalism in the nineteenth century; in the twentieth, she became an emblem of civic identity and historical continuity for the members of her community; finally, and most importantly for my argument, she is a deeply ambivalent object of pride and fascination for young women. She embodies both the radical potential for resistance to familial and social authority in defense of an ideal, and the conservative and repressive power of Catholic sexual ideology. Reine is extraordinary only in that she has continued to operate in this radically dichotomous fashion right into the twenty-first century.

The capacity of medieval women to identify more or less directly with models like that of Reine is demonstrated by the importance of the virgin martyr in the writings of Hrotsvitha, Hildegard, and Clemence of Barking, and also in the lives of women who did not write, such as Joan of Arc. For male writers, the model of the virgin martyr tends to be more problematic. Some, like Tertullian and Augustine, find it essential to prevent women from claiming the independence from social restriction that virginity appears to promise; others, like Ambrose, Aldhelm, and Wace, will link the image of the virgin martyr so intimately with suffering and death that they appear to defuse the potential of the image as a livable ideal. No matter how efficiently each attempt to deny or silence the virgin martyr may work within its own context, however, in the long run they are never more successful than those of the pagan persecutors who condemn Agnes, Margaret, or Catherine to be beaten or boiled in hot oil: the virgin martyr always manages to survive the assault and continues to preach her message of resistance. Over and over again, through nearly two thousand years of Western history, the virgin martyr has been reinvented by different writers, continually oscillating between appearances as an icon of silence and death and as one of active speech and liberation, always potentially both.

At this point it may seem that the argument I am proposing about the meaning of the virgin body and especially the martyred virgin body is naively essentialist, as essentialist as those medieval systems inherited from Aristotle that associate women with matter and men with spirit. Patristic and medieval writers were not generally so simpleminded as to mistake such idealized paradigms for either absolute or practical truth, however, and neither, I hope, am I. Virgin martyrs are not virgin martyrs because they are women; rather, they are women because they are virgin martyrs; the virgin body is always already sexed female, whatever the gender of the person inhabiting it, an apparent paradox made clear by the extreme rarity of male virgin martyrs like Hrotsvitha's Pelagius or Hildegard's Rupert, whom I discuss in chapter 5. Medieval women, on the other hand, easily identified themselves with role models characterized by their sexual condition as virgins and their physical passivity in the face of torture not because they themselves were more physical and less intellectual than men, or more passive and less active, but because they had been cast into such roles; sometimes, the most sensible thing to do in such a situation is simply to recolonize the prescribed role and turn it to one's own advantage. This is mimesis in the Irigarayan sense of the word; the subversive power of such mimesis is fully apparent in many texts written by women about women, and especially by virgins and about virgins: in Hrosvitha's subtle and ironic alterations to her (male-authored) sources, in Hildegard's cavalier rejection of the entire part of the patristic tradition concerning virginity which used it to enforce silence and humility, in Clemence of Barking's translation of the tale of Saint Catherine both into the vernacular, more available to women than Latin, and into a vehicle for sophisticated meditation on theological and political subjects.

The psychic and social mechanics that produce gendered identities in sexed bodies are, of course, enormously complex. All of us live in bodies; most of us like to believe that we have a degree of control over those bodies, although any such belief is inevitably shaken by those bodily functions over which we have little or no control, such as (to take two examples that are both deliberately loaded and especially important to medieval thought) erection or childbirth. As individuals, we may have even less control over those meanings that accrete to our bodies in the social world, since these are produced by generation after generation of cultural assumptions and attitudes; the body can sometimes come to seem like a pebble on a beach, shaped by the force of waves that it can in no way control. As the history of the twentieth century demonstrated with dreadful clarity, cultural assumptions about the body (racial body, sexed body) cannot be reformed overnight, nor can they be jettisoned at will. The body, as Foucault reminds us, has an inescapable and continuing history; within the Western tradition, the virgin body has an even more particular history, one that cannot be separated from the history of sex or from the history of women.

The virgin body, in fact, is one of the primary sites where the struggle to establish the ground of power within the entire sex–gender system takes place. The notion of virginity can be a mechanism for the enforcement of a rigidly hierarchical heterosexual ideology according to which women are valued exclusively according to their sexual status and are subjected to men for the purpose of protecting (which is to say controlling) that status. This discourse of virginity seems to arise out of male anxiety, perhaps even envy, concerning the integrity of the female body, and manifests itself in strict repression of women by men with access to legal, religious, and social power. An alternative discourse of virginity, equally ancient, as the witness of Tertullian concerning Thecla in chapter 1 demonstrates, opposes the very notion of sexual hierarchy. Woman centered, it imagines that women, and sometimes men as well, may be able to escape the dictates of both biology and society; it represents the very concept of virginity as radically liberating rather than restrictive.

In response to this feminine desire for freedom, chapter 2 argues, the narrative of virgin martyrdom itself becomes increasingly fixed. It stages another kind of desire, a masculine and aggressive desire which must be channeled in order to permit the survival of "normal" heterosexual communities. In these stories, the virgin's body calls forth the worst in men but narration permits the harnessing of that worst. Within the text, masculine aggression is projected upon the figure of the persecutor, while outside the text it is directed toward the protection of certain women within Christian society whose purity thus becomes the symbolic guarantee of the constitutive institution of that society, the Church. Thus, in the first century after the end of the Great Persecutions, we see the crystallization in the work of Ambrose and Prudentius of a particular narrative of virgin martyrdom that renders the virgin as pure symbolic object, perfectly passive and perfectly silent.[21]

When women themselves tell the story of the virgin martyr, however, the emphasis is different. Women writers tend to couple the physical passivity of the martyr under torture not with silence but with speech. For Hrotsvitha of Gandersheim, the subject of virginity becomes the excuse for exercising her own considerable eloquence to mount an attack upon male violence and vanity. For Hildegard of Bingen, the fact of physical virginity authorizes prophetic feminine speech, and becomes the ground upon which a community of women independent of the control of men may be founded. The examples of Hrotsvitha and Hildegard, which I explore extensively in chapters 3–5, suggest two of the myriad ways in which the discourse of virginity could be deployed by women who identified themselves with virgin martyrs. Indeed, for many of the women (and perhaps some of the men) who chose virginity in the Middle Ages, this choice worked rather like the choice of a queer identity at the end of the twentieth century. Writing of "the notion of 'queer,'" Judith Butler suggests that "an occupation or reterritorialization of a term that has been used to abject a population can become the site of resistance, the possibility of an enabling social and political resignification."[22] In chapter 6, I compare two vernacular saints' lives in order to demonstrate the way that, in her *Life of St. Catherine*, Clemence of Barking performs precisely this kind of reoccupation and reenergization of an identity that in Wace's *Life of St. Margaret*, had been rendered as an icon of passivity. The final chapter explores the function of these two saints within the life of a single, extraordinary historical woman, Joan of Arc, the last of the virgin martyrs.

For the women in this book, the notion of virginity becomes the site upon which female communities were founded; in real life, such communities offered, at least for short periods, education, independence from the demands of both society and biology, sometimes even political power. Nothing proves more convincingly that these communities threatened male cultural dominance than the repeated efforts of the Church to limit the power of such female institutions. Throughout the long centuries of the Middle Ages, each time a feminine alternative to masculine power within the Church arose, it was broken. Patristic writers from Tertullian on denied even virgin women access to the sacerdotal function which they tried to claim in the first centuries of Christianity. The great Anglo-Saxon double houses did not survive the Norman conquest and the power permitted to Ottonian abbesses in the tenth century was curtailed in the eleventh. The access of the nuns of Barking to education in the twelfth century was dramatically reduced by the fourteenth, when Chaucer could poke fun at the Prioress' French; during this same period monastic houses increasingly closed their doors to women, so that those few avenues to sanctity and authority still available to Hildegard and Clemence were all but cut off for later women.[23] This book does not propose to map the struggle of medieval women to claim and reclaim verbal authority and personal autonomy in any exhaustive way; to do so would require skills and energy that I simply do not possess. Just as archeology is increasingly inclined to use survey and core sampling in order to acquire information about ancient settlements, rather than committing itself to full-scale excavation, I hope to explore a few particular instances of the conflict between opposing ideologies of virginity. These instances have been lifted from what may seem like an unreasonably long period, from the late second century to the early fifteenth century. This is because the history of medieval women often seems like a cruel game of one step forward, two steps back; yet for a millennium and a half, every time there is a step toward increased independence and self-determination for women, the virgin martyr is there. If we listen very carefully, we can hear her story, not from the point of view of those male writers who sought to limit and control it, but in her own words.

A Word on Translation

In order to prevent a long book from becoming even longer, I have chosen to present prose passages in translation alone, while retaining the original language, accompanied by translation, for verse. To those who may protest that this approach privileges verse over prose, I plead guilty as charged. Translations from Latin, French, and Middle English are my own, unless otherwise noted; while most of the texts I am dealing with are available in translation, those translations are in many cases (this is especially true in the case of patristic writers) somewhat antiquated and tend to erase verbal distinctions (such as that between chastity and virginity) which I am especially concerned to preserve.

CHAPTER 1

STRANGE TRIANGLE: TERTULLIAN,
PERPETUA, THECLA

Not long ago, there was a debate between a Christian and a Jewish proselyte. They tugged back and forth on the ropes of their arguments until evening. In the end, the truth was somewhat clouded over by partisan shouting. Since, because of the uproar, the points under dispute really couldn't be made properly clear by careful examination, I have decided to finish off the questions in hand with the pen.

—Tertullian, *Against the Jews* 1.1–3

The encounter Tertullian describes at the beginning of his treatise *Against the Jews*[1] gives us a vivid glimpse of public life at Carthage at the beginning of the third century. Built upon the rubble of Rome's greatest enemy, Carthage was a city founded upon contradiction and controversy, standing in Africa but looking toward Rome, like its legendary queen, Dido. It was one of the most cosmopolitan cities of the Empire, home to people from three continents who spoke half a dozen languages and espoused an improbable variety of ideologies. If you were to walk across one of its public spaces of an afternoon, you might find yourself engaged in conversation or argument with a Stoic or Epicurean philosopher, a follower of Isis, a Rabbi, a Christian who believed in the divinity of the son of God and another who did not, or a Gnostic preaching the worship of the snake from the garden of Eden. There is no way of knowing whether Tertullian's encounter with the "Jewish proselyte" was due to chance, whether it had been set up to allow the speakers to demonstrate their rhetorical skills, or even whether it actually took place, but when Tertullian depicts the long North African afternoon fading into evening as the crowd acclaims his opponent, he brings us as close as we are likely to get to the intellectual ambience of his place and time. Carthage was an energetic and volatile city, and oratory was one of its favorite spectator

sports; public disputation could draw a crowd, could make or break a reputation. The man who won a disputation was hailed as a hero, like the
nameless Jewish proselyte—unless, of course, his opponent suffered a fit of
esprit d'escalier and continued the combat alone and in writing, ensuring
that he who lost the battle might still win the war.[2]

The milieu in which such battles took place was supposed to be a purely
masculine one. Roman rhetoric, whether in the law courts, on the floor of
the senate, or in the open spaces of the great cities, was reserved for men,
and no master of Latin rhetoric is more self-consciously masculine
than Tertullian.[3] Nonetheless, Carthage remains the city of Dido, and for
Tertullian, as for Aeneas, women in general and Carthaginian women in
particular were to prove deeply troublesome, especially in their relation to
rhetoric and public speech. Even when women are not the targets of his
tractates, as they are in *On the Veiling of Virgins* or *On Feminine Apparel*, they
appear in the margins, provoking, harassing, and distressing the apologist.
One of his earliest works, *On Baptism*, begins with the denunciation of a
female preacher, a woman who may have engaged in exactly the kind of
public religious disputation that Tertullian himself practiced. That most of
the disputatious women in Tertullian remain nameless only proves that, like
the Jewish proselyte, they lost the war; if they won a battle or two along the
way, Tertullian is not about to admit it. Even within Tertullian's own
church, there were demonstrably women who required arguing against,
which may imply that they themselves were given to argument. I have no
intention of attempting to defend Tertullian on the charge of misogyny—
his works are much too exuberant in their antifeminism for that—but I do
propose to argue that his misogyny, while genuine, is never simple, that it
can teach us a great deal about the manifold connections between rhetoric
and the virgin body at the beginning of the Christian tradition, and that if
we read through it we can catch the occasional glimpse of an actual woman
struggling against the denunciations and definitions of men like Tertullian.

In his discussion of patristic texts dealing with feminine sexuality,
R. H. Bloch claims that "much of the imagery surrounding virginity
focuses upon the notion of a bodily integrity that rhetorically holds out to
the woman willing to renounce her sexuality the promise of escaping the
consequences of the Fall. Yet, as the fathers make abundantly clear, it is not
enough merely to be chaste."[4] Bloch's larger argument involves the degree
to which patristic writers become implicated in their own rhetoric.
The virgin body itself, however, does not really exist for Bloch except as a
semantic field upon which the pens of the Fathers can play. My interest
in Tertullian is to tease out the dynamics that connect both his misogynist
rhetoric and his rarer pro-feminine statements to particular bodies and
particular women, and to question whether virginity was for him and

the women surrounding him always and exclusively a renunciation of sexuality, a negative decision. Tertullian's writings about women bear witness to an extraordinary degree of anxiety concerning the multiplicity of social, sexual, and theological meanings that the female body and particularly the virgin body could generate; virginity is suspicious to Tertullian because it is potentially not a rejection of femininity, but an affirmation of it. Nowhere are the contradictions which bedevil Tertullian's thought on the subject of femininity more evident than in his responses to the two women who stand at the beginning of the tradition of the virgin martyr: Thecla of Iconium, the legendary virgin apostle and companion of Saint Paul, is to him a dreadful example; Perpetua, on the other hand, whose public execution Tertullian almost certainly witnessed at Carthage in 203, is "the bravest martyr of Christ" (*On the Soul* 55). The situation is further complicated by Tertullian's increasing commitment to Montanism, a cult strongly invested in the prophetic utterances of women. Reading between the *Acts of Thecla*, the *Passion of Saint Perpetua*, and several texts by Tertullian thus provides an extraordinary opportunity to observe the generation of both pro- and antifeminist rhetoric around the issues of virginity, martyrdom, and feminine speech.

Neither Perpetua nor Thecla was both virgin and martyr; Perpetua was a married woman, while Thecla survived her martyrdom. Nevertheless, in these two narratives, one autobiographical and one legendary, women bear witness to their own experience in ways that are both immediate and provocative—provocative especially to writers like Tertullian, who marshals all the arguments at his disposal to silence any voice and particularly any female voice that might challenge his vision of the Church. These texts, clustered together at the cusp of the third century, demonstrate the extent to which the question of who was to control the telling of women's stories and the disposition of women's bodies was a foundational issue for the Early Church. In the centuries to follow, such battles for control would become both the subject matter and the subtext of the virgin martyr narrative.

The Cainite Woman

One of Tertullian's earliest works, probably composed not long after his conversion to Christianity, is the first authoritative exposition of the sacrament of baptism. *On Baptism* was written in response to a particular woman preacher operating in and around Carthage at the time, who taught that baptism was unnecessary. It contains a single reference to Thecla:

> If those acts ascribed to Paul give the example of Thecla in order to permit women to preach and baptize, those who cite them should know that in Asia

the presbyter who fabricated that text, in order to add to Paul's reputation with something of his own, was discovered, confessed that he had done it out of love for Paul, and was forced to resign. Indeed, how could it be true that Paul gave women the right to preach and baptize when he would not even let them learn as a matter of course? Let them be silent, he says, and consult with their menfolk at home. (*On Baptism* 1)[5]

The "acts ascribed to Paul" is the text known as the *Acts of Paul and Thecla*, or sometimes simply the *Acts of Thecla*, which tells the story of a young woman who heard Paul preach and was moved to follow him, rejecting marriage and family. Becoming separated from the apostle, she was condemned to death, and undertook to baptize herself by flinging herself into the pool of water that had been prepared as a part of her torture. The reference to "what Paul says" is to I Cor. 14, and I shall have occasion to return to this epistle later on. Here, Tertullian uses the Pauline citation in what was to become an absolutely standard way, to deny women the right to teach or preach, that is, to participate in public religious discourse. He argues that the story of Thecla, who is described in some accounts as "the first martyr of God and apostle and virgin,"[6] cannot be true because Paul would never have allowed a woman to misbehave as Thecla did; the argument is flawlessly circular. *On Baptism* also associates Thecla in a fairly explicit fashion with heresy and heretical preaching, and more subtly with sexual depravity. As Gillian Clark notes succinctly, the status of women "within any [heretical] movement was one way of attacking it, on the grounds that women are naturally more credulous than men, and that it is quite improper for them to be in authority."[7] Reading Tertullian reading Thecla permits a very specific articulation of the dialectic between feminist and antifeminist rhetoric, especially as it relates to women's right to authoritative speech, right at the beginning of the tradition of the virgin martyr. I shall suggest that the significant combination of the terms "apostle and virgin" makes Thecla a particular threat to the Church as Tertullian wishes it to be.

On Baptism opens with a brief but mordant bit of invective against the anonymous woman preacher, which betrays a marked apprehension about the dangerous effects of feminine speech:

And indeed, a certain viper of the Cainite heresy, who was in the area recently, carried off quite a few with her venomous doctrine; she began by tearing down baptism. In this, she was acting according to nature; generally speaking, vipers and asps and basilisks live in arid and waterless places. We little fishes [*pisciculi*] however, following the example of our *ichthus* Jesus Christ, are born in the water, and we remain safe nowhere else but in the water. That monster of a woman [*illa monstrosissima*], whom the law does not actually allow even to teach, knew perfectly well how to kill little fishes: by taking them out of the water. (*On Baptism* 1)

The Cainites are usually identified as a subsect of the Ophites, a gnostic group who rejected the creator God and were said to worship the serpent instead as the giver of knowledge.[8] A logical extension of this cosmology would have been a visible role for women within the sect, since Eve was the chosen interlocutor of the serpent in Eden. Tertullian takes full advantage of this association, turning the woman herself into a sort of dragon, a monster from the desert. His deft deployment of superlatives and diminutives in the opposition *monstrosissima/pisciculi* keeps the tone satirical, but the threat, as Tertullian perceives it, is very real. Nor is it limited to the denial of baptism, which certain gnostic sects indeed did preach.[9] The rejection of the sacrament is here connected intimately and repeatedly with the danger of female preaching. The Cainite woman's monstrosity, in fact, appears to be constituted not simply by the content of her poisonous doctrine but by the fact that she has violated the law (*ius*, which has the sense of natural or even divine law, in contrast to *lex*, which indicates the man-made law of the courts and assemblies) which denies her the right to preach any doctrine whatsoever. The law in question is the passage from the pseudo-Pauline first letter to Timothy: "Let the woman learn in silence, with all subjection. But I suffer not a woman to teach, nor to use authority over the man: but to be in silence" (I Tim. 2:12–13).

In a slightly later text, *The Prescription against Heretics*, Tertullian reiterates his shock at the behavior of heretical women and links their verbal excess to sexual excess: "And those heretical women, how bold [*quae procaces*] they are! They have the nerve to teach, to dispute [*contendere*], to conduct exorcisms, to undertake cures, perhaps even to baptize!" (41.5). *Procax* means shameless, and has both a sexual and a rhetorical implication; it is primarily verbal misbehavior, which provokes the epithet here, although verbal and sexual misconduct are never far apart in Tertullian. These women teach, in direct contravention of Saint Paul, and they dispute: *contendere* describes the aggressive and purely masculine speech of the law court or of philosophical argument.[10] The explicit targets of the *Prescription against Heretics* include "a virgin called Philumene, an angel of deceit" (6.6). Tertullian accuses her of seducing Apelles away from the Marcionite heresy, which was characterized by extreme sexual continence, and the seduction is clearly imagined as both verbal and sexual: "[Apelles] abandoned the continence of Marcion, falling with a woman [*lapsus in feminam*] and slipped off to Alexandria, out of the sight of his oh-so-saintly master. Upon his return a few years later, he was no better (except that he was no longer a Marcionite) and he took up with another woman, Philumene, whom

I mentioned before, who herself later became a great prostitute; inspired by her spirit [*energemate*] he wrote the *Phanerosis* based on her teaching" (30.5–6). The spiritual intercourse between Apelles and Philumene violates the Pauline law by inverting the normative hierarchy: she imposes her energetic spirit, her words and revelations upon him, rather than remaining silent and allowing him to teach her. Here, as elsewhere in Tertullian, an improper intellectual relationship between the sexes is indistinguishable from sexual depravity.[11]

In the body of *On Baptism*, Tertullian turns away from his denunciation of heresy to a lengthy exposition of the theological value of baptism. The reference to Thecla occurs immediately after the second (and last) reference to the Cainite woman preacher. Tertullian has been explaining the proper hierarchy according to which baptism should be administered. The ideal baptizer is the bishop; if he is not available, presbyters or deacons will suffice; in cases of emergency, laymen may baptize, but under no circumstances may a woman perform the rite: "Even the insolence of that woman who usurped the right to teach evidently does not include claiming the right to baptize, unless some new beast like the original one may come along, so that as one woman abolished baptism, another might administer it upon her own authority" (17). In this passage, Tertullian moves from one extreme of feminine deceit to another; the serpent-like Cainite woman taught by preaching that baptism was invalid, whereas the hypothetical "new beast" might teach that women could baptize, by appealing to Thecla. As far as Tertullian is concerned, the two are equal in monstrosity, since invalid baptism is as bad as no baptism at all; it seems not to trouble him that there is an enormous difference of doctrine between the gnostic preacher and the famous companion of Paul. The point is rather to discredit any woman who threatens the functions of men by operating in a public and authoritative sphere, either by preaching or by baptizing. Thecla thus becomes the hypothetical and misleading model for the "new beast" who might perpetrate a new form of monstrosity upon unsuspecting Christians. The authority of this model, however, rests entirely upon the canonicity of the *Acts of Paul and Thecla*. It is only after having associated the virgin apostle with the image he has already created of feminine monstrosity that Tertullian delivers the rhetorical *coup-de-grâce* by dismissing the entire textual tradition concerning her. The twentieth-century editor of *On Baptism* concurs entirely with Tertullian's move, declaring in his notes that "the so-called *Acts of Paul and Thecla* are a second century Christian romance of a thoroughly unhealthy character."[12]

What is it, precisely, that is so unhealthy about Thecla that Tertullian must first turn her into a monster and then make her disappear? The answer to this question may be easier to approach if we turn away from the legendary virgin to the historical martyr, Perpetua, who provoked a very different reaction from Tertullian.

Perpetua of Carthage

If sexuality and heresy were linked in the minds of Christians of the early third century, so were sexuality and martyrdom, and nowhere more so than in Carthage. In 203, under Septimus Severus, the city witnessed the execution of a group of Christian citizens, among them two young women. If the behavior of heretical women was evidence of feminine susceptibility to the wiles of the devil, then women's ability to suffer publicly with courage was seen as an especially clear indicator of the power of God. Nowhere was this power clearer than in the example of Perpetua.

The *Passion of Saint Perpetua* is one of the most remarkable documents of late antiquity, in content, in form, and in authorship. It tells the story of five Christian martyrs, two of whom, Perpetua and Saturus, left autobiographical accounts of their experiences in prison. An anonymous redactor, believed by some to be Tertullian himself,[13] added a brief introduction and concluded the document with what sounds like an eyewitness account of the executions, as well as a eulogy in honor of the martyrs. There seems no reason to doubt the redactor's insistence that Perpetua's prison diary is an account "in her own hand and according to her own impressions" [*mano sua et suo sensu (Perpetua* 2.3)].[14] The text thus provides an extraordinarily personal glimpse into the way the politics of gender played themselves out both in the persecution of an actual woman and in her reactions to that persecution. Most scholars concur in seeing Perpetua's narrative as the story of a woman who resists both political and patriarchal power, choosing to go to her death rather than obey the Roman governor or her father. I shall argue that while her resistance can be seen as both political and religious, it is not in any real sense of the word "feminist." That is, while Perpetua does reject the authority of her pagan father, her behavior does not in any way challenge the concept of natural masculine authority, or of normative gender roles. Perpetua redefines herself as a Christian, but she does not deny or reconfigure her femininity, or even renounce proper feminine behavior. Rather, she translates these from a pagan to a Christian context, thus remaining an ideal Roman matron even as she dies in the arena. Perpetua represents herself as a woman resistant to Imperial but not masculine control, a woman very much concerned about her father, brother, and son in this world and about her spiritual fathers and brothers in the next; she may pose a threat to the hierarchy of the pagan government, but she poses none to the ecclesiastical hierarchy in which Tertullian believed so strongly.

She does not claim the right to preach, to teach, to baptize—she claims no right at all, finally, except the right to die for her faith.

Perpetua's account of her imprisonment is written in a prose that is perfectly elegant in its simplicity; nothing could be further from the rhetorical flourishes and extravagances of Tertullian. The narrative alternates between heartrending interviews with her father and descriptions of the dream visions Perpetua experienced while awaiting execution, and this symmetry suggests a degree of literary sensibility. Perpetua may not have been consciously or deliberately shaping her narrative, but she had internalized the principles of balance characteristic of late antique narrative forms. Just as the Greek novels balance the adventures of hero and heroine, just as Tacitus balances events at Rome with events in the provinces, Perpetua balances scenes that demonstrate her ties to the ordinary life of family and civic duty with those that evoke the extraordinary rewards of Christianity. In other ways too, Perpetua seems highly aware of the power of contrast in language; her simple, paratactic style makes the rare metaphor stand out with positive radiance. When she is first arrested, she is terrified by the darkness and stifling heat of her dungeon. Once her baby is brought to her, however, the place is transformed: "The prison suddenly became a palace for me" [*et factus est mihi carcer subito praetorium* (3.3)]. The transformation is not expressed as a simile; there is no acknowledgment of the representational quality of language. Perpetua emphasizes identity, not resemblance, thus insisting on the reality of the transformation.

That Perpetua should have internalized certain dictates of narrative style is no surprise, since, according to the redactor, she was "well born and properly educated" (2.2). Her compositional style, descriptive and linear, is perfectly in keeping with what we know of the reading matter common to young Roman women.[15] It shows no mark at all of the study of rhetoric; a young woman of her class might have read Vergil or Greek novels for moral or entertainment value, but would hardly have been encouraged to read Quintilian or Seneca, essential texts for the education of young Roman men all of whom were expected to develop a certain facility in public speaking. In her attitudes toward her family, Perpetua is no less a typical product of the Roman society that produced her. While Salisbury is entirely correct in asserting that Perpetua's "rebellion and her father's sorrow point to the split in families that was occurring as Christianity spread through the empire," she overstates the case, I would argue, in claiming that "Perpetua had to forget or reject all her Roman upbringing to emerge victorious in this confrontation."[16] Inevitably, Perpetua's Christianity alters her relationship to her family, but her attitudes toward her father, her son, and her brothers remain consistent with Roman models of filial piety, and she takes great pains to emphasize her concern for her father and son.

Her mother, on the other hand, is a shadowy figure, mentioned only once. Rather than eradicating her commitment to her family, Perpetua's new religion seems to proceed from many of the same impulses, attitudes, and relations to men that characterized her as an earthly daughter, mother, and sister.

The reaction of Perpetua's father to his daughter's arrest veers between rage and despair; his emotional state is rendered with great psychological realism and with genuine compassion. Once again, Perpetua's style is characterized by a fine sense of balance; she recognizes with complete clarity that her father is moved only by love for her, and yet at the same time describes his arguments as those of the devil:

> "Father," I said, "Do you see this vase sitting here, for example, or pot, or whatever it is?" And he said, "I do." And I said to him "Could it be called by any other name than what it is?" And he said, "No." "Well then, I cannot say that I am not what I am, a Christian." Then my father, angry at this word, went for me as if he would scratch out my eyes. But he only fumed, and went away, defeated, along with the devil's arguments. (*Perpetua* 3.1–4)

Perhaps Perpetua's father is arguing that she can somehow fudge her Christianity before the judge, that she can continue to worship as she pleases but claim to be something other than a Christian. Perpetua clearly perceives his speech as sophistic in the Aristophanic sense: he is making the worse argument appear the better. She identifies his arguments (which she keeps quite separate from her father himself) as diabolical, and opts for absolute truth, rather than the manipulation of words which could make a water pot seem like a soup plate, or a Christian like a loyal follower of the imperial cult. This is both a very courageous choice, and one that utterly rejects any sort of hairsplitting, which might be useful in her defense; Perpetua will not argue, she will not dispute.

The next two encounters between father and daughter, which are narrated together, take place immediately before Perpetua's judicial hearing. Once again, she is intensely sympathetic to her father:

> This is what my father said, out of devotion to me, kissing my hands and flinging himself at my feet; and amid his tears he called me not "daughter" but "*domina*."[17] And I grieved for my father's condition. . .and I comforted him. . .and he left me, grief-stricken. Another day. . .my father appeared there with my son, and pulled me off the step, saying: "Make the sacrifice! Have pity on your child!" The governor, Hilarianus. . .chimed in: "Spare your father's old age, spare your little boy's infancy! Perform the ritual for the Emperor's welfare." And I answered: "I will not perform it." Hilarianus said, "You are a Christian then?" And I answered, "I am a Christian." And as my

father still hung about, trying to change my mind, Hilarianus ordered him to
be thrown out, and he was beaten with a stick. And I grieved for my father's
downfall as if I'd been struck myself: that's how I mourned for his pitiful old
age. (*Perpetua* 5.5–6.5)

The statement *Christiana sum* is as anti-rhetorical as anything could be.
There is nothing agonistic about Perpetua's words, even though, as she
speaks them, she knows the agony they will purchase for her in the arena.[18]
When Perpetua declares that she is a Christian, she is claiming a new identity for herself, one that is fundamentally at odds with her old one as a
pagan Roman. Both Salisbury and Dronke see this new identity as radically
replacing her old identity as her father's daughter, although Dronke goes on
to argue that her father "returns transformed. . .in several of Perpetua's
dream images," appearing "as a serene father-figure—not tormented and
tormenting, but solacing."[19] In other words, while she may not be the same
daughter to the same father, Perpetua remains a daughter, under the
authority of masculine figures such as the white-haired shepherd of her first
dream or the gigantic master of ceremonies of her final dream. Perpetua
herself admits no rupture with her father; she feels the blows rained on her
father as if she were herself being beaten, demonstrating sympathy in the
most literal sense of the word. She emphasizes this again in recounting her
final contact with her father: "When the day of the spectacle drew near, my
father came in to me, wasted and worn. He began to tear out the hair of
his beard and fling it on the ground, he hurled himself headlong and cursed
his life, and said such things as would move every living creature. I ached
for his unhappy old age" (9.2–3). Sympathy is, of course, the primary characteristic of the martyr. Perpetua's love for her father precedes her love for
Christ but is not eliminated by it; similarly, her desire to share the suffering
of Christ does not preclude her ability to share the suffering of her father.
Perpetua's obligation to her father is replaced by a more powerful obligation to her faith. The redactor of the *Perpetua* may indeed see her situation
as parallel to that of a young woman who leaves her father for a husband:
"Perpetua went along with shining countenance and calm step, as the
beloved of God, as a wife of Christ. . ." (18.2). Her entrance into martyrdom is thus figured according to a normative paradigm of gendered
behavior, the transmission of a young woman from father to bridegroom.[20]
    Perpetua's separation from her infant son is also figured as miraculous
but not unnatural, accelerating rather than abrogating the normal process
of weaning and the mother's remission of her child into other custody,
which took place fairly early in any case if the child were a boy. As in the
case of her father, Perpetua takes pains to establish her affection for her
baby. When her father refuses to return the child after Perpetua has been

condemned, she is initially desperate for his return but "somehow, through God's will, he no longer needed the breast, nor did my breasts become inflamed—so I was not tormented with worry for the child, or with soreness" (6.3). There is no indication here that Perpetua does not care for her child; she simply knows now that he can survive without her. Just as her father seems to appear transformed in her dream into the white-haired old shepherd, so her baby seems to be transformed in the dream that follows his weaning. In this vision, she sees a younger brother who had died as a child:

> I saw Dinocrates coming out of a dark place, where there were many people, very hot and thirsty, his clothes dirty and looking pale—he still had on his face the same wound as when he died. This Dinocrates had been my brother in the flesh; he was seven years old when he died horribly of cancer of the face. . . .There was a pool full of water with a rim that was higher than he was, and Dinocrates stretched up as if he wanted a drink. I was sorry that, even though the pool had water, the rim was so high that he could not drink. And I awoke, and realized that my brother was struggling. Yet I had faith that I could help him in his struggle, and I prayed for him every day. . .
> (*Perpetua* 7.4–9)

Perpetua's concern about her ability to nurse her baby is immediately replaced by a very similar concern about providing her dead brother with the spiritual drink that he needs. Her prayers are effective and when she dreams about Dinocrates again, she might just as well be dreaming of her own little son growing up into a healthy, happy child: "There was Dinocrates, clean, well-dressed, refreshed; where the wound had been I saw a scar: and the pool I'd seen before had had its rim lowered down to the boy's navel. He was drinking from the pool constantly. . .And when he had drunk his fill, he began to play with the water, as children do, full of happiness" (8.2–4).

Perpetua's final dream vision has been the subject of a great deal of analysis. In it, she finds herself in the arena, preparing to fight an Egyptian gladiator:

> A hideous Egyptian came out against me, with his seconds; he was going to fight me. Some handsome young men came alongside of me, my own seconds and supporters. And I was stripped naked, and became male [*et facta sum masculus*], and my supporters began to rub me with oil, as they do for a wrestling match. . .And a man of enormous size came out—he towered up over the top of the amphitheater. He was wearing a loose purple garment with two stripes across his chest, patterned sandals made of gold and silver, and carrying a staff like a *lanista* and a green branch with golden apples. He asked for silence, and said: "If this Egyptian defeats her [*hanc*], he will kill

her [*illa*] with his sword; if she defeats him, she will win this branch."
(*Perpetua* 10.6–9)

For Salisbury, the dream is a metaphor for "personal change" representing
Perpetua's "own baptism—the dramatic change from catechumen to bap-
tized Christian."[21] Dronke understands it as an expression of Perpetua's
desire for an heroic death; she "wants to strip herself of all that is weak, or
womanish, in her nature."[22] Rosemary Rader rejects this interpretation,
claiming "that it seems erroneous to interpret this as a belief in one's
having to become a man in order to be saved" and insists that the importance of the dream lies rather in its androgyny and in the fact that "the sexual imagery can be interchanged without the loss of essential significance."[23]
To my mind, none of these interpretations accounts fully for the oddity of
Perpetua's words, an oddity that is diminished by translation into English.
Et facta sum masculus, she says, which is generally rendered as "I had become
a man." In the English, the feminine gender has faded entirely out of the
phrase; not so in the Latin, where the feminine *facta* balances the masculine
masculus. This last word should itself cause us to pause for a moment; is it
in fact an adjective or a substantive? It can be used either way, although
it is more common as an adjective than a noun, as in *natus masculus*, a male
child, or *nomen masculum*, a masculine noun. The fact that it does not accord
with the subject seems to argue for its function as a noun, but it is worth
keeping in mind that *masculum* also had an entirely metaphorical range of
meaning when applied to nouns such as *anima* or *ingenium*: strong, bold,
heroic, manly; in any case, *factum sum masculum* would have been even more
nonsensical in the Latin. This confusion is enhanced by the words of the
lanista; he refers to the dreamer with the feminine pronouns *hanc* and *illam*.
Here, in spite of the fact that Perpetua has become *masculus*, she is recognized by the authority figure of the dream as female, and, perhaps more
importantly, presented to the crowd as such. Far from being a rejection of
her femininity, the scene thus appears to represent a profound sense of its
inalienability; even in a male body, she is still fundamentally and essentially
feminine.

This reading of the text helps to make sense of a passage in the redactor's description of Perpetua's martyrdom, which has troubled many
scholars:

> The cow tossed Perpetua first, and she landed on her back. She sat up and
> pulled at her tunic, which was ripped along one side, in order to cover her
> thighs, thinking more of her modesty than of her pain. Then she asked for a
> pin with which to put up her untidy hair, for it was not right that a martyr
> should die with her hair in disorder, in case she might seem to be mourning
> in her hour of glory. (*Perpetua* 20.3–5)

Dronke describes the details of this passage as "almost certainly fictitious" because they are incompatible with "the dream of the woman who strips naked and is anointed for combat: one who is unafraid to write like that will hardly have gone to her death in a fit of prudery."[24] Modesty and prudery, however, are not the same thing; it is of essential significance that the body that is revealed as naked in the dream is a male body (whatever the gender of the person inhabiting it) and therefore an acceptable sight in the arena, in conformity with societal expectations and even with standards of beauty. A naked female body is an entirely different matter, as the redactor's text makes clear. When Perpetua and her companion Felicity are first sent into the ring, they are naked except for nets, and the crowd is scandalized (perhaps because Felicity had visibly just given birth, possibly also because of Perpetua's rank) and insists that they be dressed. The female body, and especially the maternal female body, required or perhaps deserved the veil of modesty, even if it was destined to be torn apart by wild beasts. While it is, of course, impossible to determine whether the redactor's account reflects the reality of Perpetua's execution or rather his expectations concerning the behavior of a virtuous woman in such a situation, I see no reason to suspect that Perpetua herself would not have shared in those expectations. In maintaining her modesty, she is not behaving "prudishly" but preserving her dignity, the dignity of a triumphant Christian. It is also, of course, the dignity of a Roman *matrona*. The same combination of modesty and courage can be found in the deaths of pagan women; Tacitus's *Annals* tells the story of Pollutia, who had been unable to save her father from proscription as a traitor, and who chooses to commit suicide along with her father and grandmother: "in the same room and with the same weapon, they opened their veins and hurried into a bath, each one covered, *as modesty required*, with a single garment, the father looking steadfastly at his daughter, the grandmother at her grandchild, and she on both of them."[25]

Perpetua's final act of courage is to take the sword of her executioner and lead it to her throat. "Perhaps," the redactor muses, "such a woman could not be killed otherwise. . .unless she had wanted it" (10.10). The meaning of Perpetua, for the redactor and the audience for which he was writing (which will have included Tertullian if he was not himself the redactor) lies in her death. She is possessed of the greatest of womanly virtues, modesty and humility, and her love for her father and son is only outshone by her love for the Father and His Son. Perpetua's submission to her fate and her martyred body testify as nothing else can to the power of God; her death resounds to the glory of the nascent Carthaginian church without questioning the authority of that church. She represents the fundamental paradox of martyrdom: the greatest strength is demonstrated through ultimate passivity, by letting oneself bear witness through the body and suffer death at the hands of another.

New Prophecy and Veiled Virgins

Some scholars have seen Perpetua and her companions as followers of the Montanist New Prophecy, because of the emphasis in the text upon divine revelation through visions, and because of the eagerness of the martyrs to meet their own deaths.[26] If Tertullian is the redactor of the text, then the death of Perpetua and her companions may mark the very moment of his first interest in Montanism. In any case, the link between Perpetua and Tertullian cannot help but raise the issue of his investment in the sect, and the implications of such an investment for the subject of feminine authority. Perpetua is only mentioned once by name in the works that can be securely ascribed to Tertullian, but this is in *On the Soul*, a text belonging to his late, definitely Montanist period. In it, he asks "How is it that St. Perpetua, that bravest martyr of Christ, on the day of her death saw only the souls of the martyrs in Paradise?" (55). The evocation of her vision as reliable evidence in the vexing question of life after death is entirely in keeping with the New Prophecy movement. Since Montanism was so closely associated with the prophetic authority of two women, Prisca and Maximilla, and since Tertullian's own church seems to have been home to a number of women who were liable to Montanist fits of prophecy, one might expect a softening of antifeminist rhetoric in Tertullian's later work. The opposite is true. As his commitment to the New Prophecy grew, so evidently did Tertullian's anxiety about the function of women and women's speech within the church. Several of his most misogynist works date from this period, but *On the Veiling of Virgins* is the most revealing.

In this treatise, probably written in 213,[27] Tertullian denounces the behavior of certain young women of Carthage who insisted upon appearing in church with their heads uncovered:

> I beg you, whether you are mother or sister or virgin daughter—permit me to address you by the names appropriate to your various ages—veil your head! If you are a mother, do it for the sake of your sons, if you are a sister, for the sake of your brothers, if you are a daughter, for the sake of your father! Every age is imperiled by your person. Wear the armor of modesty, barricade yourself with the stockade of timidity, build up a rampart for your sex which will not allow your own gaze out or the gaze of others in. Wear the full dress of a woman, to preserve your virginity. (*Virgins* 2.18)

This was much more than a sartorial squabble, as the specter of incest raised in this passage suggests. As Tertullian saw it, the virgins of Carthage were rejecting Paul's command that women should veil themselves in church (I Cor. 11:3–16), and thus putting the souls of an entire community at risk by revealing far too much of their irresistibly, irredeemably sensual bodies. What Paul actually meant when he wrote to the Corinthians concerning women's head-coverings is as obscure as anything in the New Testament, but Tertullian appears convinced that he understands both the words of the apostle and the motivations of the women who rejected the veil. Since Paul had declared that women in religious assemblies must have "a sign of authority" upon their heads, these virgins, by declaring their right to go unveiled, were also declaring their freedom from masculine authority.[28] Tertullian's fundamental objection in *On the Veiling of Virgins* is twofold. First, sexual renunciation is really not possible for women; they are essentially, intrinsically, and irretrievably carnal beings, the "devil's gateway" as he puts it in another famous diatribe, and therefore a constant source of danger to the souls and bodies of men. Second, he is afraid that virgins are laying claim to some particularly feminine avenue of access to the divine, one that is not open to men. In order to counteract this double threat, Tertullian deploys a remarkable battery of arguments, and a satirical tone that often operates more like the blunt weapon of sarcasm than the rapier of irony.

One of the most remarkable elements of Tertullian's text is the enormous erotic appeal with which he invests the virgin body. It is this appeal that he fears will operate like a contaminating agent upon the men of the Christian community:

> . . .[the custom of going unveiled], which negates virginity by revealing it, is one of which no one could approve except someone of the same sort as those virgins. Indeed, those eyes which desire to see a virgin are of just the same sort as those of the virgin who desires to be seen. Eyes like that desire each other—in fact, seeing and being seen participate in the same lust. A holy man ought to blush to see a virgin, just as a holy virgin blushes if seen by a man. (*Virgins* 2.4–5)

Here Tertullian, as the revealer of the virgin's shame, becomes identified rhetorically with "eyes like that," the position of the disembodied voyeur who participates in the mutually corruptive gaze. The inalienable sexuality of the virgin is not only evident in this representation of an exchange of glances as a form of sexual congress, but throughout *On the Veiling of Virgins*. Virginity does not control, diminish, or eliminate the threat of female sexuality; it intensifies it. The sexual allure of virgin bodies is responsible for the fall of the angels themselves, Tertullian explains, interpreting Paul's much contested insistence that a woman ought to wear a "sign of authority upon her head on account of the angels" (I Cor. 11:10)[29] with the help of the *Book of Enoch*: "If indeed [the imposition of the veil] is 'on account of the angels'—that is to say, those who fell from God and Heaven on account of their lust for women—who could imagine that angels such as these would desire tainted bodies, the cast-offs of human men, rather than burning with passion for virgins, whose blossoming excuses even human lust?" (7.4).

Underlying Tertullian's very evident anxiety concerning the behavior of virgins is another concern, which may be only the more powerful for remaining unspoken. Another crux in the interpretation of I Corinthians concerns the letter's apparently contradictory dicta concerning the right of women to speak in religious assembly. On the one hand, Paul implies that women were permitted to participate in religious gatherings as long as they did so with their heads appropriately covered: "any woman that prays or prophesies with her head uncovered dishonors her head" (I Cor. 11:5); on the other, he seems to say that women should not speak in church at all: "As in all the churches of the saints, the women should keep silence in the churches. For they are not permitted to speak, but should be subordinate, as the law says" (I Cor. 14:34). The key to resolving this difficulty lies in recognizing, as Tertullian evidently did, that Paul is discussing two very different kinds of speech. Women are allowed to participate in prayer, and cannot be prevented from prophesying, for prophecy is a gift of the holy spirit, which may descend where it pleases. As Meier puts it, "all of Paul's contorted reasoning at this point may obscure the astounding fact—astounding at least for a religious group arising from the Jewish synagogue—that women were free in church to pray openly and to prophesy under charismatic inspiration."[30] Prophecy and speaking in tongues, however, are only the first part of the religious experience; prophecy, which is obscure almost by definition, must be interpreted: "If any speak in a tongue, let there be only two, or at the most by three, and each in turn; and let one interpret. But if there is no interpreter, let each keep silent in the church and speak to himself and to God" (I Cor. 14:27–28). Both men and women evidently had been prophesying in the church at Corinth, and Paul admits such prophesies regardless of the gender of the prophet. The discussion and exegesis necessary to validate prophecy, on the other hand, by relating it to scripture and doctrine, is an exclusively male domain. While the holy spirit might speak through a vessel of either sex, only men had the education and the authority to explicate what the spirit said. In making this distinction between prophetic and exegetical speech, Paul establishes himself firmly in a tradition that owes at least as much to late antique pagan culture as to Judaism; the Christian community at Corinth was, after all, not Judaic in origin, but pagan, and late antique paganism was full of religions that allowed spirit possession of female worshippers by divine influence. In the *Moralia*, Plutarch represents the prophecies of virgins as the result of a sort of spiritual intercourse with the divine, and a similar concept may well have underlain the function of the Vestal Virgins at Rome.[31] In one sense, women are open to divine inspiration precisely because they are perceived as being sexually vulnerable, appealing in their openness and perhaps in their dissociation from the rational world of masculine logic, to superhuman forces. For Tertullian, writing fifty years after Plutarch and a product of the same Graeco-Roman education and culture, it is precisely because women can prophesy ecstatically, and because ecstatic prophecy presupposes a certain kind of quasi-sexual possession, that women must cover themselves in church. Otherwise, they might compromise their potential function as the receptacles of divine truth by tempting the wrong kind of angels.

The issue of prophetic speech in general and feminine prophetic speech in particular was if anything more complex in the late second and early third century than it had been when Paul was writing, because of the spread of what came to be known as the Montanist heresy. Catholic Christianity maintained that the era of divine prophecy had come to an end with the Revelation of John; the Holy Spirit had spoken only to the apostles, and now all that remained was for the faithful to await the fulfillment of those prophecies. By the middle of the second century, however, the age of apostolic prophecy seemed rather long ago, and in about 170, Phrygia, part of what is now Turkey, became the epicenter of a movement known as the New Prophecy. The New Prophecy was not a heretical sect in the sense that Valentinianism or Arianism was, since its adherents manifested no doctrinal differences from Catholics; their only point of divergence from the increasingly established church was, in fact, their insistence that prophecy continued in the present day. Nonetheless, the followers of the prophets Montanus, Prisca, and Maximilla posed a clear threat to Catholicism because of their emphasis on charismatic gifts: if the spirit could still speak to individuals directly, there seemed to be little need for an organized and hierarchical church. Early on, the position of women within the movement became the focus of arguments against it. Elizabeth Schussler Fiorenza makes it very clear that some of the same objections that Tertullian leveled at the virgins of Carthage were also made with regard to the Montanists:

> Since the Montanists' opponents could not refute the movement on doctrinal grounds, they attacked it by slandering it for its prophetic women leaders. According to Origen, "those disciples of women, who choose as their master Priscilla and Maximilla, not Christ" appeal to the succession of women prophets in Scripture to authorize women's leadership. Origen seeks to refute their claim by arguing to the contrary that the biblical women prophets did not speak in public or in the *ekklesia* but only in private.[32]

On the face of it, the Montanists seem a rather odd group for Tertullian to have attached himself to, and indeed it is difficult not to suspect that his long and slow movement from Catholicism to Montanism may have been in part due to his misgivings about the role of women in any church. Nevertheless, by the time he was composing *On the Veiling of Virgins*, Tertullian was a wholehearted supporter of the New Prophecy;[33] indeed, he may have been for almost a decade. In at least one sense, the concern he betrays about the behavior of virgins fits in precisely with his concern about the authority of charismatic prophecy. Prisca and Maximilla, who were both (according to one tradition[34]) married women who had left their husbands, were divinely inspired; that is, they spoke the word of God in spite of themselves. The virgins of Tertullian's North African church, in contrast, claimed a special avenue to sanctity without the benefit of having been chosen by God to speak for Him. Rather than submitting themselves to God's will, they appeared to be demanding that he pay special attention to them. In his *Exhortation to Chastity*, Tertullian reports one of Prisca's pronouncements dealing with the experience of prophecy: "Purification [*purificantia*] creates harmony; then they see visions, and if they bow their heads, they hear clear voices, wholesome and mysterious."[35] As Jensen notes, *purificantia* is often translated as "sexual purity," although this may not have been what Prisca intended; importantly, however, *purificantia*, sexual or otherwise, is at least imaginably available to both sexes, to the chastely married and to the widowed, while Tertullian's objection to the behavior of the unveiled virgins is founded in their claim for a status separate from and superior to those others. Prisca's dictum also emphasizes humility—those who see visions bow their heads—which is precisely what Tertullian accuses the virgins of Carthage of lacking. It is thus less surprising than it may initially appear that Tertullian reports this particular saying. Similarly, it is worth noting that there were certain charismatically gifted female members of the Carthaginian community of whom Tertullian clearly approved wholeheartedly. In *On the Soul* he describes "a sister who has been given the grace to receive revelations, which she experiences in church during the celebration to the glory of the Lord through ecstasy in the Spirit"; this woman, however, does not speak during the divine service, but only sees and hears. She functions as a receptacle for divine inspiration rather than as a mouthpiece for it. The mouthpiece, in fact, will prove to be Tertullian himself: "When the congregation was dismissed after the completion of worship, she said, in accordance with her custom of reporting to us what she saw (this is, you see, also very carefully described so that it can also be tested): 'Among other things, the soul was shown to me. . .' " (9). Tertullian authorizes her visions by writing them down, just as she authorizes his teaching on the soul by seeing it. Jensen notes that both in this text and in

On the Veiling of Virgins, accepted revelations are remarkably convenient for the author: "the prophetesses are shown exactly what Tertullian would like to prove: in one case the 'corporeality' of the soul, in the other the duty of veiling—even the exact length of the veil is 'revealed'! Apparently Tertullian reserved for himself the testing of the prophecies. By what authority he derives this right for himself remains unclear."[36] The authority by which Tertullian derives this power is actually quite clear, if we glance back once more to Paul, who admits that a woman may prophesy, but forbids her from discussing her prophecies, or those of others, in church: "As in all the churches of the saints, the women should keep silence in the churches...If they want to learn anything, they should ask their menfolk at home" (I Cor. 14:34–35).

Tertullian's objection to special status for virgins is based not only on his sense of their inalienable sexuality, or on his reading of Paul, however, but on what sometimes seems to be an almost personal sense of injustice:

It would be really unfair, if women, who are in all things subject to men, were to display an honorific mark of their virginity, which would encourage our brothers to admire and ogle and praise them, while so many male virgins, voluntary eunuchs [*viri autem tot virgines, tot spadones voluntarii*] must go along with their virtue concealed, bearing no sign which would make them, too, remarkable...[here follows satirical speculation on what outward signs male virgins might choose—rooster feathers, tattoos, *veils* perhaps?]...I am certain that if the Holy Spirit had approved such a mark, it would have done so for men and not women, since above and beyond the [natural] authority of sex, it would have been more appropriate to honor males for the quality of their chastity itself. Because the male sex is more eager [for sex] and hotter than the female, the effort of restraining this greater passion would be more worthy of display, if display of virginity were an honor. Indeed, is not chastity superior to virginity, both that of widows and that of those who have mutually agreed to renounce the shared injury? Virginity is maintained by grace, after all, chastity by virtue. It is a great struggle for anyone who has had sex to give it up. On the other hand, if you have never known the pleasures which result from desire, it is easy not to feel desire at all, since the experience of those pleasures is not there to work against you like an enemy [*cuius autem concupiscendi ignoraveris fructum, facile non concupisces, adversarium non habens, concupiscentiam fructus*]. So why would God not have approved some such honor for men rather than for women, either because they are closer to Him, "in this own image," or because they work harder at it? If He has decreed nothing to the male, even less should there be anything for the female. (*Virgins* 10.1–5)

At this point it may be salutary to review the progress of Tertullian's argument: women should wear veils in church "on account of the angels," that is, because they are sexual beings; virgins, far from being exempted from this command, need veils more than most, because they are even more sexually appealing; if women were not to wear veils, this would be tantamount to granting them some special mark of honor; if any one were to have some special mark of honor, it should be men, both because they are truly in God's image, and because their desires are more powerful than those of women, and they therefore deserve more credit for overcoming them; and besides, God likes men better. Even in a discursive culture that understood logic to be only one of a range of possible modes of persuasion, and far from the most useful, the mental gymnastics of this argument are breathtaking. Tertullian bases his case upon two paradoxical assertions; to begin with, the absence of a veil, that is the absence of the sign of a certain condition, becomes itself a sign, one that can only unfairly be denied to men. Then, in a curious reflection of this process, Tertullian creates a hypothetical category of male virgins, "voluntary eunuchs" who, if they existed, ought to be allowed to claim the same distinction as female virgins. Just as the absence of the veil becomes itself a sign, male virgins are created by a sort of reifying invocation of lack. Female virgins are, by a definition that comes to us from the Latin, intact, untouched; male virgins, *spadones voluntarii*, are equally definitively touched, mutilated.[37] Tertullian quickly abandons the rather slippery parallel he has established (his imaginary voluntary eunuchs are rapidly turning into drag queens, wearing veils and feathers) and retreats to firmer ground: all women are subject to men in every way, and therefore have no right to claim special status in any circumstances.

Behind Tertullian's verbal pyrotechnics lies what seems to be a very real fear that claiming one special honor might lead to more. If virgins could reject the veil, arguing that they were not subject to one of the Pauline injunctions, there was nothing to prevent them rejecting the rest and claiming, in the name of their virginity, a greater role in the church: " 'It is not permitted for a woman to speak in church', or to teach, or to baptize, or to make the offering, or to claim for herself a role in any other masculine office, that is to say in any priestly function. Are any of these offices then permitted to a virgin?. . .Clearly, no honor of this sort is granted to the virgin on account of her position" (9.1–3). Even more powerfully than *On Baptism*, *On the Veiling of Virgins* suggests that there may have been those in Tertullian's milieu who were arguing or even agitating for feminine access to sacerdotal function. Having successfully associated Thecla with the monstrous Cainite woman and then used the rumor of interpolation in the Pauline canon to dismiss her, here he turns to arguments based on grammar (a standard rhetorical move) to make his case that "virgin" is merely a subset of "woman" and therefore not excused from the apostle's dictate: "If indeed 'man is the head of woman' the same goes for the virgin, from whom the married woman is derived—unless the virgin is some sort of monstrous third sex with a head of its own" (*Virgins* 7.2). The technique is the same; first he makes the threatening female a monster, and then he makes her disappear by invoking the authority of the word, of the rhetorical skills that are his by right both as an educated Roman male and as a Christian practitioner of exegesis. Tertullian's solution in *On the Veiling of Virgins* is admirably simple: if women are making such dangerous claims on the basis of their virginity, render them no longer virgin and they will no longer be a problem; if a virgin revealed is no longer a virgin, then reveal her. When Tertullian has finished with them, the virgins of Carthage are virgins no more: "Every public exposure of a good virgin is a rape. And yet, it is less awful to suffer a physical rape, because that at least is in the nature of things" (3.7). Where, one wonders, does rhetorical rape stand on the continuum of awfulness?

Throughout later works such as *On the Veiling of Virgins* and *On the Soul*, Tertullian appears to be trying to reconcile the actuality of the New Prophecy with what he understands to be the proper and natural ordering of a religious society. As Susanna Elm notes, "what marks the early Montanist movement is its egalitarianism: both women and men were engaged in its leadership."[38] Catholicism, meanwhile, was "developing into an episcopal imperial church" characterized by hierarchy in all realms of life, but especially by hierarchies of gender.[39] Tertullian, a true believer both in the continuing possibility of prophecy and in the "natural" or God-given hierarchies that subordinated women to men, seems to have been struggling hard to bring these two perspectives into balance. Perhaps the near-hysterical tone of some of his late works can be best understood as the expression of Tertullian's sense of being trapped between his devotion to the radically antinomian New Prophecy on the one hand and his own strong impulses toward category, order, and hierarchy on the other; the first of these could not help but threaten the second, although this is a conflict that Tertullian nowhere admits or confronts.

Virgin Apostle

If we return after this long excursus to consider the dreadful example of Thecla in greater detail, it becomes clear that Tertullian's movement away from Catholicism and toward Montanism would in no way have altered his early assessment of the virgin apostle. In sharp contradistinction to Perpetua, the (probably) legendary Thecla submits to no one at all, not even to death. Thecla survives her martyrdom. Nor does she submit herself to divine inspiration by speaking as an inspired prophetess, laying claim instead to a different kind of verbal authority. Thecla, in fact, violates all late antique models for proper feminine behavior and thus challenges the socially conservative ecclesiastical hierarchy which Tertullian was trying so hard to establish in the first years after his conversion to Christianity, and which, as we have seen, he did not renounce even after embracing the New Prophecy.

The popularity of the *Acts of Thecla* is demonstrated by its wide distribution; over forty Greek manuscripts survive, as well as Latin translations and Syriac, Armenian and Slavonic versions.[40] The tale tells how Thecla, a noble girl engaged to be married to a suitable young man, sits at her window and hears the Apostle Paul preach in a courtyard below. Moved by his words, she abandons her family to join Paul in prison. She is condemned to be burnt at the stake, but delivered by a miraculous hailstorm. Without being invited, she accompanies Paul on his journey to Antioch, though he refuses to baptize her. In Antioch, she rejects and humiliates an important citizen who has fallen in love with her, and is condemned again, this time to be eaten by wild animals; believing herself to be about to die, she baptizes herself by leaping into a pool full of man-eating seals. A flash of lightning kills the seals, and Thecla rejoins Paul briefly before embarking on a long and glorious career as an apostle, although this career is not recounted in any detail.

In *The Revolt of the Widows*, Stevan Davies describes the triple nature of Thecla's trials: "First, she must avoid the advances of her betrothed husband and the Syrian Alexander, who desire her as a female. Second, she must endure the torments of civil authorities, who punish her because of her determined sexual continence. Third, she must struggle to break through Paul's misapprehension of her as nothing more than a beautiful woman, weak and subject to temptation."[41] This description overlooks the emphasis placed upon Thecla's struggle to gain an independent and authoritative voice, a struggle that may have seemed particularly meaningful if the original author of the *Acts of Thecla* was, as Davies argues, a woman.[42] The story of Thecla is the story of a young woman who, by suffering publicly for her religion, gains the right to speak publicly concerning that religion, to function as a missionary and apostle.

To be an apostle is by definition to be a public figure, one who speaks and suffers in front of witnesses and as a witness. Public speech in the defense of one abstract ideal or another was, as we have seen, a common, even a definitive feature of late antique urban life. Public disputation was both a spectator sport and a profession, and the Christian prophets and preachers who began to multiply at the end of the first century were only one subset of a whole culture of peripatetic speakers. What made the Christians different was their willingness to suffer more than humiliation for the sake of their point of view. From the very origin of the genre, the canonical Acts of the Apostles, two concepts are linked: the aggressive and powerful use of words is balanced by a complete physical passivity under punishment and torture. Stephen, the very first martyr, dies because of what he says and how he says it: "Now Stephen, filled with grace and power, was working great wonders and signs among the people. Certain members of the so-called Synagogue of Freedmen, Cyrenaians and Alexandrians, and people from Cilicia and Asia, came forward debating [*sudzetountes*] with Stephen, but they could not withstand the spirit with which he spoke" (Acts 6:8–10). The verb *sudzeteo* means to search or to examine in the sense of looking for truth or examining a statement; it also means to dispute, and thus identifies Stephen's discourse with the norms of philosophical contention. Stephen's long speech on the Holy Spirit, however, with its citations of Old Testament instances of the persecution of prophets, is not a defense or an attempt at persuasion but a calculated provocation, which infuriates his accusers: "they cried out with a loud voice and stopped their ears and rushed together upon him. Then they cast him out of the city and stoned him. . ." (Acts 7:57–58).

The connection between physical passivity and verbal authority is made even more strongly in the *Apocryphal Acts*. While Paul submits with complete humility to decapitation, bending his neck to make the executioner's blow easier, a gesture we have already noted in the case of Perpetua, his words have enormous power. They convince the Romans, Cestus and Longus, that he will rise from the dead, and, when he does, they even affect the mad Emperor Nero. The text makes it very clear that it is Paul's words more than his appearance that inspire the emperor to release other Christian prisoners: "when Nero heard [it] he was greatly troubled, and commanded the prisoners to be set free" (*Paul* 263). The *Acts of Peter* makes an even clearer connection between verbal power and actual passivity. The martyr addresses himself: "The hour has come for you, Peter, to deliver your body to those who are taking it. Take it, whose business it is. Of you, executioners, I ask to crucify me with head downwards and not otherwise. And the reason I shall explain to those who listen" (425).[43] His explanation, which begins only after he has been crucified as requested, links the revelation he is about to make to his complete lack of physical power; he goes on to make absolutely explicit the connection between his words, the Word, and martyrdom: "For you ought to come to the cross of Christ, who is the extended Word, the one and only, concerning whom the Spirit says, 'For what else is Christ than the Word, the sound of God?' The Word is this upright tree on which I am crucified; the sound, however, is the crossbeam, namely the nature of man; and the nail which holds the crossbeam to the upright in the middle is the conversion and repentance of man" (425). Peter's final words stress once and for all the verbal quality of

Christian devotion: "we praise you, we thank you, we confess you in glorifying you, though we are weak" (426). Because we are weak would have been even more accurate.

Peter and Paul in the *Apocryphal Acts* start out as apostles, as public speakers, and thinkers, engaging in intellectual and moral debate with pagans in the open spaces of the ancient world. Paul, in the canonical Acts, is represented as speaking not only in synagogues from Antioch to Jerusalem, but in much more public places such as the Areopagus in Athens, where he is said to have preached to Epicurean and Stoic philosophers (Acts 17:16–33); whether Paul actually engaged in such disputation or not, "the author of Luke-Acts thought it useful to depict the Apostle of the Gentiles in such a light."[44] In the context of the late first century, Christian missionaries must have seemed little different from any of the other philosophers whose voices were part of the public discourse and often bore witness to a particular philosophical truth. Nero and Domitian, both infamous in the Christian tradition as persecutors of the apostles, also persecuted philosophers.[45]

Public disputation, whether engaged in by philosophers of the Second Sophistic movement or by early Christians, was and always had been a masculine realm of discourse. The names of a handful of female philosophers survive from antiquity, but they are always curiosities rather than models, viewed with suspicion and an inevitably prurient interest from Aspasia, Pericles' concubine, to Hypatia, head of the philosophical school at Alexandria in the fourth century, murdered under obscure circumstances by a Christian mob.[46] Like the agora or forum, the law courts, that other arena of public speech, were forbidden to women. Ulpian, a contemporary of Tertullian, insisted in his exhaustive encyclopedia of Roman Law that women should not appear in court because to do so would be to infringe upon the functions of men; he traces this prohibition back to the dreadful example of a certain "Carfania, who by brazenly making applications and annoying the magistrate gave rise to the edict."[47] While the Roman and Hellenistic worlds were certainly not without important and powerful women who might even function as patrons of civic games or civic building projects, and who might in private display extraordinary learning, they were effectively banned from any form of public speech, by the overwhelming power of social convention. With the advent of Christianity, however, the issue of women and public speech became much more complex. As Gillian Clark puts it, "the [Graeco-Roman] philosopher could take for granted that his audience thought that women should be given the same moral training as men, but not the same education in gymnastics and rhetoric. . .But Christian philosophers could not escape so easily."[48] Because of its emphasis on spiritual equality before God, Christianity appeared to offer women access to a form of public existence and verbal authority that they could never possess under classical paganism or Judaism. This is the power to which Thecla aspires in the *Acts of Thecla*, and the power that Tertullian is so determined to deny to her and to all women.

It is commonplace to argue that the passion of the virgin martyr is more affecting than that of her male counterpart because of her greater physical weakness; the fragility conferred upon her by her gender is supposed to make her more pathetic. While this may be partially true in the *Passion of Perpetua*, at least in the redactor's account of Perpetua's death, it is not the case for Thecla. The connection between passive martyrdom and aggressive eloquence works differently for Thecla than it does for Peter and Paul, and her gender lies at the root of this difference, but not in any essentializing way. For Peter and Paul, the progression of the narrative is from the marketplace to the arena; their speech brings about their martyrdom. For Thecla, excluded because she is a woman from the scene of public discourse, the process cannot operate in the same way. In order for her to become a witness to divine truth, she must be transformed and the transformation is a social one, marked by a movement from silence to speech through martyrdom, rather than ending in martyrdom.

Thecla begins as a passive listener, as the recipient of another's words almost by accident: "while Paul was thus speaking in the midst of the assembly in the house of Onesiphorus, a virgin (named) Thecla—her mother was Theocleia—who was betrothed to a man (named) Thamyris, sat at a nearby window and listened night and day to the word of the virgin life as it was spoken by Paul" (*Acts of Thecla* 240). Paul's words produce an almost trance-like silence in Thecla; her mother worries because she "sticks to the window like a spider, is (moved) by his words and gripped by a new desire and a fearful passion" (240). She does not respond at all when her mother or her fiancé address her, and so they have Paul arrested. The first independent action Thecla takes in the story is wordless: "Thecla in the night took off her bracelets and gave them to the door-keeper, and when the door was opened for her she went off to the prison. To the gaoler she gave a silver mirror and so went in to Paul and sat at his feet and heard (him proclaim) the mighty acts of God" (242). By giving away her bracelets and her mirror, objects which are strongly identified both with her social class and her gender, Thecla purchases the right to go on listening to Paul's words. She has not yet, apparently, earned the right to speak words of her own. When the two of them are brought before the tribunal on the following day, once again it is Paul who speaks; Thecla, when asked why she will not marry Thamyris, remains silent. This silence stands in curiously marked contrast to Perpetua's *Christiana sum* and suggests that Thecla's way of bearing witness will be equally different from that of the historical martyr. The narrative continues: "And when she did not answer, Theocleia her mother cried out, saying: 'Burn the lawless one! Burn her that is no bride in the midst of the theatre, that all the women who have been taught by this man may be afraid!' " (242). Throughout the whole *auto-da-fé* that follows, Thecla does not betray a moment of weakness; rather, it is the governor who weeps, moved not by her pathos but because he "marveled at the power that was in her" (243). Nor does she speak, except to comment to herself (and apparently *sotto voce*) upon the appearance of "the Lord sitting in the form of Paul. . .she looked steadily at him; but he departed into the heavens" (242). This apparition provides one of the first indications of just what a failure Paul will be as a mentor to Thecla, and can even be read as her own unconscious recognition of his lack of commitment to her. Throughout the narrative, as many readers before me have noted, Paul will desert Thecla in her moment of need, forcing her to rely upon herself and God.[49] Sure enough, the rain comes down, the fire is put out, and Thecla escapes to join Paul in the desert. Only now does she gain the power of speech, and her very first line in the text refers back to her incomplete (but not failed?) martyrdom: "I am seeking after Paul, for I was saved from the fire" (243).

Paul's reaction when Thecla is restored to him indicates a shift in the relationship which the text has previously established between the two major characters and their access to divine knowledge:

> But when she came to the tomb, Paul had bent his knees and was praying and saying: "Father of Christ, let not the fire touch Thecla, but be merciful to her for she is thine!" But she standing behind him, cried out: "Father, who didst make heaven and earth, the Father of thy beloved Son [Jesus Christ], I praise thee that thou didst save me from the fire, that I might see Paul!" And as Paul arose he saw her and said: "O God the knower of hearts, Father of our Lord Jesus Christ, I praise thee that thou hast so speedily [accomplished] what I asked, and hast hearkened unto me." (*Acts of Thecla* 243)

Paul has received no foreknowledge of Thecla's release, a fact that the narrator highlights by having her appear behind him: it is difficult not to imagine the apostle starting at the sound of Thecla's voice. Moreover, his prayer of thanksgiving is not only perfunctory, it betrays a somewhat desperate attempt to reestablish control over the situation; the narration of the scene, in which Paul's praise of the speed with which his prayer has been answered is juxtaposed with the reader's knowledge that Thecla has in fact been free for some time before the prayer was made, seems deliberately ironic, and even slightly comical. From this point on, Thecla is an active verbal participant in her own destiny. She declares her intentions, and will not be dissuaded, even by the objections of her unwilling mentor. Paul's words, on the other hand, go from being ineffectual against the will of Thecla, to downright deceitful. In Antioch, a Syrian named Alexander attempts to buy Thecla from Paul (presumably mistaking her for his concubine). Paul's denial of Thecla here ("I do not know the woman of whom thou dost speak, nor is she mine" (243)) has clear echoes of Peter's denial of Christ; the second half of the statement, at least, is true, but this hardly redeems Paul, who vanishes when Alexander embraces Thecla. Her words, on the other hand, appeal publicly to her social and religious status: " 'Force not the stranger, force not the handmaid of God! Among the Iconians I am one of the first, and because I did not wish to marry Thamyris I have been cast out of the city.' And taking hold of Alexander she ripped his cloak, took off the crown from his head, and made him a laughing-stock" (243). This moment crystallizes the threat to the social order that Thecla embodies, but it also emphasizes her verbal autonomy. She claims an identity for herself, stranger and handmaid of God, which establishes her as a missionary, she asserts her power to choose her own destiny ("I did not wish to marry Thamyris") and she draws from this assertion the power to physically assault Alexander. The power to define herself in words is immediately linked to the ability to defend herself from the threat of assault.

If Thecla's first failed martyrdom in Iconium marks the moment from which she will claim the right to speak publicly, then her second, in Antioch, serves not only to confirm her personal power and authority but to demonstrate the potential power of the unified speech of women in a group.[50] The confrontation, as scarcely a reader of the text has failed to notice, is set up as a veritable battle between the sexes: a lioness carries Thecla on her back and defends her against the male beasts, and the lecherous Alexander provides, as a clear substitute for himself, a pair of bad-tempered bulls "with red-hot irons beneath their bellies" to tear Thecla apart.[51] The women in the audience form a sort of chorus of dismay, shouting when Thecla is condemned to the beasts, and weeping when the brave lioness dies.

The reactions of the women in the audience suggest something more than sympathy, however. They function as a *conclamatio*, an acclamation, which was in the Roman world of late antiquity a very specific form of public speech with definite religious and civic implications:

> The most widely attested function of acclamations. . .is that properly described as acclamation—the honoring of an individual. The simplest form of such acclamations gives a man a particular epithet, just as in the formulae honoring the gods—so-and-so is great, or good, or patriotic, *philopatris*; it can be shown how such acclamations by public assemblies underlie the

terminology of the abundant decrees with which the cities of the Greek East honored prominent citizens.[52]

Acclamation of individuals was a well-established practice under the empire, especially in Asia Minor from the second to the fifth centuries. Emperors might be acclaimed (more or less spontaneously) when they appeared in the circus, as might the governor of a city or province, someone who had built a new aqueduct, or a gladiator who had performed particularly well in the arena. Public acclamations were often recorded by stenographers and appended to records of legislative proceedings, or inscribed on monuments or milestones.[53] Acclamation is constituted by voices speaking in unison, often in ritual and repetitive language, and indicated in description or transcription by phrases such as *mia phone*, "in one voice." As Roueché notes, such unanimity is understood to be divinely inspired, and attested in both pagan and Christian settings: "it is as manifestations of a divine impulse, as well as of public opinion, that acclamations are significant; and this is most important of all in the validation of the authority of leaders, both secular and ecclesiastical."[54] The language of Thecla's female partisans demonstrates exactly the kind of repetition and unison characteristic of *conclamatio*:

> "An evil judgment! A godless judgment!. . .O god, an impious judgment is come to pass in this city. . .May the city perish for this lawlessness! Slay us all, Proconsul! A bitter sight, an evil judgment!". . .And the crowd of the women raised a great shout. . . .And straightway the governor issued a decree, saying: "I release to you Thecla, the pious handmaid of God." But all the women cried out with a loud voice, and *as with one mouth* gave praise to God, saying: "One is God, who has delivered Thecla!," *so that all the city was shaken by the sound.* (244–45)

The locution *eis theos*, God is one, is a common opening for acclamations "over a long period in pagan, Jewish and Christian contexts."[55] In the real world of the second century, of course, the acclamation of a woman by women would not have carried any political weight at all. Thecla's recognition by the women of Antioch is purest fantasy, wishful thinking, perhaps, on the part of the (female?) author of the *Acts of Thecla*. It is the sort of fantasy that would have seemed like a nightmare to Tertullian.

Thecla makes her longest speech in the text after she has been recalled from the arena, as though her sufferings there have authorized it. For the first time, in response to the governor's question as to who and what she is, her words take the form of something more than a prayer:

> I am a handmaid of the living God. . .I have believed in him in whom God is well pleased, His Son. For his sake not one of the beasts touched me.

For he alone is the goal of salvation and the foundation of immortal life. To the storm-tossed he is a refuge, to the oppressed relief, to the despairing shelter; in a word, whoever does not believe in him shall not live, but die forever. (245–46)

Thecla is beginning to preach, beginning to use language designed to move and affect her hearers, using metaphor to make her point. It is essential here to note that not only does Thecla convert the audience (this will become standard in later virgin martyr tales) and the procurator, who recognizes her status as "handmaid of God" (this will be unheard of in later virgin martyr tales), but that the acclamatory formula carries with it a public recognition that is immediately ratified by Queen Tryphaena, who supplies Thecla with the other essential component of civic authority, money: "Come inside, and I will assign to thee all that is mine" (246). Thecla's ministry will be well funded.

If the acclamation of the women and her adoption by Queen Tryphaena suggests a degree of civic recognition for Thecla, the clothing she assumes implies another form of authority. The governor offers her garments and tells her to put them on, as a mark of her release from punishment. Thecla makes it perfectly clear, however, that he is not the one who is clothing her: "But she said: 'He who clothed me when I was naked among the beasts shall clothe me with salvation in the day of judgment.' And taking the garments, she put them on" (246). In the house of Tryphaena, she makes another significant sartorial statement, transforming "her mantle into a cloak after the fashion of men" (246) before setting out on her mission. This assumption of clothing "in the fashion of men" has nothing to do with a rejection of femininity; rather, what Thecla is doing is assuming the *tribon*, the mantle of the philosopher. Justin Martyr wore such a cloak after his conversion, to indicate that Christianity was the true philosophy; Tertullian advised the (male) Christians of Carthage to assume a similar garment in *On the Mantle*; and Hypatia of Alexandria wore one to indicate her position as head of the School of Platonic Philosophy. The mantle is an identifying mark, a provocation and invitation to disputation and philosophical discourse, the polar opposite to the virgin's veil that separates her from society and symbolically muffles her voice as it hides her body. The philosopher's cloak, especially one converted from a woman's dress, is the only imaginable garb for a virgin-apostle, and when Paul sees her wearing it, and surrounded by a crowd "of young men and maidservants," he is taken aback. She announces her intention ("I am going to Iconium") and he finally, albeit reluctantly, gives her his blessing: "Go and teach the word of God." Paul is never at ease with the phenomenon he has created in Thecla, although all she has done is to take literally the words she heard him pronounce long ago in Iconium: "Blessed are the bodies of virgins, for they shall be well pleasing to God, and shall not lose the reward of their purity. For the word of the Father shall be for them a work of salvation in the day of his Son, and they shall have rest for ever and ever" (246). Thecla evidently understands these words as authorizing her to undertake a work of salvation in the temporal world, in the name of her virginity, much as the virgins of Carthage saw their virginity as granting them a particular status in Tertullian's church. It seems not to have occurred to Paul that talking about women might have been construed as talking to them, as giving them a mission. The Paul of the *Acts of Thecla* is more comfortable with the abstract concept of the virgin body than with an actual, embodied virgin.

Having at last received a formal apostolic mission, Thecla returns to Iconium where she confronts her mother, and to the cell where she first sat at Paul's feet, as though laying the ghosts of her past. Then she carries on, right out of the story, into Seleucia where she converts multitudes and lives to a very old age. Later versions of the story add embellishments: the aged Thecla is pursued by rapists and swallowed up by the living rock, or envied by pagan doctors whose livelihood she threatens by performing cures. In the fourth century, the *Acts of Thecla* were rewritten into a Greek *Life of Thecla*, which alters the narrative in small ways, which nonetheless amount to bowdlerization and indicate the particular aspects of the tale that appeared subversive or threatening. Tertullian might not have objected so strenuously to this retelling, which softens the attitude and muffles the voice of its protagonist: "While the proconsul tried, with such gentleness and good will, to make the young girl change her mind, Thecla said not a word, believing that it was against womanly decency and virginal shame to speak a word in public and make a virgin's voice heard among such a lot of people."[56] When the women in the audience exclaim at Thecla's struggles, they are not making a coherent political statement, but reacting out of titillation: "And the female sex could not be silent when it saw this marvel, for the sex rushes to meet pleasure and flees fear."[57] Perhaps most significantly of all, the crowd that roars out to save Thecla is no longer a crowd of women, but one indicated by more neutral pronouns. The editor of the text, who carefully points out the *Life*'s misogynist elaborations on the *Acts of Thecla*, believes that they exist to prevent Thecla from becoming a model who might inspire other women to preach or baptize.[58] Such revisions, in other words, are necessary precisely because of the power inherent in a figure as transgressive as Thecla.

The *Life* tells the story of Thecla as someone like Tertullian might have rewritten it. While the *Acts of Thecla* represents the saint's choice of virginity as both socially and politically radical in its challenge both to the heterosocial norms of marriage and family and to the spiritual and temporal authority of men, the *Life* makes its heroine a much more conventionally feminine figure, modest, silent, and submissive. This version of the saint resurfaces in even more adulterated form in *Les Vierges Martyres*, a beautiful, red-bound volume from 1903, which came into my possession a year or two ago. In this book, which was presented, according to the bookplate, to a fourteen-year-old convent schoolgirl for excelling in religion class, Thecla does not baptize herself; she does not undertake a preaching mission; she is nothing but a virtuous and beautiful Christian girl rescued in the arena by an affectionate and gentle lioness. In chapter 2, I will chart the limitations and definitions imposed upon the idea of the virgin martyr by male writers of the fourth and fifth centuries, limitations that defined a genre by reinscribing masculinist and heterosexist social norms; such stories, told and retold through the centuries, would eventually culminate in bowdlerized narratives appropriate for pious children. Successive chapters explore the perennial tension and oscillation between the image of the silent and sentimentalized martyr whose representation serves the interests of patriarchy, and the voice of the aggressively eloquent virgin, which is more rarely and much less systematically raised to tell her own tale in her own interest. I cannot resist, however, taking a moment to imagine the career of Thecla as the author of the *Acts of Thecla* might have continued it. One can almost see her, wrapped in her philosopher's cloak, sitting by a fountain in one of the small Seleucian cities. She is disputing the meaning of the life of Christ with some chance met opponent, pagan, Christian, or Jew, and her supporters, male and female, sit around her, muttering approval for a point well made, as the heat of the day finally fades and the stars begin to come out.

CHAPTER 2

ANDROGYNOUS VIRGINS AND THE THREAT OF RAPE IN THE FOURTH CENTURY

In Caesarea, in Palestine, in 308 or 309, a virgin from Gaza was arrested and publicly tortured, not for being a Christian, although she was one, but because, horrified by stories of women sexually abused by the Roman authorities, she had dared to suggest that any emperor who appointed such ministers was a tyrant. Her crime, in other words, was political and not religious; she had spoken treason. In the crowd that witnessed her torture stood another virgin named Valentina. She shouted out to the executioners, demanding to know how long her "sister" was to be brutalized. As she must have known would happen, she too was arrested and dragged up to the tribunal, where she kicked over the altar, scattering the coals from the brazier upon which Christians were invited to cast incense in honor of the emperor. Evidently, this gave the authorities an idea: Valentina and the woman from Gaza were burned to death together.[1]

The sufferings of Valentina and her companion are recounted by Eusebius; if he was not an eyewitness to these particular deaths, he knew people who were, and he composed *The Martyrs of Palestine* at least in part as a memorial to those friends and acquaintances of his who had died during the Great Persecution of Diocletian.[2] His account, in other words, is as close as we are likely to get to the actual martyrdom of real virgins, and it has several features that ought to claim our attention.[3] To begin with, what is completely intolerable to these women is not the threat of death but what Eusebius calls "the threat of prostitution" (*Martyrs* 8.5). One method of intimidation employed by the Roman authorities against the Christian minority was evidently sexual humiliation, almost certainly including rape. Virgins were inevitably most vulnerable to this particular form of torture, because their virginity itself constituted both a provocation and a prohibition; violating a virgin was, then as now, not just the violation of a body but of an entire system of religious or cultural taboos.[4] Next, neither woman is initially arrested for being a Christian, but rather for criticizing, either implicitly or explicitly, imperial abuse of power. Valentina reveals herself as a Christian once she is on the dais, but she accuses well before she confesses; like the virgin from Gaza, she is motivated by sympathy on behalf of another woman. Finally, these two very public deaths imply lives with a public aspect as well. The treason of the woman from Gaza was spoken in some place where it could be overheard, and Valentina was no recluse but someone who chose to be in the marketplace at this particular time and under these circumstances. There were many who hid during the persecutions, or who fled the cities only to return when it was safe, but Valentina chose to stay and chose to die, publicly and independently. For Eusebius, such women are "female in body, male in determination" (8.5); he has no other vocabulary with which to indicate this kind of courage, and his approving promotion of the two martyrs to the rank of honorary men will be echoed in the works of many later writers.[5] A different way of understanding such heroism, however, would be to see Valentina and her companion as part of the tradition established by Thecla who, as I argued in chapter 1, asserted her right to public speech and public presence by rejecting the restrictions placed by patriarchal society upon her gender, and not by rejecting her identity as woman. Valentina speaks up for her "sister" very much as Tryphaena and the anonymous women in the crowd spoke up on behalf of the heroine of the *Acts of Thecla*. They do not deny that they are women; rather, they participate in the spirit of the legendary Thecla, moving freely in public spaces, claiming kinship with each other and the right to denounce crimes committed against other members of their sex precisely because they are women.

By the end of the fourth century, when persecution had been replaced by increasingly acrid theological controversy and Christians had developed the habit of denouncing each other as viciously as the pagans had ever done,[6] the life of the virgin had been irrevocably altered. It is impossible to imagine a virgin's voice ringing out in accusatory tones in any public meeting place in Rome in the 380s or 390s; she has been relegated to the private world and her voice effectively muffled. For Ambrose, author of several tracts on virginity and brother of the professed virgin Marcellina, the modesty of the virgin can only be expressed through silence. For Jerome, the virgin must at all costs avoid the outside world. "Ever let the privacy of your chamber guard you. . .Dinah went out, and she was corrupted" (Letter 22.25),[7] he wrote to the sixteen-year-old Eustochium. To the mother of an infant who had been promised to the virgin life before her conception, he wrote in even more insistent terms: "Never let her go out, or those who roam the city may find her and strike and wound her and tearing away the garment of her modesty leave her naked in her blood" (Letter 107.7). Rome may indeed have been a dangerous city in 400 C.E., but there is more at work here than concern for a young girl's physical safety. In the course of the fourth century, the role and meaning of the virgin, like almost everything else about Christianity, had changed. In the days of the Church triumphant, the active virgin apostle in the mold of Thecla was superseded, albeit never completely, by the passive virgin martyr who would be represented by Agnes in Ambrose's *On Virgins*, the first Latin tract on virginity in more than a century.

One reason for this transformation is obvious. In Greek, *martureo* means "I bear witness"; the victims of pagan persecution, male and female, bore witness both verbally and physically not only to the power of their convictions and their God, but also to the injustice of the temporal powers that oppressed them. After 312, when toleration was established by Constantine's Edict of Milan, and even more after 325, when the emperor himself presided over the Council of Nicaea, Christian men like Eusebius, who became bishop of Caesarea, were no longer in opposition to temporal powers. Rather, they had become the agents of temporal power. There were still, under Constantine and his successors, officials who inflicted savage punishment; but now it was as likely as not that both judge and prisoner would be Christian. This curious state of affairs was acknowledged in the mid-fourth century by a papal decree barring those who had served as magistrates from the priesthood because they would inevitably have been involved in the shedding of blood.[8] Women, of course, were never eligible to become magistrates, although they might still be victims; Jerome tells the tale of a Christian woman unjustly accused of adultery who survived mutilations quite as dreadful as those of the martyrs of Palestine. But in a world where justice was administered, often savagely, by Christian men, the image of Christian women denouncing judicial injustice was increasingly problematic. As Tertullian had discovered a century earlier, the very "manly" qualities that might be admirable in the arena could be disconcerting within one's congregation.

The triumph of Christianity created other problems as well. The Church had always positioned itself in opposition to society; now, virtually overnight, it *was* society. Martyrdom had been a radical but unmistakable way of separating *us* from *them*, true Christians from mere poseurs. In the fourth century, something else was needed to fulfill that function, and that something else would be asceticism, a discipline based in withdrawal from the world and mortification of the flesh. Asceticism, whether practiced in the Egyptian desert or in the back bedrooms of wealthy women at Rome, set a particularly high value on sexual renunciation. The ideal of virginity, however, was to prove deeply perplexing for men and women alike. On the one hand, Christian writers were determined to make virginity something it never had been in the pagan world, a state that could characterize both men and women; on the other, they fetishized the absolute quality of female virginity over and above such conditional qualities as chastity and continence, imagining an ideal Christian body that was mapped upon female rather than male biology. The two modes of discourse which evolve out of this paradoxical emphasis on the virgin body are always in tension with each other even when they are not explicitly oppositional. The first, which we will find exemplified by Methodius of Olympus, attempted to reimagine the concept of virginity, making it a fully androgynous quality. In Methodius's *Symposium*, the figure of Thecla, who had embodied a radical reimagining of the capacity of women at the end of the second century, embodies what is perhaps an even more radical imagining of gender itself. Implicit in Methodius's revision of virginity is the assumption that gender is not essential, does not define the nature of human souls, and is fully transcendable. In the Latin West after 312, on the other hand, virginity, with its implicit promise of equality between the sexes, increasingly became what it had been for Tertullian, a threat to ecclesiastical hierarchy. It was all very well for women to behave like men when facing imminent death; now that the Church was not only legal but also powerful, however, the possibility that women might claim, on the grounds of their virgin status, the right of self-determination or even some active role in ecclesiastic life, as Thecla had done, was unthinkable. By the end of the fourth century, the legend of the virgin martyr had been rewritten from one that promised freedom from male domination to one that inculcated female submission to male authority, and especially female silence. The Latin Fathers, uncomfortable with reimagining virginity as radically as Methodius did, would content themselves instead with reimagining the virgin. The result would be the transposition of the experience of martyrdom into the literary genre of hagiography, a genre that created categories so overdetermined that neither Thecla nor Perpetua would be able to fit the ideal paradigm of feminine martyrdom.

Reimagining Virginity

In the ancient world, virginity (*parthenia* in the Greek, *virginitas* in the Latin) was an essentially social or even economic quality that enhanced the value of pagan girls on the marriage market. It was also a term almost entirely without relevance to the male of the species.[9] Classical authors had few illusions on the subject, and even in late antiquity, virginity in the pagan male is never more than an approximation. Foucault's discussion of the Hellenistic romance reproduces the double standard accepted by the

Greeks. For him, *Leucippe and Clitophon* is about "virginity exposed, assailed, doubted, slandered, safeguarded—except for an honorable, minor lapse that Clitophon allowed himself—and finally justified and certified in a sort of divine ordeal," and he goes on, apparently without irony, to note that when the lovers are reunited, "Clitophon can also say, in a symmetrical fashion: 'You will find that I have imitated your virginity, if there be any virginity in men.' "[10] Where, one might ask, is the symmetry? Leucippe's virginity is absolute, intact. Clitophon's virginity, on the other hand, is heavily qualified, both by Achilles Tatius's use of the hypothetical, and by Foucault's parenthetical admission of his "honorable, minor lapse." Male virginity is, in fact, meaningless in the context of a social world where virginity defined the marriageability of girls, but never of boys.[11] Longus's *Daphnis and Chloe* represents virginity even more clearly as a definitive physical state. Daphnis is warned by the older, married woman who initiates him into sex (this is another example of what Foucault would call an honorable lapse; it involves complete sexual intercourse and the pleasure of both parties) that, unlike her, the virgin Chloe will bleed and feel pain upon penetration.

Greek and Roman medical writers described a variety of physical differences between the bodies of virgins and those of married women, and they were especially interested in determining precisely what it was that provoked pain and bleeding upon defloration. Soranus, a Greek writing in Asia Minor in the second century C.E., explains that the entrance to the vagina is narrow in virgins; penetration stretches this narrow opening and causes bleeding and pain. Soranus's description of this narrow entrance with its folds (the word he uses is *stolis, -idos* which also describes a fold in a woman's dress, as well as other folds in the flesh, such as wrinkles on the forehead) is less than perfectly explicit; he is, however, both explicit and emphatic in describing what the female genitalia do not possess:

> Some believe that a fine membrane stretched across the vagina obstructs it and that the rupture of this occurs during defloration and causes pain, or that this occurs when menstruation begins before defloration; they believe that if this remains in position, becoming thick and hard, it causes the pathological condition known as *atresis*. This is untrue. First of all, no such thing is found during dissection; second, in the case of virgins, one ought to sense it when using a vaginal probe, whereas actually the probe enters deeply.[12]

The word Soranus uses to describe the barrier whose existence he denies is *hymên*; he uses the term in the normal, Greek medical sense, familiar from Aristotle's *Natural History*, in which the word means nothing more or less than membrane: "All blooded animals possess hymens. A hymen resembles a fine textured skin. . .Hymens surround every one of the bones and every one of the viscera both in the larger and in the smaller animals. . .If cut apart, a bared hymen does not grow together again."[13] In his dismissal of the hypothetical vaginal hymen, Soranus is arguing against a contemporary belief, perhaps popular, perhaps Roman, for the existence of such a membrane stretching across the vagina on the inside. Perhaps his arguments did not appear relevant to Roman physicians. For one thing, the early age at which Roman girls were married may have permitted a belief that girls did not menstruate until intercourse had ruptured the hymen; Aline Rousselle suggests that because Roman girls might be "married at twelve, sometimes even younger, and were immediately deflowered, some of them becoming pregnant before they had had a menstrual period [the] Romans were. . . able to mistake for a universal anatomical feature what is in fact a rare malformation," that is, an imperforate hymen.[14] Soranus was unusual in that he appears to have based his anatomical descriptions upon actual observation; traditionally, physical examination was not necessarily part of diagnosis. Especially (but not exclusively) in the case of women, doctors proceeded by asking questions of their patients and by observing such external evidence as the clarity of urine or the color of the complexion.[15] In both Greece and Rome, obstetrics and gynecology were generally the province of midwives and not doctors, since feminine modesty forbade the attentions of a male doctor in intimate situations.[16] It is difficult to imagine the circumstance that might lead a girl under the age of twelve or thirteen, or her parents, for that matter, to seek the advice of a physician in a social climate in which menstruation before marriage could be interpreted as proof of loss of virginity.

Soranus's methods were not all that separated him from his contemporaries; he was unusual in his belief that young women should not be married until after they had begun to menstruate, and in fact described lifelong virginity (*diênekês parthenia*) as a healthy lifestyle, even dedicating a chapter of his book to the subject. He distinguishes between celibacy such as that of the widow or temporarily continent wife, which he calls *enkrateia*, and *diênekês parthenia*, but for him the distinction is based not upon the definitive, singular rupture of a single organ, but on a more gradual process according to which the vagina becomes accustomed to intercourse.[17] For Roman doctors, on the other hand, the virgin body was both more definite, since they imagined it as being totally sealed and defined by a single organ, and less so, since their experience of the actual bodies of real virgins seems to have been largely inferential rather than experiential.

In general, sexual moderation was recommended for both sexes in pagan late antiquity. Virginity was valuable in unmarried girls, because it laid the foundation for female chastity in marriage and thus guaranteed the legitimacy of offspring, but it was seen as a temporary condition, even in the case of the Vestal Virgins, and it was a condition exclusive to female bodies.[18] For Christians, it very quickly became something much more complicated, a state in which both the physical and the metaphysical were implicated, an ideal to which both sexes were expected to aspire, a physical condition to be permanently maintained and guarded. The shift from a moderate to an extreme vision of sexual renunciation is evident in the very first generation of Christian writing, in the asymmetry between Paul's half-hearted approval of marriage for those who can do no better—"if they are not practicing self-control, they should marry. For it is better to marry than to be aflame with passion" (I Cor. 7:9)—and his clear preference for continence—"he who refrains from marriage will do better" (I Cor. 7:38). A few decades later, the *Revelation* of John described the reward of the hundred and forty-four thousand virgins who have not "defiled themselves with women" (Rev. 14:4) and created a new ideal of masculine continence. That this ideal was modeled on one hitherto only appropriate to the female body is indicated by the fact that it could only be described in Greek by a word that had never indicated any other sort of body before: *parthenos*. Once virginity became an ideal for men as well as for women, however, the equation that had operated in the classical world, according to which virginity was a bodily category typical of the female of the species for a certain period of her life, had to be recalculated. This recalculation could move in two different directions; either one might reimagine the category of virginity as separate from that of sex, as essentially androgynous, or one might reimagine the virgin herself in such a way that, in spite of her bodily conformity with the ideal of virginity, she was barred from whatever authority or power that same ideal conferred upon men.

If anyone in the third century succeeded in imagining the androgynous virgin, it was Methodius of Olympus. We know next to nothing about Methodius. He was from Lycia, in southern Asia Minor, and Jerome described him almost a century after he died as both a bishop and a martyr. If this is true, he will have died at about the same time as Valentina and her companion.[19] His *Symposium* is both a *jeu d'esprit* in homage to Plato's text of the same name, and a serious exposition of a fairly complex and not always consistent theology. The structure of the text is more sophisticated than has generally been acknowledged, and within it sex and gender become largely irrelevant categories. The *Symposium* begins with the arrival of a woman named Gregorion at the house of her friend, Euboulion. She brings news of a debate between virgins judged by Arete, or virtue.[20] Gregorion wasn't there herself, but she has heard all the details from her friend Theopatra, who was, and so she proceeds to enlighten Euboulion. Gregorion and Euboulion pop up at irregular intervals in the text, providing occasional commentary on the arguments of the contestants, and then, in the epilogue, engage in a minor debate of their own, which Euboulion wins. The text thus establishes a *mise-en-abyme* which appears to unmoor the opinions stated from any single authority or author, but the situation is complicated by the fact that Euboulion is the feminine of Euboulios, the pseudonym Methodius regularly adopted for his narrative persona in other works.[21] The instability of gender is thus a feature of the text from the very beginning, and this instability is heightened by the fact that all of the surviving manuscripts have at least occasional masculine participles associated with the name Euboulion.[22] Methodius appears to underline the distinction between author and auditor (Gregorion is the narrator) with an exchange in the epilogue. Euboulion asks her informant whether a "lady from Telmessos" was present at the dinner party. "No," replies Gregorion, "the report is that she was with Methodius when he was questioning Arete about this matter. It is indeed a good and blessed thing to have a guide and teacher like Arete" (*Symposium*, epilogue). Methodius thus simultaneously separates himself from his narrators and recalls his existence to the reader, along with that of the mysterious lady of Telmessos who may have been a friend or patron.[23] The author of the text, in other words, is inscribed in the text itself, but in drag and as one of his own characters.

The *Symposium* of the title is thus carefully established at several removes from the "real" world of the author. Within the debate itself, Methodius takes great pains to give the virgins various discursive styles, and the debate as a whole is rather more lively and subtle than most commentators on the text would lead one to imagine. The exchange between the first two speakers is dramatic. Marcilla explains her evolutionary understanding of virginity, which incorporates a fairly severe judgment of marriage; Theophila gives a more generous reading of "increase and multiply," which provokes Marcilla to interrupt and contradict her. Theophila is flustered, but regains her composure and eventually silences Marcilla. The whole exchange not only recalls the Platonic dialogues, but also suggests that we should be cautious about automatically confusing the positions of the characters with that of the author, as Musurillo tends to in his commentary. The narrator does not record the reception of Marcilla's argument; Theophila, on the other hand, is rewarded with "a delightful burst of applause as the maidens complimented her on her discourse" (2.6). While Marcilla's vision of virginity as the endpoint of a process of gradual perfection may also be Methodius's vision, he appears to be distancing himself, disingenuously perhaps, from her excessively encratic tendencies. Thalia's speech too is presented in a manner that invites something less than automatic approval. Her exegesis of Genesis makes sex almost completely metaphorical, and it is very long. This provokes the first interruption by Euboulion, who, in what may be a sly dig at Origen, author of a famously long *Homily on Genesis*, declares the speech longwinded: "My dear Gregorion, Thalia said a good deal, although after measuring and crossing an enormous sea of words, she scarcely got to the point at issue" (4.3).[24] Gregorion agrees.

Thecla's speech is even longer, but it is identified by the appreciations preceding and following it as entirely admirable; once Arete has welcomed Thecla, the outcome of the contest is a foregone conclusion. "I am very happy, Thecla," she says, "to accept your spontaneous offering, and I feel confident that you will give us a suitable discourse to the best of your ability. We know that you are second to none in your grasp of philosophy and universal culture [*Philosophías te gàr tês egkuklíou paideías oudenòs hustereˆseis*] and I need hardly mention that you were instructed in divine and evangelical doctrine by Paul himself" (6.1). This is not the Thecla of the *Apocryphal Acts*, constantly struggling against the restrictions imposed upon her by her society because of her gender, but one who no longer even recognizes the existence of such restrictions. Arete's words recognize Thecla as one who transcends the normal social boundaries of her sex, as someone who can and does compete in the masculine world of philosophy and who has been shaped by *paideia*, the rhetorically based system of education, which Gleason, writing of the Second Sophistic movement of the previous century, describes as a "calisthenics of manhood" that "made boys into men."[25] Just as Euboulion/Methodius is gendered feminine by name and revealed as masculine by the slippage of participles, Thecla is feminine in her identity as virgin and masculine in her identity as skilled orator. Because of this skill, she is allowed to make what amounts to two speeches; having finished with the issue of virginity, which she explores through exegesis of the figure of the Woman clothed in the sun from *Revelation*, she asks and receives permission to make a second argument concerning astrology and predestination. It may not seem entirely fair that Thecla should win a debate on virginity by making a speech on free will, but it makes a certain sort of sense; throughout the *Symposium*, Methodius has been determined to represent virginity as a virtue that is both chosen by free will and that transports its practitioners to the heavens (1.1). Thecla's virginity has given her the authority to distinguish the heavens of the pagan prognosticators from the celestial realms of the Christians. Her profound knowledge of astronomy and mathematics are both transcended and rendered transcendent by her faith; she thus embodies the victory of Christian truth over pagan learning. At the same time, she translates the pagan system of education, *paideia*, into a Christian context. Educated by Paul, as Plato was educated by Socrates, she appears to exemplify not just the kind of equality between the sexes that early Christianity promised, but also the eradication of difference based upon gender and confirmed through education.

Indeed, for a text entirely populated by virgin women, the *Symposium* is oddly without a feminine perspective. The ideal of virginity it develops is almost perfectly androgynous, by which I mean without characteristics that identify it with one gender or the other, and is expressed in pain-stakingly neutral language. Eusebius, writing admiringly of Valentina's courage, could only describe her determination as manly; Tertullian, strug-gling with the concept of the male virgin, found himself able to imagine him only as a eunuch. Methodius, on the other hand, neither makes his women honorary men nor worries that men may become like women; when Thecla establishes a series of binary oppositions between intemper-ance and temperance, wrongdoing and righteousness, the analogous first terms, often translated as "effeminate and manly" are actually *kinaidôn kai andreiôn* (8.15). *Andreia* is indeed manly virtue, but its companion term has nothing to do with women, indicating instead the passive partner in a male homosexual act, and this erasure of the feminine proves characteristic of the whole text. A phrase from Domnina's speech shows the method by which sexual difference is eroded: "In order to achieve Beauty (*to kalòn*, in the Platonic sense of that which is essentially, eternally, and universally beauti-ful) nothing can so help mankind (*tòn anthrôpon*), o lovely virgins (*ô kalipárthenoi*) as purity (*hagneía*, purity beyond the merely sexual)" (10.1). In the Greek, the universal "mankind" immediately precedes the vocative *kalipárthenoi*, thus emphasizing through propinquity the appropriateness of the virtue of virginity for all members of the human race. Domnina insists also that "everyone should celebrate virginity, some because practicing virginity has married them to the Word, others because on account of virginity they are freed from the law that says 'you are dust and to dust you shall return' " (10.6). The pronouns for "some" and "others" are not feminine, as one might reasonably expect in the discourse of a woman speaking to women about a condition so normatively feminine as virginity. They are masculine (*toùs mèn...toùs dè*), and thus evidently intended as universal. Methodius's favorite periphrasis for Christ, "the Logos," increases the ungendered, asexual quality of the relationship that is being imagined; desire for the "Word" implies an entirely disembodied erotics. Virginity is represented as fundamentally metaphysical rather than physical. It is what allows the human to be identified with the divine. As Agatha claims in her speech, mankind was made in the image of (*kat eikóna*) God, but can only become *like* God (*homoíôsin*) through virginity (6.1).

In keeping with this project of gender neutrality in which virginity is imagined as a condition divorced from bodily sex and therefore available to the human person regardless of gender, the speech of Thallousa develops a pragmatics of virginity that is illustrated by predominantly masculine examples, both positive and negative. Her initial premise is that "the perfect person (*tòn téleion*) must offer up all, both of his body and of his soul, that he may be complete and not deficient" (5.2). Thallousa's ideal is virginity maintained from childhood: "Whosoever strives to keep his flesh undefiled from childhood by the practice of virginity is the one who offers himself perfectly to God" (5.4). She acknowledges that sexual purity is a part of the recipe, but does not dwell upon it: "I have then completely consecrated myself to God when I struggle to preserve my flesh not only untouched by actual intercourse, but unsullied also by any other offence" (5.3). She cites Paul on "the unmarried woman" (I Cor. 7:34), but aside from this her examples are of men. The image of perfection is Abraham, whose marital status is irrelevant because of his willingness to sacrifice his son, and the images of its opposite are Noah, the men of Sodom, and Cain; all embody loss of control, albeit not always nor exclusively sexual. It is as though, having made the ten virgins who participate in the debate the mouthpieces of virginity, and imagining them as women because the word *parthenos* automatically signifies femininity to a Greek reader, Methodius is particularly concerned to make space in what they said for the profession of virginity by men; he therefore erases the details of virgin biology as fully as possible. Even when Arete speaks in passing of the "actual organs of generation" [*ta tês paidopoiêseôs órgana* (11.1)] she keeps them sexually nonspecific. Just how unusual a rhetorical strategy this is becomes fully evident if we compare Methodius to Tertullian. For Tertullian, as I argued in chapter 1, the problem of the virgin body is that it cannot be separated from the female sexual body: "a virgin ceases to be a virgin from the time when it becomes possible for her not to be one. And accordingly, among the Jews, it is unlawful to deliver a girl to her husband except after the proof by blood of her maturity. . .already her voice is changed, her limbs are fully shaped, her shame clothes itself, the months pay their tributes" (*Virgins* 11). The inevitable fact of menstruation suggests a loss of integrity, an almost ritual uncleanness that undoes the purity claimed by the virgins of Carthage.

One of the most remarkable features of the *Symposium* is the way it deals with actual sexuality, in detail and in positive, almost glowing terms. There is none of the disgust that Tertullian felt for the betrayal of the soul by the flesh, none of the melodramatic descriptions of fallen virgins betrayed by swelling bellies which become so common in the work of later writers, no representations of women as inevitably carnal temptresses.[26] There is, in fact, almost no reference to female sexuality at all. When sexual desire is evoked, it is male. The delight of male erotic experience is evoked with romanticizing nostalgia by Theophila, who imagines the creation of Eve both as a pre-Lapsarian nocturnal emission and as the measure of man's desire for fatherhood:

> For under the stimulation of intercourse, the body's harmony—so we are told by those who have consummated the rites of marriage—is greatly disturbed, and all the marrow-like generative part of the blood, which is liquid bone, gathers from all parts of the body, curdled and worked into a foam, and then rushes through the generative organs into the living soil of the woman. Hence rightly is it said that therefore a man leave his father and his mother: for man made one with woman in the embrace of love is overcome by a desire for children and completely forgets everything else; he offers his rib to his divine Creator, to be removed that he himself, the father, may appear once again in a son. (*Symposium* 2.2)

Women are never represented as suffering from (or enjoying, for that matter) sexual desire, either procreational or otherwise. They are the soil that receives the seed or, in an image Theophila develops at length, the kiln where the human being is cooked:

> . . .the process of our birth into this world [is] something like a house with its entrance lying near to steep mountains. . .there is a modeler sitting inside making many statues and the material of clay is constantly being handed in to him through the windows from the outside by a number of men, none of whom see the artisan. . . . Each of the men working together to supply the clay has assigned to him one special opening to which alone he must bring and deposit his clay; he must not touch the other openings. . . . The artisan within the house, going round to each of the windows in turn, takes the clay he finds there and separately moulds it in each case; and after a period of some months of modeling, he gives back the finished product through the respective windows to those on the outside. . .But the one who, contrary to the command and ordinance, deposited the clay at the window belonging to another, is to be punished as a wretched transgressor. (*Symposium* 2.4)

In case we don't get it, Theophila explains that the windows refer to the female sex and "those who bring the clay are the male sex who, desirous of offspring, are brought to deposit their seed in the woman's channels as provided by nature, just as the men above did with the clay in the windows" (2.5). Again, desire is masculine; what is more, the analogy seems to make adultery entirely a problem of misdirected male sexuality. Throughout the text, in fact, when sexuality is evoked and even more notably, when it is problematized, it is male; the only reference to female desire comes in a passing reference to Potiphar's wife in Thecla's hymn.

The ideal of sexual renunciation embodied in Arete and the ten virgins and imitated by Euboulion, Gregorion, and the Lady of Telmessos, is feminine; in the universe of the text, this is an ideal that is unproblematic (if not easy) for women to imitate. But the energy expended upon male *exempla* of virginal behavior and the emphasis upon the delights of male sexuality that must be renounced imply an intended audience, which is composed of both men and women. If Methodius was writing for a particular spiritual community, it was most likely of the sort that John Chrysostom was later to denounce emphatically in *On the Necessity of Guarding Virginity*, one in which men and women together pursued an ascetic ideal, granting each other spiritual rather than physical love. Such a community, in which sexual difference was seen as irrelevant, fits the tone of Methodius's work much better than a single-sex community which made sexual difference absolute by the very fact of excluding men. After Methodius's death in the last days of the Great Persecution, however, asceticism was to develop in ways that made this androgynous and egalitarian ideal not just a curiosity but also an apparent threat to the natural order of things, especially in the Latin West. In the face of a Christian society evolving toward increasingly hierarchical power structures, the androgynous virgin, who might have facilitated a way of imagining true equality between the sexes, never stood a chance.

The Monastic Ideal

The practice of extreme asceticism by complete retreat from the world, which began in the third century in the deserts of Egypt, was intended to refine the body into an ideal state in which it would become dry, hard, and translucent like a precious metal. In the body of a monk like Abba John, whom Pseleusius described to Paphnutius, author of the *History of the Monks of Egypt*, the flesh had been entirely mortified: "he likened him to the brilliance of silver on account of the purity of prayers and to the pale-green color of gold on account of the pallor caused by his asceticism."[27] What was left was so ethereal and rarefied that it seemed almost ready to blow away, as indeed the body of another monk encountered by Paphnutius did: "I took hold of his arm and it came off in my hands and disintegrated into dust."[28] The incident provokes not horror but religious awe. This was a human creature who had achieved the pinnacle of asceticism, who had controlled his body so that even after death it did not demonstrate rot or decay but simply fell into atoms, like the clean sand of the desert itself. When John Cassian, who had lived as a monk in Egypt in the last decades of the fourth century, undertook to write a handbook for ascetics in Gaul, where the cenobitic lifestyle was something new, he too used the metaphor of precious metals to describe the ascetics. In the preface to his first book, the *Institutes of the Cenobitic Life*, he imagines his patron, Pope Castor, commissioning from him an edifice like the temple of

Solomon, decorated not with objects of ordinary, "voiceless" gold and silver, but with ornaments "cast from holy souls, shining with the integrity of their innocence, justice and chastity."[29] In this book and that which followed it, the *Conferences*, Cassian tried to teach by instruction and by the example of the great ascetics of Egypt a method of transforming the unruly human flesh into the purified monastic body by submitting it to the absolute and unremitting control of the spirit.

The task of the monk, according to Cassian, is to "leave the flesh while staying in the body" (*Institutes* 6.6) by achieving a condition of radical purity. Such purity manifests itself by the kind of luminosity Paphnutius witnessed in Abba John, or Cassian in Abbot Serenus, and it is intensely difficult to achieve, because it depends upon submitting every aspect of life to the power of the spirit, so that the purified body becomes the reflection and receptacle of the purified soul. The ideal monastic body would exist in a state of perfect equilibrium, a kind of suspension between life and death, sleeping only to wake again almost immediately and pray, laboring only to feed itself sparingly, consuming only enough food to maintain life, but so little that even the natural processes of excretion were virtually suspended. Cassian's *Institutes* is a primer on asceticism for beginners. In it, John identifies the eight principal vices that will afflict the monk and provides advice on how to overcome them. Given that the monks of Provence had no desert into which to withdraw but would be living in one of the most fertile provinces of the Late Roman period, famous for both oysters and wine, one might expect that John would expend particular energy on the sin of gluttony; he insists, however, that fornication is the most tenacious and difficult vice to overcome (*Institutes* 6.1), and condemns gluttony primarily because it contributes to fornication. In complete concordance with contemporary medical theory, he sees sperm as a by-product of the digestive processes and limiting one's intake of food as key to limiting one's sexual desires. Indeed, both this book and the *Conferences*, which consist of a series of recollected conversations with the monks Cassian knew as a young man in Egypt, deal obsessively with the way that sex continues to haunt those men of God who have renounced the world and the works of the flesh. When John speaks of fornication, however, he does not generally mean sex with women or even with men, he means something much more inescapable and morally perplexing, those sexual acts that occur when the monk is alone except for the company of his own thoughts. If slapping a mosquito deserved six months of penance in a swamp, what was a monk to make of those inevitable and involuntary movements of his penis? Book Six of the *Institutes* deals primarily with the problems of involuntary erection and nocturnal emissions, which marked the final frontier of bodily control.

Cassian, like many other Latin writers, makes a clear distinction between virginity and chastity, although his distinction, unlike that of Tertullian, is not based upon gender: "there is a difference between continence, that is *encrateia*, and chastity in which one passes into that state of integrity and incorruption called *hagneia*, a virtue which is granted only to those who remain virgins in both flesh and mind (*virgines vel carne vel mente perdurant*), like the two Johns we know of from the New Testament, and in the Old Testament Elias, Jeremiah and Daniel" (*Institutes* 6.4).[30] *Encrateia* was presumed to be within the reach of all men, if they were willing enough. *Hagneia*, complete impassivity of body, was a gift from God, extremely rare and generally only achieved by the very ancient; one measure of the success of such men was that nothing, not even the erotic dreams confessed to them by younger men, could produce in them the "movement of lust" [*motus concupiscentiae* (*Institutes* 6.11)]. This kind of masculine virginity exists conceptually as an inversion of feminine virginity. The body of either sex, as Mary Douglas puts it, is a container: "Females are correctly seen as, literally, the entry by which the pure content may be adulterated. Males are treated as pores through which the precious stuff may ooze out and be lost."[31] Cassian describes at length the methods used by the Egyptian monks to prevent any such oozing out. Some, "fearing that they may perhaps be deceived while sleeping by nocturnal illusions which would diminish the strength built up over so long, cover their hips with sheets of lead so that the stiffness of the metal applied to the genital area will inhibit obscene humors" (*Institutes* 6.7), but the preferred method of eliminating those "obscene humors" that produced unwanted sperm was extreme fasting.

Both the *Institutes* and the *Conferences* betray an inconsistent attitude to the problem of involuntary erections. On the one hand, Cassian and his mentors seem to have realized that some movements of the penis are both inevitable and natural, since they occur in infants and in deep sleep. On the other, they were intensely aware of the role of sexual fantasy in the lives of the monks, and the fact that even eunuchs experienced erection could be adduced as evidence that male arousal was entirely to do with lust, which was purely sinful, rather than procreation, which was at least natural if not admirable (*Conferences* 2.10). Every nocturnal emission, therefore, had to be closely scrutinized, and the monk is warned against misrepresentation, either to himself or to his confessors. The physical fact of having ejaculated could perhaps be hidden from the brethren, but if the monk had "polluted himself by secret connivance" by participating in his own fantasy, then God and his angels at least would know (*Institutes* 6.20). If the monk could be absolutely sure that he had neither invited nor enjoyed the experience, then he had not sinned seriously enough to require abstinence from communion; emissions were a regrettable fact of nature, like excretion, and even the experienced monk could expect to experience them once in a while, perhaps every other month, if he was careful about what he ate (*Institutes* 6.20). If, however, he entertained improper thoughts, either before falling asleep or upon awakening and finding himself aroused, then he must do penance. The possibility of demonic temptation was ever present, and it is not always clear whether the devil is to be seen as an exterior force, an assault from outside, or one that merely takes advantage of indwelling weakness.[32] Cassian recounts the troubling case of a man gifted with near perfect chastity who never experienced any difficulty in controlling his body except on the night before he was to receive communion, when he would infallibly have a nocturnal emission. For a while, he abstained from communion, out of shame, but eventually he decided to seek the advice of the elders of the community. They questioned him thoroughly: was he eating too much, and thus causing his body to produce superfluous humors that were being converted into sperm? Was he falling into the sin of pride by mistaking his chastity for something that he had won for himself, rather than as evidence of divine grace? His answers on these points satisfied the elders, who reached the only possible conclusion: he was being tempted by the devil, and the evidence of this was precisely the fact that his nocturnal emissions occurred only on the eve of taking communion. They permitted him to partake of the Eucharist, since this was obviously what the devil was trying to prevent, and the problem vanished immediately (*Conferences* 22.6).

Cassian's books and Paphnutius's *History of the Monks of Egypt* provide a glimpse into a world where female sexuality was almost irrelevant. Even outside of the monastic communities of Egypt, Palestine, and Syria, the unruly quality of male sexuality made it difficult for men to claim physical virginity: "I have never known a woman, and yet I am no virgin" [*et mulierem ignoro, et virgo non sum* (*Institutes* 6.19)]. Basil of Caesarea's words, quoted by John, indicate the ascetic man's deep sense of futility faced with the uncontrollable nature of his own body. Augustine, who came to asceticism late, was similarly distressed by the willful independence that seemed to him to characterize male sexual organs. The *City of God* includes a famous rumination on pre-Lapsarian sex, which reveals Augustine's profound distrust of the erection. The idea that a single organ might direct the will of man rather than being subject to it strikes him as both undignified and subversive. If horses can twitch their flesh to get rid of flies, if some people can wiggle their ears, or produce musical and odorless farts or even swallow and regurgitate sharp objects, he argues, the intractability of the penis can only be understood as a mark of original sin. In punishment for the original failure of man's will, that will is eternally vulnerable to being overruled by a single obstreperous organ (*City* 14.24).[33] When Augustine imagines procreation as it would have been before the Fall, he sees both partners as remaining virgin: the woman would retain her maidenhead and the man would not experience erection (*City* 14.26). For Cassian, for Basil, and for Augustine, physical male virginity is measured not by contact with the opposite sex, or even the same sex, but by freedom from ejaculation and erection. The male virgin was thus virtually a mythical beast.

Reimagining the Virgin

In the face of such uncertainty about the possibility of maintaining virginity, or even approximating it, in a male body, the body of the female virgin was an object of admiration to male ascetics and, inevitably, of envy: "Here was a wellshaft of deep certainty for which they themselves thirsted."[34] In the later half of the fourth century, virginity, which had been an occasional topic for earlier generations, became something akin to an obligatory subject for theologians. Gregory of Nyssa, Basil of Ancyra, and John Chrysostom all wrote treatises on virginity, and the subject was, if possible, even more popular in the Latin West, which produced texts about virgins to suit every possible taste; Jerome's letters and diatribes are the most combative, Ambrose's sermons the most lyrical, and Augustine's meditations on virginity in the *City of God* the most theologically complex. To these enormously influential works must be added a great number of anonymous treatises and asides which crop up more or less in passing in works primarily devoted to other topics. In Peter Brown's words, the virgin's "physical integrity came to carry an exceptionally high charge of meaning."[35] Patristic praise of the virgin body cast a long shadow, however; precisely because these bodies were so significant, so conceptually powerful, the issue of who was to control them was paramount. As Averil Cameron reminds us, "just as real women were denied an answer to the rhetoric of their portrayal, so a male author ostensibly writing about women was writing about authority and control and about the reconciliation of irreconcilable polarities."[36] This separation between real women and what women might mean for masculine authority is particularly evident in the letters of Jerome, who was genuinely fond of a group of Roman ascetic women who were equally devoted to him—"some of my best friends are women!" one can hear him protesting to those critics who accuse him of misogyny. Jerome's letters to and about women demonstrate with perfect clarity both how and why the virgin had to be subjected to physical, intellectual, and social control.

Jerome is one of the most fascinating figures of his time, if only because he was never lukewarm about anything.[37] His involvement in the development of asceticism and in the lives of ascetic women was immediate and personal. He had lived as a monk in Syria for a few years and had managed, even in that remote corner of the world, to make enemies and to get involved in one of those theological controversies that, in the fourth century, so quickly turned into political disputes. Returning to Rome in 382, he became the friend and mentor of a group of wealthy Roman women descended from some of the most famous senatorial families (a fact that never failed to impress him) who had chosen to follow the ascetic way of life. He was fascinated by them and they by him, and the fascination grew into a lifelong and mutual affection in the case of Paula and her daughter Eustochium. Jerome is one of the very few patristic writers who was involved on a daily basis with powerful and intelligent women.

Jerome was entirely convinced of the intellectual capacity of women, and did not see this as in any way contradicting their moral and ontological inferiority. He encouraged Paula to learn Hebrew (Letter 108.26) and clearly enjoyed establishing curricula for the young women who placed themselves or were placed by their mothers under his spiritual direction. In his letter to Paula's daughter-in-law Laeta who had vowed her own daughter to virginity when she was still in the womb, he lays out a challenging and surprisingly liberal course of study. She is to master the Old and New Testaments, and "only then can she finally read the Song of Songs without danger; if she were to read it first, it would harm her, for she would not be able to understand that a hymn to spiritual marriage is conveyed beneath such fleshly words" (107.12). Jerome's method of education never forbids a text outright, although he may warn against it, or recommend that it be delayed until the virgin in question is mentally mature enough to comprehend it. Such a course of study is not simply a matter of creating kindred spirits, although Jerome clearly derived great pleasure from intellectual exchange with women like Marcella, Paula, and Eustochium, but a defensive measure. Women's minds, while educable, are morally inferior, easily swayed, and have an unfortunate tendency to degenerate into heretical thought if left unguided, preferably by Jerome himself (130.17).[38] In a letter to Ctesiphon condemning the teachings of Pelagius, he represents women not as the victims of heretical teachings but as active disseminators of unorthodoxy. Jerome draws upon both Tertullian and Epiphanius to make his case, which is founded upon a citation from Paul's letter to the Ephesians: "Of women who are thus presumptuous the apostle says that they 'are carried about with every wind of doctrine, ever learning and never able to come to the knowledge of the truth' " (133.4). He associates every major heresy (and some for which this passage is the only witness) with the misleading speech of women.

The ideal woman, for Jerome, is one who expands her mind while keeping a careful guard on her tongue. Eustochium is to read extensively but to be careful about her speech: "Don't try to seem excessively eloquent, don't play around with poetry. . .and don't imitate the affectation of married women who close their teeth, open their lips, lisp and drop the endings of their words. . .engaging in adultery of the tongue" (22.29). He praises Paula for referring heretics who pose troubling questions to him rather than answering them herself, although she could have, and provides an unintentionally revealing portrayal of Marcella's verbal discretion in his eulogy for her: "She gave her opinion not as her own but as from me or someone else, admitting that what she taught she had herself learned from others. She knew that the apostle had said: 'I suffer not a woman to teach' and she did not want to seem to injure the male sex, many of whom (including some priests) questioned her on doubtful and obscure points" (12.7). It is perhaps no surprise that Marcella resisted all of Jerome's invitations to join him and Paula in Palestine, preferring to maintain the relative intellectual independence of an ascetic existence within the walls of her great house in Rome.

Jerome's virgins are not only women who must open their minds while closing their mouths, but also precious objects to be locked away from the world, for "no gold or silver cup was ever as precious to God as the temple of the virgin's body" (22.23). The virgin is not to go out, not even to visit the baths, but must remain isolated, confined to her room. Just as Marcella's education did not give her the right to challenge the authority of a man like Jerome, the virgin's complete freedom from the sexual contract did not and must not confer social freedom upon her. She might have liberated herself from the authority of a bridegroom—Jerome pictures Demetrias, the greatest heiress of her day, laying claim to freedom and courage as she decides to break her engagement—but it was absolutely essential that she submit herself to some other form of masculine authority. Nowhere is this need for submission more clearly demonstrated than the letter "To a Mother and Daughter living in Gaul." Here, Jerome undertakes to address the female relatives of a young man who has traveled all the way to Bethlehem from Gaul to complain of their misbehavior. The situation as the young monk depicts it is dire: not only do his sister and his widowed mother refuse to live together and keep an eye on each other, but the older woman wears makeup and goes to parties, while the younger woman has taken up with a holy man with whom she lives in what she claims is a spiritual marriage. The daughter is the primary target of Jerome's letter, and he depicts her as the perfect antithesis to the modest and withdrawn Eustochium: she goes around the town to visit her relatives, attends dinner parties, and even goes to the baths, trusting to her professed virginity to protect her and to guarantee her reputation. Jerome takes a hard line with this woman he has never met. He lingers over the image of her various indiscretions in a positively prurient manner: "What are you doing, girl, with your healthy, beautiful, plump pink body, heated up by the pleasures of the flesh, by wine, by the baths, consorting with married women, and with young men?" (117.7). He imagines her responding, demanding to know whether it is a sin to live with a holy man; Jerome's answer is a resounding "yes," and he goes so far as to recommend that she marry the man in question because regardless of what sins her body may or may not have committed, her good name is already compromised beyond salvation. She has made an elementary and very serious mistake, says Jerome, confusing liberty with license [*procacitatem libertatem vocas* (117.5)]. This cleverly turned phrase shows just what is at stake. Like the Carthaginian virgins at whom Tertullian took umbrage, this young woman and those like her assume that professed virginity puts them beyond the reach of masculine authority.

Letter 117 is usually dismissed as a rhetorical exercise, and indeed the society virgin Jerome depicts in it is clearly the product of his always fertile mind. It seems unlikely, certainly, that any monk would have traveled all the way from Gaul to solicit a letter from an aging ascetic, no matter how famous. One brief passage, however, suggests that the brother himself may have existed; perhaps he was visiting Palestine on pilgrimage, and merely happened to unburden himself while visiting Jerome's monastery. In any case, the description of the source of the brother's distress suggests a very real and very pragmatic reason for the restrictions imposed upon the social lives of virgins: "[your brother] is indignant that you prefer another young man to him, not, admittedly, some long-haired dandy dressed in silk, but one of those tough guys who looks good in grubby clothes, who holds the purse strings, takes care of the weaving, assigns the household tasks, looks after the slaves and takes care of all purchasing" (117.8). This virgin, in other words, is not only misbehaving with regard to her person, which would be bad enough, but with regard to her property; her brother's anxiety is suddenly revealed as deeply self-interested. He may (or may not) as a monk, have given up any claim on his inheritance, but he cannot bear to see it in the hands of another. The irony of the situation is apparently entirely wasted upon Jerome, who had for years lived closely (albeit not under the same roof) with Paula and whose monastery had been founded with her money. Money, in fact, is one of the constant themes of texts written to and about virgins. In his letter to Demetrias, Jerome takes it upon himself to give the heiress a little financial advice, suggesting that she get rid of her burdensome worldly wealth not by decorating churches but by contributing to struggling monasteries (130.14). He stops just short of pointing out that his own foundation has been, since the death of Paula some years earlier, rather short of cash. In his eulogy for Paula, addressed to Eustochium, he went so far as to congratulate the daughter on the fact that there was not a penny of her mother's enormous fortune left for her to live on, but a mountain of debt instead (108.30).

The issue of money emerges even more clearly when we look back toward Italy, where in the 370s Ambrose found himself invested, against his will, he insists, as bishop of Milan. Ambrose was to become a famous advocate of the formal profession of virgins as one of the definitive features of Catholic Christianity; Brown evokes the Milanese ceremony of veiling powerfully: "Their presence defined the Catholic basilica as a privileged, sacred space. . .In a crowded church, blazing with light and with the shimmer of white triumphal robes, a burst of rhythmic shouting marked the moment when the consecrated woman took up her position behind a special pure white marble railing that marked her off from the rest of the basilica as clearly as did the chancel rail around the sanctuary"; he goes on to note, however, that "with the formal consecration of each virgin, a portion of the wealth of each family found itself frozen. . .in the treasuries of the Catholic Church."[39] This must have been especially important in a see such as Milan that had been, up until Ambrose's sudden promotion to the episcopacy, in the hands of Arian Christians under the notorious Auxentius. Ambrose was also, no doubt, influenced by his older sister Marcellina, who had taken the veil when he was still an adolescent, thus becoming one of the first professed virgins at Rome. In Ambrose's first treatise, *On Virgins*, personal conviction and episcopal politics came together to produce the most extended and powerful identification yet of the virgin with the martyr.

This text, which marks the beginning of a prolific writing career, combines the substance of three sermons, two by Ambrose and one that he ascribes to the bishop from whom his sister received the veil twenty years earlier. Ambrose transforms the virgin from an active female hero in the model of Thecla, associated even in the context of Methodius's androgynous vision with free will and persuasive speech, into something both enormously potent and enormously oppressive: a symbol of the church itself. The virgin martyr, represented by Agnes and a nameless virgin of Antioch, becomes an erotically supercharged figure, the receptacle of masculine desires both licit and illicit; in Ambrose's work, and in the poems of Prudentius, which build upon it at the beginning of the fifth century, it will no longer be the speech of the virgin martyr that testifies, but her beautiful, passive, vulnerable body. The virgins of Jerome's letters, in spite of the rhetorical and actual restrictions laid upon them, are always actual people. Eustochium had a life outside of his letters, and we can occasionally glimpse her living it, tending her mother's deathbed along with Jerome. Paula the younger, who grew up to join her grandmother and Jerome in the Holy Land, appears independently in the *Life of Melania*, seeking advice from the more celebrated ascetic. Even in the case of the hypothetical woman from Gaul, Jerome imagines the responses that she might have made, and they are often surprisingly persuasive to the twentieth-century reader, if not to Jerome himself. The young women of Ambrose's *On Virgins*, on the other hand, are fully mythologized, always already metaphorical, heavily laden with meaning but denied any voice of their own, any possibility of responding to their representation. Symbolically, the virgin martyr is the sacrificial victim upon whom the identity of an imagined faith depends, just as the professed virgin's inheritance guaranteed the more mundane requirements of the actual Christian community; as victim, the virgin martyr is identified intimately with silence, voyeurism, and death.

On Virgins is addressed to Marcellina, but Ambrose forestalls any imaginable response from her, identifying her as a sounding board and nothing more. "The love of chastity, and you too, holy sister, even though you are silent because of your subdued way of life, now beckon us to say something about virginity" (*On Virgins* 1.3.10)[40] he says, making it clear that he is speaking not so much for but instead of Marcellina. The silence of the virgin is one of the dominant themes of the book, in fact, especially in the final volume in which Ambrose reports the instructions of Liberius, who officiated at Marcellina's veiling. "If women are ordered to be silent in church concerning divine matters and to ask their husbands at home, how cautious do we think virgins should be, in whom modesty is an adornment of their age and silence a recommendation of their modesty?" (3.3.9). Ambrose has Liberius say, inverting the emphasis of the apostle's words, which implied that outside of church women might indeed speak. Ambrose/Liberius goes on to drive the point home, painting a colorful picture of a church in which the readings are drowned out by chattering women and telling the fable of a bishop who silenced a pond full of croaking frogs so that his sermon might be heard. "Let virginity be signaled first by the voice, let modesty close the mouth, let religion exclude weakness, let custom instruct nature" (3.3.13), he insists; the voice of the virgin, in fact, is no voice at all but a state of perennial voicelessness.

At the beginning of the treatise, Ambrose figures himself as the precise opposite of the voiceless virgin; the first four paragraphs of the text represent its author as impelled to speak against his will and tormented by hesitation:

> Although I distrust my own abilities, to be sure, nonetheless I am spurred on by tokens of the divine mercy and dare to give thought to a discourse, for when God willed it even an ass spoke. If an angel stands by me as I labor under the burdens of this world, I too shall open the mouth that has been closed for so long a time, for he who removed the hindrances of nature in the case of that ass can remove those of inexperience as well. In the Ark of the Old Testament the priest's staff blossomed; it is easy for God to bring forth flowers in his holy Church from our knotty wood also. Why should

we despair that the Lord would speak in human beings when he spoke in thornbushes? God did not disdain a bramblebush. If only he would cast light on my thorns too! (*On Virgins* 1.1)

This is perhaps the most tortuous use of the modesty *topos* in its long history, but it is curiously appropriate to a book characterized by "a combination of the spectacular and the tentative with an admixture of guile."[41] The agonized opening of the text allows Ambrose simultaneously to participate in the silent sanctity of the virgin, and to evade it. He wishes to be as silent as Marcellina, even rather ostentatiously envies her subdued way of life; upon being acclaimed as bishop, he initially insisted that he intended to pursue a quiet life of philosophical speculation.[42] The will of God, however, forces him to break his silence and, incidentally, put his extensive rhetorical training to divine use. Virginity was to prove his most compelling theme; on the body of the virgin, whether consecrated woman, martyr, or Mary herself, Ambrose was to build a great deal: his credentials as theologian, the prosperity of his bishopric, and a compelling ideology of the church as sacred space.[43] Precisely because she would come to bear such enormous symbolic weight, it was essential to his project that the virgin should be silent. She was not a person any more, but a sacrificial victim, an object of veneration, inspiration, and interpretation, like the equally speechless relics of Protase and Gervasius, which were also instrumental in establishing Ambrose's authority at Milan.

Having established his inability to speak, Ambrose proceeds to speak with enormous eloquence on his chosen subject, beginning by recounting the story of Saint Agnes: "In devotion beyond her age, in virtue above nature. She seems to me to have borne not so much a human name as a token of martyrdom whereby she showed what she was to be [i.e. a lamb, *agnus*, to the sacrifice]" (1.2.5). The tale itself will have been familiar to his audience; Agnes had been venerated at Rome for some time, although her historicity is dubious.[44] Ambrose's account is a *tour-de-force*, juggling sensational paradoxes: aged twelve at her death, Agnes bears witness to Christ before she could legally bear witness in court; a mere child, she is wiser than her elders; and she goes to her death as if to a marriage. Like the virgins in Tertullian's *On the Veiling of Virgins*, Agnes is invested with enormous physical appeal, but unlike Tertullian, Ambrose seems to revel in it. His initial description of Agnes is inexorably focused upon the appealing frailty of her flesh:

> Could there be, in such a tiny body, space for a wound? Yet she who had no place to receive the sword had what it takes to vanquish the sword. At that age, most girls cannot even bear parental scowls, and if you prick them with a pin they weep as though wounded. She was not afraid of the bloody hand

of the executioner, she was unmoved by the pressure of clanking chains, ignorant of death but ready to offer her whole body to the sword of a raving soldier, ready, if she were dragged against her will to the altar, to stretch out her hands to Christ from the midst of the flames and to signal the victory of her conquering Lord from the sacrilegious furnaces themselves, ready to put her neck and her hands into fetters of iron, even though no bonds could confine such slender limbs. (*On Virgins* 1.2.7)

The initial evocation of a body too childish to have space for a wound both denies and inevitably recalls the fact that young Christian women of Agnes's age were often obliged to suffer a more mundane wound on their wedding night; Melania the Younger was married, against her will, at the almost equally tender age of fourteen. The image of the young girl pricked with a pin reinforces our awareness of her as a physical creature, subject to incomprehensible injury, and the final evocation of limbs too slight to be restrained, except voluntarily, has an explicitly masochistic quality. Ambrose goes on to emphasize again and again the quasi-sexual quality of Agnes's immolation: "No bride would hurry to her marriage bed as joyfully as the virgin proceeded with eager step to the place of torture!" (1.2.8). Although he has represented her as a child, once she ascends the tribunal she is immediately the object of desire: "How fearfully the executioner acted in order to intimidate her, how he flattered her in order to persuade her [to make the sacrifice]! And how many men desired that she would come to them in marriage!" (1.2.9). The child becomes a nubile woman at the very moment when she is publicly exposed to the crowd and threatened with torture. The erotic charge built up around her is released, however, not through sex but through her death, which is represented as consummation, as Agnes bows her neck to the executioner's sword. Ambrose does not provide a description of the execution itself; rather, like an old-fashioned movie director showing waves crashing on a beach or fireworks exploding, he redirects his audience's attention to an alternative climax, a set of those paradoxical *sententiae* in which he takes such delight: "You have then a twofold martyrdom in one victim—that of modesty and that of religion. She both remained a virgin and obtained martyrdom. . .For virginity is not praiseworthy because it is found in martyrs but because it makes martyrs" (1.3.9–10). Virginity is valuable, desirable, precisely because it leads to death, because, in a metaphorical sense, it is death.

The connection of virginity to death is emphasized again in the examples of suicidal virgins with which Ambrose ends his tract. He mentions Saint Pelagia of Antioch who, during the persecution, found herself "surrounded by those who would rob her of her faith and her chastity" (3.3.8); here, the violation of virginity is clearly understood also to be a violation of religious status; losing her virginity will be equivalent to losing her faith.

Pelagia thus chooses to die, not by execution but by her own hand. She dresses herself in wedding clothes before throwing herself off the roof. Her mother and sisters in their turn fling themselves into a river. Miraculously, their bodies are found with their clothing still decorously arranged. As the last in this series of victims of self-immolation, Ambrose cites Marcellina's ancestress Soteris, who: "offered her face—which, when the entire body is tortured, is usually untouched and looks upon the torment instead of suffering it—to the executioner. . . . She did not flinch, her countenance did not yield, lamentation did not overcome her nor did she give way to tears. Finally. . .she found the sword that she was searching for" (3.7.38).[45] Soteris desires not simply to suffer for her religion, but to suffer in new and extreme ways in order to prove the extent of her devotion. The question of whether suggesting such spectacular forms of torture for herself might be in some sense hubristic, evidence of a desire to be outstanding among martyrs, does not seem to occur to Ambrose, but it is quite marked if we compare Soteris to Perpetua or other historical martyrs whose acceptance of death did not extend to stage-managing their own tortures to greatest effect.

Ambrose's rhetoric, however, like Soteris's martyrdom, is calculated precisely to create powerful emotional effects in the service of establishing a very particular relationship between the Catholic and the image of the virgin martyr. His story of Agnes defines the virgin martyr as an almost irresistible object of desire, and the story of the virgin of Antioch, which forms the centerpiece of the second volume of the treatise, intensifies this appeal, associates it with a near magical untouchability, and creates a curiously imbricated relationship between the virgin and the audience. "Not long ago," Ambrose begins, "there was a certain virgin at Antioch who kept from public view. But the more she avoided the gaze of men, the more she inflamed them. For a beauty that is heard of but not seen is all the more desirable. . ." (2.4.22). If, for Tertullian, a virgin exposed was a virgin no more, for Ambrose the very fact of withdrawing herself from the gaze of men renders the virgin's allure all the more intense. When persecution breaks out, the situation of the virgin of Antioch becomes even more impossible: "When they saw the firmness of her profession, her concern for her purity, her readiness to suffer and her modesty in the face of their stares, they began to reflect how they might strike at her religion by way of her chastity so that, once having removed what was more important, they might also snatch away what they had left. They ordered the virgin either to sacrifice or to be sent to a brothel" (2.4.23). While the virgin debates internally at some length as to the choice she must make, her resistance to her persecutors takes the outward form only of silence: "She wept and was silent, lest an adulterer so much as heard her speaking. . .consider whether she who did not submit her voice to adultery would have been able to submit her body to adultery" (2.4.24). The contrast between this virgin and Valentina and her companion from Eusebius's *Martyrs of Palestine* is especially marked here. Valentina's virginity granted her a moral authority that allowed her to challenge unjust punishment meted out by secular authorities without any concern for what others might think; the virgin of Antioch, on the other hand, is silenced by her own virginity, paralyzed by shame and fear of public opinion.

In the paragraph that immediately follows the virgin's choice of silence, Ambrose deploys another of his systems of paradoxes, which, in this case, establishes the readers or auditors of his text in a very ambivalent relationship with the martyr:

> All at once my discourse is ashamed and fears, as it were, to enter upon and relate the wicked course of events. Stop your ears, virgins of God: a young woman of God is being led to a brothel. But open your ears, virgins of God: a virgin can be forced to prostitute herself, but not to commit adultery. Wherever a virgin of God is, there is a temple of God. Brothels not only do not bring chastity into disrepute, but chastity even does away with the disrepute of such places. (*On Virgins* 2.4.25)

This sudden appeal to an audience of virgins outside of the text serves to create a degree of suspense, encouraging the audience to imagine a chaste young woman in a brothel even while it promises implicitly that the worst will not happen. Here, Ambrose acknowledges the heightened degree of interest and sympathy he has created on behalf of the virgin of Antioch. Problematically, this interest is not fully separable from that of the "huge crowd of curiosity seekers" (2.4.24) inside the story who rush to the brothel to see what will happen. "Learn the miracles of the martyrs, holy virgins, but unlearn the vocabulary of these places" (2.4.25), Ambrose instructs, but it is too late. Suspense, and the possibility that the virgin may indeed suffer a "fate worse than death" is maintained until the last possible moment, when a soldier bursts into the brothel. This man, however, turns out to be a fellow Christian, who exchanges his clothing with the virgin, allowing her to escape. Once again, her behavior both reflects and distorts that of Valentina; Valentina spoke out in defense of another woman; the virgin of Antioch must be saved by, and in her turn fail to save, a man. When he is sentenced to be put to death in her place, she insists upon joining him, thus gaining, like Agnes, the "double crown" of virginity and martyrdom. The question of whether one can remain virgin in spirit even after being violated in body is thus indefinitely deferred. The virgin had come to the conclusion that "it is more tolerable to have a virgin mind than virgin flesh" (2.4.28), thus opening the possibility that a woman might be judged by some standard independent of the condition of her body, but the possibility is immediately foreclosed by her rescue and subsequent death. The two circles of Ambrose's double crown become inseparable; each guarantees the other. Similarly, the circle of nonbelieving witnesses within the narrative is intimately connected to the circle of believing witnesses outside of it, to Ambrose's auditors.

The identification of virginity and martyrdom is even more absolute in the poems of Prudentius, composed around 420, which also intensify the voyeuristic participation of the audience in martyrdom. In his accounts of the deaths of Eulalia and Agnes, Prudentius does not avoid, as Ambrose had, direct description of the actual executions. His commitment to poetic language increases our interest in the physical quality of the suffering body; the torment of the martyr becomes, in the case of Eulalia, quite literally graphic:

> nec mora, carnifices gemini
> uncea pectora dilacerant
> et latus ungula virgineum
> pulsat utrimque et ad ossa secat
> Eulalia numerante notas.
> "scriberis ecce mihi, domine.
> quam iuvat hos apices legere
> qui tua, Christe, tropaea notant!
> nomen et ipsa sacrum loquitur
> purpura sanguinis eliciti." (*Peristephanon* 3, 131–40)[46]

Immediately, twin executioners tore into her slim breast, striking with iron claws the virgin's chest on both her sides and cutting to the bone. Eulalia counts the marks. "See, Lord," she cries, "You're written on me now! How good it is to read these letters spelling our Your victories; the purple blood drawn forth itself declares Your holy name."

Prudentius's description is both sensual and highly artificial; it turns Eulalia into a work of art, her limbs painted [*picta*] with her own blood. When she is burned at the stake, the virgin's sexual modesty is preserved by her long hair, but the image of her "fragrant locks" catching fire first and blanketing her in flame is itself entirely erotic. To hurry her death, she breathes in the flame, and breathes out her soul in the form of a snow-white dove. Prudentius's language is often deliberately Vergilian, and the image of Eulalia can hardly help but recall that of Dido, burning both literally and figuratively for a different kind of love.[47]

In his hymn to Agnes, Prudentius adapts Ambrose's epithalamic mode, making the analogy between sex and death even more explicit:

> ut vidit Agnes stare trucem virum
> mucrone nudo, laetior haec ait:
> "exulto talis quod potius venit

vesanus, atrox, turbidus armiger,
quam si veniret languidus ac tener
mollisque ephebus tinctus aromate,
qui me pudoris funere perderet.
hic, hic amator iam, fateor, placet:
ibo inruentis gressibus obviam,
nec demorabor vota calentia:
ferrum in papillas omne recepero
pectusque ad imum vim gladii traham." *(Peristephanon* 14, 69–78)

When Agnes saw a grim-faced man stand forth with naked sword, she joyfully exclaimed, "I'm glad that it's a man like this who comes, a raging, cruel,
violent man-at-arms and not some delicate, tender, gentle youth, perfume-
scented, who would destroy me with the death of chastity. This lover, this one
at last, I confess, pleases me; I will go forth to meet him with hastening steps,
I will not deny his burning desire. I will take his blade into my breast, I will
draw the force of the stroke of his sword into the depths of my heart."

Prudentius's reworking of Ambrose's text also clarifies the role of the audience in relation to the virgin martyr, by collapsing the stories of Agnes and
the virgin of Antioch. The *trux tyrannis* [savage tyrant] condemns Agnes
to the brothel, but unlike the virgin of Antioch, she is not in the least
dismayed; she has no need to debate with herself about the relative values
of a virgin soul and a virgin body, because she already knows that her body
cannot be violated; the tradition of the inviolability of the virgin body is
an established fact both for Prudentius, writing more than a generation
after Ambrose, and for the virgin herself as he represents her:

"haud," inquit Agnes, "inmemor est ita
Christus suorum, perdat ut aureum
nobis pudorem, nos quoque deserat.
praesto est pudicis nec patitur sacrae
Integritatis munera pollui.
ferrum inpiabis sanguine, si voles,
non inquinabis membra libidine." *(Peristephanon* 14, 31–37)

"Christ is not so thoughtless of his own" she said "as to abandon us and let
our precious chastity be lost. He stands by the chaste and will not suffer the
gift of holy virginity to be defiled. You may, if you wish, pollute your sword
with blood, but you will not soil [a virgin's] limbs with lust."

These lines are significantly difficult to translate since neither the blood nor
the limbs are specifically identified as belonging to Agnes; she is already out
of her body, speaking not for herself but for the entire community that
she has come to represent, a community of virgins and by extension
a community of Christians who believe in the sacred value of virginity

even when they are not themselves virgin. This community is implicit in the crowd of people who refuse to look at Agnes when she is publicly exposed; the young man who does dare to look, on the other hand, is a more problematic figure:

intendit unus forte procaciter
os in puellam nec trepidat sacram
spectare formam lumine lubrico.
en ales ignis fulminis in modum
vibratur ardens atque oculos ferit.
caecus corusco lumine corruit
atque in plateae pulvere palpitat. (*Peristephanon* 14, 44–49)

One of them, it happened, cast a shameless glance upon the maiden and did not fear to look upon her sacred beauty with a lustful eye; a flame winged like a thunderbolt with shivering heat smote his eye and he fell blind from the blazing light and lay twitching in the dust of the square.

Prudentius's narrative technique, even more than that of Ambrose, invites the reader to behave just like this young man, to cast a desiring eye upon the body of the virgin martyr and to have that desire instantly and irrevocably reconfigured for the good of the community.

Several significant transformations have occurred in the story of the virgin martyr as retold by Ambrose and Prudentius. First, the narrative has become generic, as has its heroine, who becomes, in tales like these, very much a store brand rather than a name brand, her identity almost entirely effaced by the function she fulfills. The plot of the narrative becomes formulaic, and one of its constitutive elements is the threat of rape, never fulfilled. Irresistibly desirable, the virgin martyr must be raped; defined by her virginity, she cannot be raped. Instead of penetration by a penis, she will inevitably suffer penetration by a sword. The threat of rape is a way of reconfiguring the virgin rather than virginity; it is imagined as peculiar to women, just as virginity was once a condition peculiar to women; the threat of rape, in fact, becomes a way of making female virginity more fragile than the male equivalent, even though the experience of the desert fathers had suggested that nothing in this world was more tenuous than male chastity, which could be undone by the involuntary movement of a single, rebellious organ. The virgin's speech in these accounts is equally paradoxical, simultaneously combative and powerless; her words cannot convert her tormentor, but can annoy him severely. Her silence can only, finally, be ensured by decapitation. The generic impression created by these virgin martyr narratives (the most significant distinction between Agnes and Eulalia in Prudentius's telling is metrical) is in large part produced by the self-conscious qualities of the texts themselves, by Ambrose's rich rhetoric and Prudentius's pseudo-Vergilian poetics, both of which focus attention on the telling rather than the tale. The virgin becomes merely the object upon which such rhetoric can deploy itself, the blank screen rendered meaningful by a play of colored lights projected onto it. As Bloch notes, within the aestheticizing rhetoric of patristic discourse, "virginity, as absolute, has no substance, does not exist. . .the abstraction that virginity implies is destroyed by its articulation."[48] To this formulation, itself as absolute as any patristic *sententia*, I would add one important qualification: patristic discourse was not, however much it tried to be, universal. Struggle though it might to make virginity a "concept. . .emptied of sense,"[49] virgins themselves had consistently challenged or even, in some cases, openly refused patristic overdetermination in the first few centuries of the Christian era. The existence of the virgins of Carthage demonstrates this impulse, while Eusebius's narrative invites us to see virginity in pragmatic, political terms, as a form of resistance against corrupt and unjust temporal authorities, and especially as a bond between women.

In the century that separates Prudentius's Agnes from Eusebius's Valentina, the literary virgin martyr has become the victim of sacrifice rather than execution, a sacrifice that is reenacted each time an actual virgin takes the veil, choosing to live her virginity as martyrdom. This ritual is presided over not by the agents of the imperial government but by the agents of the imperial church. It is the transformation of the virgin from willing victim in the cause of politico-religious resistance into even more willing lamb to the slaughter in the cause of spiritual authority that provokes the definitive emptying out of sense which Bloch describes. The generic narrative pioneered by Ambrose and Prudentius was to prove enormously powerful and genuinely repressive; it worked to enshrine the virgin martyr and her imitators as ideal figures within a system both normatively heterosexual and heterosexually hierarchical.[50] The perfect virgin, defined in terms inseparable from her biological femaleness, is absolutely subject to the masculine authority of the church, an authority that invoked her intact body as talismanic and foundational, even while severely controlling the range of meaning that fetishized body could convey. In the centuries to come, even the stories of Ambrose and Prudentius were occasionally revisited and reinvested with alternative meanings, refilled with sense, especially in retellings by women. Before turning to such revisions, however, it seems necessary to consider the inevitable implication of the male author in a narrative in which revelation, as Bloch points out, is always violation.[51] In both Ambrose and Prudentius, the author who describes the passion of the virgin, thus putting her on show before a fascinated audience, takes up a role uncomfortably close to that of the *trux tyrannis*. Once again, my analysis will attempt to read through the paradoxical structures

Bloch maps so compellingly, and to look for the virgins hidden behind the discourse of virginity.

Violating Virgins

Late in his career, when he was well established as the leading advocate of consecrated virginity in Italy, if not in the Christian world, Ambrose became involved in a legal case regarding a virgin named Indicia, who was accused of unchastity by her brother-in-law and brought to trial.[52] The letter he wrote concerning the case to Bishop Syagrius of Verona demonstrates both a passionate commitment to the concept of chastity as a moral rather than physical condition, and deep ambivalence about the potentially metaphysical nature of virginity. It is unclear exactly how the charge against Indicia arose (it seems likely that the brother-in-law desired greater control over both the virgin and her inheritance) but the two bishops seem to have been united in believing Indicia innocent. Where they differed was in their attitudes toward how this innocence could be proven. Syagrius had wanted to avoid a public trial by having Indicia examined by a midwife in order to prove or disprove her virginity; Ambrose objected strenuously, maintaining that such a procedure was both immodest and inconclusive, and that in any case a professed virgin's chastity was sufficiently demonstrated by her manner of conducting herself. Even while arguing that virginity is a condition determined by moral criteria, however, Ambrose worries also that a gynecological examination might "damage the seal [nota] of intact virginity" (Letter 5.9). A nota is a mark, sign, or signal imprinted (perhaps with a signet ring) or attached in order to identify a body, a book, or any object; it is also, figuratively, a mark of character or quality. Ambrose's use of this particular word invests the hymen with a quasi-legal status and implies that the presence or absence of this remarkable mark has everything to do not only with the morality of the woman in the case, but with the question of who possesses her. If the seal that identifies her as belonging to the church is tampered with, then the goods themselves, in other words, immediately become suspect. While an intact hymen could not make an immoral woman chaste, the rupture of the hymen even by accident might open the perfectly closed body of a moral woman, thus undoing her virginity. In this incident, medical and theological concepts concerning virginity conflict, revealing the degree to which the hymen, however it was defined by medical writers, was an necessary generator of metaphor and paradox for theological writers. Ambrose needs the idea of the hymen as sign, mark, or seal, if only to undo its meaning. In the case of a real woman like Indicia, virginity is never fully dissociable from female biology; her virginity is, in Ambrose's mind, intimately associated with although never guaranteed by her intact hymen, an organ whose very intactness can only be disproved and never proved. The story of the virgin martyr as Ambrose tells it, in which a virgin is always the object of sexual desire, reinforces this essentialism. If the virgin of Antioch had been raped and then put to death, would she have been any less a holy martyr? It is a question that Ambrose resists confronting; both Agnes and the virgin of Antioch remain absolutely untouchable objects of desire. Death always guarantees virginity, and virginity death.

The elaborate metaphorical connections established between virginity, rape, and death by Ambrose and Prudentius became dreadfully literal in 410, by which time both bishop and poet were dead. After besieging Rome for the better part of two years, and reducing it (according to Jerome's report, which may not be entirely trustworthy) to cannibalism, Alaric and his Goths breached the walls and sacked the city. The Goths were Arian Christians, and they spared the great churches on Alaric's orders; they were not so considerate of consecrated Christian women, many of whom were raped or threatened with rape. Jerome recounts the courage of Marcella, an old woman herself, defending a younger and more appealing protégée of hers from the soldiers who irrupted into her house (Letter 127). For this one success, however, there were many failures; some of the consecrated women who suffered rape killed themselves. The sack of Rome, the ancient imperial city, untouched by foreign armies since the fourth century B.C.E., was an unimaginable shock to the entire culture of late antiquity. Some pagans insisted that the sack was a punishment for having abandoned the worship of the ancient, Roman gods in favor of an imported near-eastern religion like Christianity; many Christians wondered how such a violation could have been visited upon the city, which was the center of the Catholic world, home to the tombs of both Peter and Paul. That Barbarians should have attacked Christian virgins and not been blasted by thunderbolts, that virgins should be sexually humiliated and left alive, bereft of what was to most people their defining characteristic of physical integrity, was enough to shake the faith of all but the most pious. In order to restore and refine that faith, Augustine undertook the composition of the *City of God*, a book in which the situation of the virgin will become even more paradoxical than it was for the bishop of Milan. If, for Ambrose, the only good virgin was a dead virgin, for Augustine even death does not guarantee chastity. For him, virginity is vulnerable even to a thought and the hymen, the sign of virginity, is always already ruptured from the very moment that any question concerning it can be raised.

Augustine's attitude toward the cult of virginity espoused by Ambrose had always been ambivalent; while Ambrose surrounded himself with consecrated virgins like a sort of holy bodyguard, Augustine's life at Hippo was severely masculine. Nor was he particularly enthusiastic about extremes of feminine asceticism; his letter to Ecdicia, a woman who had pressured her husband into accepting a continent marriage, blames her severely for her husband's subsequent adultery. She had no right, according to Augustine, to lay claim to physical independence in the name of spiritual devotion. Ambrose, in contrast, had described with approval a girl who defied her family, publicly seizing the altar and declaring her virginity although they wished her to marry (*On Virgins* 1.11.65–66). In his attitudes toward virginity, in fact, Augustine is very much the inheritor of that earlier North African, Tertullian; he is profoundly wary of encouraging the virgin to mistake her physical integrity for moral superiority. Nor would he have accepted Ambrose's equation of martyrdom with virginity; for Augustine, the two were of entirely different orders. Martyrdom is a much greater gift than virginity, and it depends upon humility, a humility with which the virtuous married woman must of necessity be very familiar. For this reason, as he makes clear in *On Holy Virginity*, the married woman might actually have an edge over the virgin, when it came to displaying the humility essential to the martyr: "[the virgin] may not yet be a Thecla, but perhaps [the married woman] is already a Crispina" (*Holy Virginity* 45). Crispina, like Perpetua, was a married martyr.

For Augustine, virginity is admirable only so long as it does not allow the inappropriate exaltation of the virgin, either by herself or by others, in any way that would threaten the natural and appropriate hierarchy that subordinated women to men. For him, bodies are signs, always pointing toward but never revealing the truth, which is the image of God. The female body is an especially inefficient and limited sign, because

> in their bodily sex, [women] do not signify [the image of God]. Therefore they are ordered to be veiled. The part which they, as women, signify, may be called the concupiscent part, over which the mind subject to God, is dominant, so long as it lives in an upright and orderly way. Thus the mind and the concupiscent part of a single human being (one ruling, the other ruled, one dominant, the other subject) are represented by two beings, man and woman, as regards bodily sex. (*Monks* 594)

In this characteristically complex formulation, the feminine, expressed as "woman," represents the weakness and sensuality inherent in all human beings, male and female. Male sexuality may be a constant reminder of the Fall of Man, but this formulation of concupiscence itself as womanly displaces even the unmanageable erection, as a manifestation of the "concupiscent part," onto the feminine. Whereas Ambrose is willing, even eager to imagine the virgin as ritually pure, untouchable, possessed of a moral superiority manifested through her intact flesh, Augustine distrusts the condition of virginity defined according to either physical or meta-physical terms, precisely because it is associated with a bodily sex that cannot fully signify the image of God.

In his discussion of the violated virgins of Rome in the City of God, Augustine elaborates a typical "double bind,"[53] which severely limits the ability of women to claim either physical or moral virginity. He begins by admitting that no one is responsible for an act of lust committed upon her body by another: "As long as the spirit through which the body earns its sanctity remains constant, the violence of another's lust does not deprive even the body of its holiness, which is safeguarded by the maintenance of its own self-control" (City 1.18). As a counterexample, Augustine imagines the case of a consecrated virgin who is on her way to meet her lover, hav-ing already decided to give herself to him; from the moment when that decision is reached, the physical intactness of her body means nothing. Virginity is now defined as a purely metaphysical value. There is a catch, however. Augustine goes on to consider the case of women who killed themselves for shame in the aftermath of rape, taking Lucretia as his model. There are, according to him, two ways of interpreting her behavior: either she suffered from the sin of pride, and therefore could not bear to live with her humiliation, or, just possibly, Lucretia, was not really innocent: "What if (although she alone could know this) she was seduced by her own lust and, although the youth did violently attack her, she consented, and then was so remorseful when she came to punish that act that death seemed to her the only expiation?" (1.19). A potentially liberating argument is thus trans-formed into a way of making women if not actually responsible for their own rape, at least responsible for the loss of their chastity.

Augustine expands the argument to include Christian women by revis-iting Ambrose's example of Pelagia and her companions: "As far as these women are concerned, I do not dare give any rash judgment. Indeed, I do not know whether divine authority may have given the church some valid witness according to which their memory is thus honored; perhaps it is so" (1.26). But perhaps not; the insinuations Augustine has already made con-cerning Lucretia, whom he sees as at worst an adulteress, at best excessively greedy for praise, continue to resonate in his doubt about authoritative wit-ness to the divine inspiration of the suicide of Pelagia and her sisters. The possibility of having, on some level, consented to rape is always present in Augustine's discussion of the matter, even when, explicitly, he denies it; during a rape, while "chastity may not be expelled, still shame may be injected, for fear that the mind may be believed to have consented to the will of another in an act which might not perhaps have taken place with-out some carnal pleasure" (1.16). One way or another, the virgin's chastity, of mind as well as of body, cannot escape undamaged. Virginity is thus transferred from the realm of the physical into the realm of the moral, and since women are inevitably associated with the physical, as images not of God but of the "concupiscent part," spiritual purity becomes for them a virtual impossibility. Augustine establishes an ideal of moral virginity distinct from the physical only to call it into question by insisting on the inseparability of flesh and spirit in the body of woman. Like Tertullian, he thus enacts on a rhetorical level the rape that is always only threatened in the stories of the virgin martyrs as recounted by Ambrose or Prudentius. Augustine, in fact, by violating Lucretia's chastity verbally, casts himself rather paradoxically in the role of the Arian barbarians whose violence he professes to deplore. It is worth remembering that while Lucretia was a fictional character, the Christian women whose rape provided part of the impetus for the *City of God* were real women, contemporaries of Augustine even though personally unknown to him; the potential effect of his rhetoric upon lived lives, therefore, was enormous.

In essence, for both Augustine and Ambrose, virginity is a quality that can only be disproved and never proved. It is always a vanishing virtue, so precarious, in fact, that it can only be asserted in the negative. The consecrated woman who suffers rape has lost something, even if she consented neither in mind nor in body; what she had in the first place can never be properly observed or defined. Only the legendary virgin martyr is unequivocally virgin. Only in the case of Eulalia can the interior *nota* be read on the exterior, in the bloody letters of Christ's name inscribed upon virgin flesh. As Agnes exposed in the brothel, the virgin martyr is something to behold, which may inspire awe, devotion, even conversion; she is herself the sign or seal of the community of Christians, but she is not its voice. Even Thecla, in a brief appearance in Ambrose's *On Virgins*, is no longer a voice denouncing injustice or preaching the word of the Lord, but the inviolable object of the averted gaze of a male lion:"They saw the creature crouched on the ground and licking her feet, silent witness to the fact that it could not violate the virgin's sacred body. . .By adoring the martyr, the lions taught the meaning of religion; they taught chastity, for they kissed only the virgin's feet and lowered their eyes modestly to the ground, so to speak, so that no male, not even an animal, might see a virgin naked" (1.3.20). The virgin's body now holds the gaze of pagan persecutor and Christian worshipper alike in a sort of erotic stasis. The erotic is, as Bataille and the Marquis De Sade have taught us, congruent with but not necessarily contiguous to the sexual:"There is no better way to know death than to link it with some licentious image. . .Eroticism, unlike simple sexual activity, is a psychological quest independent of the natural goal."[54] The sexual, which was something to be actively resisted in the *Acts of Thecla*, is here transcended by voyeuristic eroticism. It is not simply repressed, it is sublimated, a more complex process producing a diffusion rather than a denial of desire and one that creates a sensual experience all the more heightened for being liberated from the merely genital. The equation of death with sex not sex with death subtly alters the nature of martyrdom: it transforms an execution into a sacrifice, and in so doing creates an intimate relationship not only between the female victim and the male executioner, but also between the virgin and the male author, which extends to include the observer or auditor, both within and outside the text. The radiant and pathetic figure of Agnes can arouse an emotion on the part of Ambrose's congregation which is both akin to and distinct from sexual desire, enormously powerful and yet licit, and it depends upon the voicelessness of the virgin herself, on her willingness to testify through her body rather than her words. While Thecla was cited disapprovingly as an imitable model for feminine speech by Tertullian, the experience of the violated virgins of Rome demonstrates that only the voicelessness of the reimagined virgin could be imitated; her inviolability was impossible in the real world.

The models of Agnes, Eulalia, and the virgin of Antioch would define the legend of the virgin martyr for the next five hundred years. "In male-supremacist cultures," as Andrea Dworkin remarks, "women are believed to embody carnality: women are sex."[55] The definition of female virtue exclusively in terms of sexual purity reinforces this notion; the virgin becomes the exception that proves the rule, and as such a mechanism for the enforcement of normative notions of hierarchical heterosexuality, which subjected women to men while erasing the possibility of the kind of female to female connection expressed by the story of Valentina and the woman of Gaza.[56] The examples of these women, like Methodius's experiments in radical androgyny, suggest that the reduction of the virgin martyr narrative to such a restrictive paradigm was required precisely *because* the ideal of virginity seemed capable of becoming the ground either of an exclusively feminine access to sanctity or a radical equality between the sexes. It is difficult otherwise to explain why narratives with so little basis in historical fact, not to mention so little plot development, incident, or suspense, continued to be told and retold through the ages. Virgin martyrs had no obvious, immediate relevance to the lives of those holy women, some of them queens and most of them nuns, who achieved sainthood during the sixth to tenth centuries. The virgin martyr narrative, in fact, remained curiously aloof from the lived lives of actual Christian women, who lacked the opportunity to demonstrate their faith by dying for it, and this is part of the point. The tales of legendary martyrs functioned to create a closed circle of impossibly idealized virgins to whose rank a young mother like Perpetua could not be admitted, nor a peripatetic preacher like Thecla whose virginity had not been granted the ultimate seal of approval in death. Not until Hrotsvitha in the tenth century and Hildegard in the twelfth began to rewrite the martyrologies in their own words and even more importantly in their own images would the repressive paradigm of virgin martyrdom be undone in ways that permitted the premises of gender hierarchy to be rethought.

CHAPTER 3

FROM THE SUBLIME TO THE RIDICULOUS IN
THE WORKS OF HROTSVITHA

The preface to Hrotsvitha of Gandersheim's first work, a collection of six *Legends*, invites us to imagine the author as a timid young woman, uncertain of her literary skills and anxious about the reception of her book:

> I need the help of many to defend this little work now that it is finished, all the more so since at the beginning I was not sustained by much strength of my own; I was not yet mature in years, nor advanced in my studies. But I did not dare to reveal the direction of my intent by asking the advice of someone wiser, for fear that I might be forbidden to write on account of my down-home way of speaking [*rusticitas*]. So, in total secrecy and almost furtively, struggling alone to write, and sometimes tearing up what was poorly written, I worked away as best I could to put together a text which might be of some slight value, woven from passages of other writings which I gathered together in the granary of our foundation of Gandersheim. (Pref. I: 5–6)[1]

Rusticitas derives from *rus*, the Latin word for the countryside, and wakes a series of literary echoes resonating all the way back to Horace, who had written an engaging satire on the adventures of a country mouse and a city mouse, in which the country mouse came out ahead. In the context of most classical Latin rhetoric, however, *rusticitas* was not a desirable quality. It described speech that was provincial, rural, boorish, uncouth, the antithesis of *urbanitas*, the polished eloquence to which all rhetors must aspire.[2] In contrast to their classical and late antique predecessors, medieval writers, painfully aware of the differences between their own Latin and the eloquence of patristic writers like the "honey-tongued" Ambrose and the great Augustine, let alone that of models like Vergil and Cicero, tried to make a virtue of simplicity. "Why should I be afraid of my ignorance," asks Gregory of Tours at the beginning of his *Life of St. Martin*, "when the Lord, our Redeemer and our God, selected fishermen instead of orators and countryfolk instead of philosophers. . .?"[3] By implying familiarity with this long rhetorical tradition, Hrotsvitha's protestation of *rusticitas* thus immediately begins to undermine itself. The process is completed by the image elaborated in the following sentence, in which the writer is represented not as an author, with all the connotations of authority built into that term, but as a collator, one who gathers up and organizes the bounty of Gandersheim's library. The image of the writer as mere laborer in the monastic granary neatly recognizes the original, literal sense of *rusticitas* and thus reinvents the word in its positive metaphorical sense, as country simplicity. The representation of her own professed literary naïveté thus paradoxically becomes the ultimate proof of Hrotsvitha's sophisticated ability to manipulate language; it would be difficult to imagine a more disingenuous apology.

Nor does Hrotsvitha's method of gathering together texts for her collection of saints' lives prove to be simple; instead of limiting herself to choosing and transcribing her sources, Hrotsvitha recast them into verse, into dactylic hexameters or elegiac couplets, embellished with leonine rhymes. She defends her use of meter in the following terms:

> Although composing in meter is supposed to be laborious and difficult for the fragile female sex, by relying upon the exclusive help of merciful grace from on high, I have tried to put the songs of this little work into dactylic meters. I have done this not with any confidence in my own powers, but so that the little imaginative talent granted me should not lie sluggish in the dark cave of my heart and be destroyed by the rust of neglect, but rather be struck by the hammer of earnest devotion and give forth a little chime of divine praise so that even if the occasion never arose for any further profit to come of it, still the sound itself might in the end be transformed into a useful instrument. (Pref. I: 8)

Hrotsvitha's use of the modesty *topos* is keenly double-edged here, as many readers before me have noted.[4] Having admitted that metrical composition is supposed to be too taxing for the feminine intellect, Hrotsvitha goes on to say that she has chosen to write in verse nonetheless, not for any pragmatic reason, not, for instance, because verse has the power to be more persuasive than prose, an argument with which she would have been familiar from classical sources such as Horace's *Ars Poetica*, but because she has a divine gift for meter (albeit a slight one) and it would be a sin to let it go unused. This statement neatly separates poetic ability, represented by the God-given capacity to make a pleasing sound, from the poet herself, thus maintaining her pose of humility (nearly) intact.

Earlier Christian writers had struggled with the question of whether it was permissible to use the forms and language of pagan literature to convey Christian truth. "What does Horace have to do with the Psalter, or Vergil with the Gospels?" Jerome had demanded in his letter to Eustochium.[5] For Prudentius, however, Christian subjects could only revitalize the ancient forms of Roman poetry, and much of his work is designed to prove precisely this; in his work, the *carmen* (poem or song) that praised Roman power when voiced by Vergil or Horace will now devote itself to the glory of the martyrs and the praise of the apostles.[6] As late antiquity faded imperceptibly into the early Middle Ages, the appropriateness of poetry as a vehicle for divine praise began to be taken for granted. When the Anglo-Saxon abbot of Malmesbury, Aldhelm, undertook to compose a work on virginity in the late seventh century, he did so in the form of a *liber geminatus*, a twinned book, written once in prose and once in verse to demonstrate his own virtuosity, his ability to reinvent Latin poetry in a Christian context.[7]

Aldhelm was much admired in Britain—Bede called him "a shining example of style, admirable for his literary as well as his ecclesiastical erudition"[8]—and his influence was felt at a very early date on the Continent. Boniface, a central figure in the evangelization of Germany during the eighth century, carried the works of Aldhelm with him to monasteries at Fulda, Würzburg, and Mainz; in fact, the earliest copy of the prose *Letter on Virginity* is a ninth-century manuscript from Würzburg while other copies of his work were made at Reichenau, Saint Riquier, and Saint Gallen.[9] The accessibility of insular texts to tenth-century German writers, the fact that several of the same stories are told by Aldhelm and Hrotsvitha, and the verbal echoes from the *Poem on Virginity*, which emerge here and there in both her *Legends* and *Plays*, suggest powerfully that Aldhelm was one of the authors represented in Gandersheim's comprehensive library. Any comparison of Hrotsvitha's work with Aldhelm's, however, can only serve to emphasize the continental author's originality in dealing with her source materials. Aldhelm's two books on virginity look back self-consciously to the attitudes of Ambrose and especially Jerome, representing women like Agnes, Eulalia, and Thecla in static and objective terms, as icons of passive suffering and absolute humility before the Divine Will, completely without will of their own. Both the message of his text and its medium, with its Vergilian flourishes, establish him as an author with impeccable literary and theological forefathers. Hrotsvitha, on the other hand, weaves themes of virginity, eloquence, and power together in quite different patterns from those of her predecessors. As a member of the "fragile" female sex, she cannot insert herself effortlessly into the masculine genealogy of authority as Aldhelm does, but the sly subtext of her preface suggests that she is perfectly aware that the grounds of her exclusion have nothing to do with lack of ability.

Hrotsvitha's voice is the first female voice we have heard since the very different one of Perpetua; she is the first woman to take up the stories

institutionalized by Ambrose and Prudentius, and in her retellings the
virgin martyr will no longer be an icon of silence for holy women, a
metonym for the Christian Church, or the voiceless and compelling object
of an erotic gaze. Hrotsvitha's virgins are characterized not by silence
but by a forensic eloquence, which is both passionate and intellectual.
While Ambrose would have acknowledged his Agnes reborn in Aldhelm's
poem and Jerome would probably have been pleased at the afterlife there
of Demetrias and Eustochium, the personalities woven from Hrotsvitha's
gleanings in the Gandersheim library would be scarcely recognizable to the
authors who told their stories in earlier centuries. The problem of authority is, nonetheless, a serious one for Hrotsvitha. Her work is full of citations
and allusions that demonstrate an intimate familiarity with the Latin tradition of the virgin martyr, a tradition that, as I argued in chapter 2, is
conducive to feminine silence rather than to chimes of divine praise, however faint. If there was, as I suggested in chapter 1, an early alternative to
the tradition of the patristic writers, embodied in the figure of Thecla and
modeling feminine independence and eloquence, it was completely lost to
Hrotsvitha. Like most of the medieval women writers who succeeded her,
she probably felt herself to be alone in her attempt to invent modes of
resisting the overdetermination of virginity and of rescuing the virgin
martyr from the no-woman's land to which the Fathers had banished her.
This makes Hrotsvitha's accomplishment even more extraordinary; in her
work, founded though it is in the repressive models of the fourth century, the
virgin martyr for the first time develops not only subjectivity but attitude.

Aldhelm and the Second Sex

The first part of Aldhelm's twinned book, the *Letter*, is addressed to Abbess
Hildelith and her community of nuns at Barking, an institution that was to
have a long and glorious career as a center of feminine devotion and education: "To the most reverend virgins of Christ, who should be revered
with every affection of devoted brotherhood, and celebrated not only for
the distinction of their corporeal chastity, which many achieve, but also
to be glorified on account of their spiritual purity, which few maintain"
(*Letter*, Dedicatio, pp. 228–29). The *Poem* was also probably intended for
the women of Barking; indeed Aldhelm promises in the *Letter* that, having
established a foundation in prose, he will go on to give it a poetic roof,
with trochaic tiles and dactylic shingles (*Letter* 60). The demands of the
epistolary genre mean that we get a clearer picture of the text's intended
audience in the *Letter* than in the *Poem*, and the essential characteristic of
that audience, as Aldhelm imagines it, is its high level of education. He
commends Abbess Hildelith for the "rich eloquence of her words and her

virginal expression of sophistication" (*Letter* 2), high praise indeed from a man whose own elaborate style gives the lie to the common assumption that medieval Latin is simple and easy to read. He imagines the nuns at Barking "growing learned in divine teaching through the motherly care of the Church" (*Letter* 2), and develops a string of classical athletic metaphors to convey their studious diligence: the ladies of Barking are like wrestlers, javelin casters, archers, riders, and rowers, competing in the contest for the ultimate prize of divine truth. Their zeal for study covers not only scripture, but also allegory, history, grammar, and prosody (*Letter* 4). They are also, finally, like bees, symbols both of diligence and of chastity, who generate wisdom instead of offspring (*Letter* 4–5).[10]

While recognizing the intellectual abilities of his audience, however, Aldhelm is also convinced of the secondary status of women in the divine order of things. The first catalog of examples in the *Letter* (and in the *Poem*, whose structure follows that of the letter fairly closely) is devoted to male virgins, beginning with figures from the Old Testament and continuing through representatives from the New Testament and more recent history. Only after this does he turn to women:

> Having, therefore, completed my summary of the examples of the masculine sex, who supported the structure of chaste behavior with a foundation of integrity which is in no way cracked, and moving on in gradual verbal steps to the equally distinguished members of the second sex [*ad inclitas itidem secundi sexus personas*] who continually endured in the preservation of holy virginity with an inflexible strength of mind, I shall endeavor to pluck successfully the loveliest flowers of purity from these women so that I may be able to embroider with a braid that cannot be unwoven the crown of eternal beatitude. (*Letter* 39)[11]

The imagery of this passage is somewhat at odds with Aldhelm's assertion that the distinction of women in the pursuit of chastity may be the same as that of men. It is not simply that he places men first and women second, thus implying an essential inequity; more problematic is the trope that makes men the foundation of an edifice of sanctity based upon spiritual integrity, since this makes men essential to the entire structure, while the role of women remains undefined. The first use of the building metaphor in the *Letter* established prose as a foundation to be roofed with poetry; if this second metaphor is taken as operating in parallel, so that women are imagined as the roof of a temple to chastity, then they are essential components of the structure, even though one may be moved to wonder just how well dactyls and trochees will keep out the rain and snow. The possibility that women constitute mere ornaments, however, finials, friezes, or decorative ironwork upon a fundamental edifice of masculine chastity, is not excluded. As Bloch reminds us, "the contrast between the straight, forceful, truthful language of man and the gracious, curvaceous, refined language of women is more than simply a contrast between styles";[12] it is always already a moral judgment. Aldhelm's association of women with ornament becomes explicit in the last part of the letter, a paraphrase of Cyprian's *On the Dress of Virgins*, in which he cautions the nuns of Barking against excessive vanity. This warning is nominally addressed to religious of both sexes, but the instances of sartorial excess he cites, long polished fingernails, dresses with embroidered hems, and so on, are clearly directed at women.

The final metaphor of the passage, in which Aldhelm proposes to "pluck the flowers of purity" from his female examples, is equally ambivalent. It is presumably intended to recall the literary activity of poets like Prudentius, whose *Peristephanon* is a floral crown or garland of tales of the martyrs, but, particularly given Aldhelm's classicizing impulse, it can hardly help but recall the language of Latin love poetry in which plucking flowers is almost inevitably associated with sexual pleasure, with the loss of female chastity. Aldhelm could not have known the most famous classical example, Catullus's image of the flower cut by the plow in one of the bitterest of his poems to Lesbia, but Ovid's account of the rape of Persephone by Pluto, in which the virgin is plucked by the god as she herself plucks spring flowers, was certainly available to him.[13] Just as the object of the elegist's sexual and textual desire is his mistress' body, so the object of Aldhelm's praise when he turns his attention to women is a purity that, for all his equivocation, is never entirely independent of the female body.

In fact, it is precisely the limitation of women to and by the body that allows men to be the primary, foundational models for virginity in Aldhelm's scheme. His male examples are generally and often even primarily associated with virtues and abilities that may be grounded in sexual purity but which transcend it. The Old Testament figures, Elijah, Elisha, Jeremiah, and Daniel are all prophets; in the case of Daniel (and Jeremiah in the *Poem*) prophecy is explicitly described as the reward of virginity. Among the "modern" male virgins, John the Baptist, John the Evangelist, John the Abbot, and Silvester are all also identified as prophets. Some have even more extraordinary powers, implicitly made possible because of their virgin status: John the Evangelist, Martin of Tours, and Julian can all raise the dead, while other male virgins perform a variety of miracles from healing the sick to living underwater for twenty-four hours. All these men are more than simply virgins; some are martyrs, some are hermits, some are bishops, and a few combine all of these roles; some, like Ambrose, Jerome, and Basil of Caesarea, are Fathers of the Church and precursors of Aldhelm in the literary pursuit of virginity. In spite of his deep familiarity with their works, however, Aldhelm never betrays the kind of anxiety about the physical indefiniteness of male virginity, which was so obsessive in the works of fourth- and fifth-century writers; in fact, he turns Basil's mournful *et feminam non cognosco et virgo non sum* [Woman I know not, and yet I am no virgin] completely inside out:

> . . .Basil, in fact, lived without corruption of the flesh, by virtue of his integrity; I know this from interpreting his own aphorism, "Woman I know not, and yet I am no virgin." Indeed, it is said to be a traditional practice of accomplished orators who, standing up high on the rostrum address crowds of people and, in the presence of a diverse audience composed of both sexes, they sometimes assume a different persona from their own. . .the bishop I mentioned before is thus presumed to be speaking in this oratorical mode, claiming that the spotlessness of bodily chastity, which is only external, is in no way sufficient for the acquisition of the distinction of genuine integrity. (*Letter* 27)

Basil's admission of the inevitable carnality of the male, which we have seen reflected in the works of Augustine and Cassian, is here transformed into a demonstration of consummate rhetorical virtuosity, on a par with the demonstration of poetic skill that Aldhelm himself displays in, for instance, the metered double acrostic that forms the preface to his *Poem*.

Aldhelm thus succeeds in separating virginity almost entirely from corporeality in the case of his male virgins. In the case of women, on the other hand, virginity is defined not simply by corporeality but by the erotic charge that the female virgin body inevitably arouses; these flowers of chastity are here for Aldhelm to pluck precisely *because* the women whom he praises escaped having their flowers plucked by less high-minded admirers during their brief lives. The narratives attached to women in both *Letter* and *Poem* are strictly limited in comparison to those attached to men. The majority of Aldhelm's female virgins are martyrs, and not a single one of them raises anyone from the dead, nor are any of them gifted with prophecy. A quantitative analysis makes the difference between the sexes strikingly clear: Aldhelm's male exempla consist of thirty-one male virgins and five Old Testament figures of dubious relevance to the main argument (Joseph, David, Samson, Abel, and Melchizadech, of whom only Abel is an obvious contender for the title of virgin); of these, only seven are martyrs. On the women's side, there are twenty-two virgins and one Old Testament nonvirgin, Judith, who is cited as an example of how alluring and dangerous female adornment can be (albeit in a good cause); fourteen of these women, or almost two-thirds of them, are martyrs. What is more, they are all martyrs for virginity, by which I mean that their virgin state is the proximate cause of their martyrdom. They all follow the paradigm established by Ambrose in his story of Agnes, dying because they will not renounce their chastity, which is essentially equated with their faith. Of the male martyrs, only one, Malchus, who is captured by pirates and sold into slavery, dies "rather than profane his chastity" (*Letter* 31).[14] Aldhelm's catalog of virgins thus reveals a distinction between masculine and feminine experience, which is both quantitative and qualitative. Virginity is only one aspect of sanctity for men; for women, it is virtually the only one, and it is not associated with supernatural or prophetic power. Even the rare exceptions to the rule are instructive. Mary, of course, is *sui generis*. Eugenia, who dresses as a man and becomes a monk, achieves holiness by denying her gender. Eustochium and Demetrias, familiar to Aldhelm from Jerome's *Letters*, are praised for their learning, but even more for inspiring dedications from such a learned man; their virginity inspires a devotion that mirrors desire. Constantina converts a pagan general by means of her unassailable virginity, which is indistinguishable from her beauty; again, the virgin is the object of desire. Thecla, finally, is represented as a somewhat defective model, precisely because she does *not* make the supreme sacrifice—Aldhelm praises Eulalia, who follows Thecla in his catalog, as superior because she is both virgin *and* martyr. Men may overthrow pagan sanctuaries, like Martin, stop tidal waves, like Hilarion, or be wafted across rivers without incurring the shame of undressing, like Amos; what women do best is to arouse the lust of pagan persecutors and die in defense of their chastity.[15]

The Strong Voice of Gandersheim

Hrotsvitha's *Legends* were evidently a success, the first stage of what was to be an extraordinary literary career. They were followed by her most famous work, a collection of plays on holy subjects, and by a couple of epic poems in praise of the Ottonian dynasty. In the preface to her plays, Hrotsvitha puns on her own Germanic name, calling herself the "strong voice of Gandersheim" [*clamor validus Gandershemensis*]. The Saxon monastery of Gandersheim of which she was a member was an institution that must almost naturally have produced such a voice. It had been founded in the mid-ninth century by Liodolf and Oda of Saxony, not coincidentally also the founders of the Ottonian imperial house, a dynasty that in its political ambitions and cultural sophistication belies the "Dark Ages" label so often applied to the tenth century. Gandersheim was a canonical rather than Benedictine institution.[16] In practice, this meant that Gandersheim had many of the powers and privileges of an independent principality. Its abbesses, mostly princesses of the blood, were also princesses of the Church and the nascent Saxon state; they could participate with other prelates in the imperial council and were even addressed as *metropolitana*, a feminine equivalent of the title granted to bishops.[17] In the mid-tenth century, Gandersheim benefited from both royal and papal protection, paid no tithe to bishops, minted its own money, and maintained a small private army.[18] Women living under the canonical system were not cloistered as were those who lived by a stricter version of the Benedictine rule; while they were not exactly free to renounce their vows (to do so would have been scandalous at the very least) they retained property upon entering the order, although it normally had to be administered on their behalf by a male relative. They were permitted to write to and receive letters from friends outside of the institution, to own books, and have servants.[19] Perhaps most importantly, they were not separated from the life of the court, and were in some cases intimately involved in that life; Otto II had made his sister Mathilda, abbess of Quedlinburg, regent when he went to war in Italy, and when Otto III went south to Rome to be crowned Holy Roman Emperor in 996, he took his sister Sophia out of Gandersheim to accompany him.[20] The French historian Labande makes it clear just how intimately connected the secular and religious worlds were for women in such positions: "One should see here the result of a realist dynastic politics: by refusing to marry its daughters, the imperial house avoided inviting troublesome and factional sons-in-law onto the edges of the succession; by making these daughters nuns or canonesses, and eventually abbesses, they established invaluable political adjuncts in the spiritual, intellectual and political strongholds which constituted the great monasteries of the Empire."[21] This is the world of which Hrotsvitha was a part, and it is probable that, like the emperor's niece Gerberga, her abbess and probably her friend, she was familiar with the Ottonian court, which was highly devout but also cosmopolitan and luxurious. Otto II was an amateur of clerical disputation; his mother was a Burgundian princess whose first marriage had connected her to the ruling families in Italy; his wife, Theophano, was a Byzantine princess who had brought with her to Aachen upon her marriage a collection of extraordinary silks as well as the Greek language, the relics of several Greek saints, and quite possibly books containing hagiographical material unfamiliar in the West, which eventually found its way into Hrotsvitha's work.[22]

Even in the *Legends*, Hrotsvitha demonstrates not only familiarity with a wide range of texts, but also a sharp critical awareness concerning them:

> If indeed the objection is made that some of these works are based upon sources which are, according to the opinion of some at least, apocryphal, this is not a crime of evil-minded presumption but rather the error of ignorance, for when I began to weave the threads of this braid, I did not know that some of the sources with which I was working were dubious.

> When I discovered this, I decided not to undo my work, because although things may seem false now, they may yet be proven true. (Pref. I: 2–4)

This passage at first reads like a modest disclaimer, of the sort that remains fashionable today in the prefaces to scholarly works ("any errors which remain are my own"). Beneath its apologetic surface, however, it is really a statement of confidence, and also a description of Hrotsvitha's method. The source of her *Maria*, the Apocryphal *Gospel of Matthew*, which may have been a Byzantine text that traveled West with Theophano and then circulated within the intellectual community of the Ottonian court, included elements that were certainly dubious by Catholic standards, while several of Hrotsvitha's other stories were at best noncanonical. The author, however, while not rejecting expert opinion outright, reserves judgment as to the truth value of such texts: the future may "prove" them.

A similar attitude toward the contextual nature of authority may be distinguished in Hrotsvitha's choice of source material for her life of Agnes, which contains reminiscences of a variety of earlier texts. Hrotsvitha's first line, *Virgo quae, vanas mundi pompas ruituri / Et luxus fragilis cupiens contempnere carnis* [A virgin who, desiring to flee the empty shows of the world and spurn the pleasure of the fragile flesh (*Agnes* 1)] echoes a line from Aldhelm's *Poem on Virginity*: *qui falsas mundi contemnunt pectore pompas* [in heart they spurn the false shows of the world (*Poem* 116)].[23] Half-lines and phrases from Prudentius's *Peristephanon* and *Psychomachia* also resonate through the poem, along with tags from a variety of other sources. These casual citations, most of which are not foregrounded or flagged in any way, suggest that Hrotsvitha had read widely and absorbed her reading thoroughly, without necessarily feeling the need to advertise it. The proximate source of her *Agnes*, however, is not Aldhelm, whose account of the Roman virgin is extremely brief, nor Prudentius, although Hrotsvitha clearly admired his style, but a prose letter mistakenly ascribed to Ambrose, which she renders quite closely into verse.[24] This choice of source is revealing; in contrast to Prudentius' depiction of Agnes, or that of Ambrose in *On Virgins*, both of which, as we have seen, concentrate on the pathetic passivity of the martyr, the Pseudo-Ambrosian letter provided Hrotsvitha with a representation of the virgin martyr conveyed through direct speech. This allows her to represent Agnes not as a suffering body but as an eloquent and rational voice, a woman who defends her choice of virginity as a talented lawyer might defend any other unusual but legally binding contract.

In general, Hrotsvitha respects the contents of the speeches she inherited from Pseudo-Ambrose. In the letter, for instance, Agnes argues in her initial rejection of her unwanted suitor that he must leave her alone because she is betrothed already to another lover, Christ, whose parentage is not only superior to his but dazzlingly paradoxical, who is more glorious than the sun or moon, who comes accompanied by choirs of angels rather than rowdy friends, who can offer her brighter jewels, feed her on milk and honey, and permit her the extraordinary privilege of loving and being loved in a heavenly bedroom while remaining a virgin.[25] Hrotsvitha resumes all these points, altering the order only slightly, but where Pseudo-Ambrose lingers upon an extended comparison between the worldly riches offered by the young aristocrat and the heavenly gifts promised to a bride of Christ, Hrotsvitha diminishes this element of the argument, perhaps uncomfortable with what sometimes feels like an appeal to a divinely oriented venality. From the beginning of the speech, Hrotsvitha places the emphasis not so much on the rewards of virginity but on the nature of the bond between herself and Christ:

> Nec credas a te posse meum pervertere purum
> Cor, quod amatoris praevenit nobilioris
> Dulcis amor, pulchrum cuius fidei fero signum
> In facie summa necnon in corpore toto,
> Quo me signavit strictimque sibi religavit. (*Agnes* 64–68)

> Do not think that you can pervert my pure heart, for it is protected by the sweet love of a nobler lover, and I bear upon my face and even in my body the beautiful sign of his faith, with which he has marked me and tied me tightly to him.

The leonine rhymes *pulchrum/signum* and *signavit/religavit* drive home the importance of the mysterious sign that marks Agnes as the betrothed of Christ. Borne upon her face, Agnes's "sign" is the manifestation through her beauty of something that is visible and yet at the same time hidden in her body. The word itself, *signum*, recalls the term Ambrose used when referring to Indicia's simultaneously meaningful and meaningless maidenhead, her *nota*. In Hrotsvitha's text, however, the permanence and validity of the seal impressed upon the body as a signet ring may be pressed into wax is neither questioned nor limited. It is a mark that is both physical and metaphysical, which quickly transcends the corporeal as the word *signum* itself is expanded into a constellation of related concepts. The mark upon Agnes's face and body is both the reason Christ loves her, and the guarantee or token (*pignus*) of that love: *Ille quidem talis me desponsavit amoris / Pignore ceu sponsam clara dotando corona* [He has engaged himself to me with a pledge of such love, giving me as though I were a bride a shining crown (*Agnes* 90–91)]. Maintaining the love that binds the virgin to Christ, however, is not an easy thing; it demands a concerted exercise of the will on her part: *Cui debebo fidem soli servare perennem: / Ipsi me toto cordis conamine credo*

[I must preserve my faith eternally for him. I believe myself to be his with the effort of my entire heart (*Agnes* 109–10)]. The importance of the *signum* and its multiplicity of meaning, are established at the very beginning of the poem, in Hrotsvitha's advice to those who may wish to follow Agnes:

> Conservet pure sincero cordis amore
> Signum laudabilis, quod portat, virginitatis;
> Quae<que> caput Christo signat velamine sacro. . . (*Agnes* 7–10)

> Let her preserve with the pure and sincere love of her heart the sign which she bears of her praiseworthy virginity, she who marks her head with the veil sacred to Christ.

Here again the sign is both the seal of her virginity and the external expression of it. The virgin marks herself with the veil; it is not imposed upon her by any external force.

For Agnes, of course, marking herself as a bride of Christ also means marking herself out for death, and Hrotsvitha makes it perfectly clear that her heroine is aware that this too is a free if difficult choice:

> Cuius amore quidem ferventes congrue pridem
> Perplures sacrae constanti corde puellae
> Elegere mori saevis poenisque necari,
> Quam decus insignis corrumpere virginitatis. (*Agnes* 15–18)

> Indeed, burning with love of him, many holy virgins with constant heart choose death and to be killed in savage ways rather than corrupt the honor of their remarkable virginity.

Insignis contains *signum* much as remarkable contains mark, and reminds the reader that the choice of the mark is inseparable from the choice of death. Confronted with the voice of Roman authority, which attempts through threats and intimidation to make her renounce her God, Agnes emphasizes the binding nature of her previous promise to Christ. In her first exchange with Simphronius, the mark of her faith, the sign that both preserves and condemns her, becomes increasingly identified with her word:

> Sed virgo Christi nec suppliciis superari
> Nec blandimentis potuit devincier ullis,
> Quin servaret amatori sine fraude priori,
> Quod pepigit, pactum, signo fidei stabilitum. (*Agnes* 150–54)

> But Christ's virgin would not be overcome by torture, nor could any sweet words dissuade her from preserving for her first love without deception the firm pact she had made with him as a mark of her faith.

The *pactum stabilitum* (once again the leonine rhyme reinforces the point Hrotsvitha is making) is an unbreakable promise, a legally binding agreement. The verb that controls this *pactum*, *pepigit*, from *pango*, has a rich and relevant range of meanings, including to fasten or fix, to determine, to contract, and also to compose, write, or record; it thus not only reinforces our sense that the bond between Agnes and Christ has the force of a formal contract, but makes Agnes the author of that contract. Guaranteed in this manner, Agnes's own words become increasingly effective from this point on, and begin to generate a new kind of sign, visible miracles. When Simphronius threatens her with the brothel, she dares him boldly (*audacter*) to carry out his threat, asserting that Christ will protect her. Sure enough, once she is stripped, her hair grows miraculously to cover her. Hrotsvitha has transposed this incident from Prudentius's account of the martyrdom of Eulalia, but her rendition of the miracle works hard to undo the sensuality with which the Roman poet invested it. Where Eulalia's miraculously growing hair gave forth a seductive fragrance, the sweet smell in Hrotsvitha's poem is completely disembodied and concomitantly de-eroticized. Rather than focusing attention on the naked body beneath the hair, Hrotsvitha arrests her reader's gaze by making the hair itself a curiously abstract covering so heavy as to be opaque. Thickening her verse itself, she notes the density of Agnes's hair and repeats the related words *tegumen* (a cover) and *tegere* (to cover) four times in five lines:

> Ast, ubi distracto nudatur **tegmine** toto,
> Continuo bene densati crevere capilli,
> Qui, ductu longo lapsi de vertice summo,
> Descendendo pedum plantas **tetigere** tenellas,
> Corpus et omne comis **tegitur** ceu **tegmine** vestis. (*Agnes* 215–19)

> But when she was naked, stripped of all her clothing, her hair grew so thick that, falling all the way from the top of her head, it descended to cover the tender soles of her feet, so that her entire body was covered with hair as though with a covering garment.

Where in Prudentius's poem the reader's gaze is invited to follow that of the martyr as she looks down on her own breasts being tormented, and the saint's shoulders and throat are revealed by the poet even as the hair grows to cover them, all that Hrotsvitha allows us to glimpse of Agnes is the tender soles of her feet.

This miracle is quickly followed by another, the appearance of an angel who clothes Agnes even more effectively in a radiant garment that is actually identified by the first man to enter the brothel as a *signum stupendum*, an astonishing sign. The transformation of the sign, which is a promise of fidelity and chastity, into a garment that preserves fidelity and chastity both reinforces the mutual nature of the contract between Christ and the virgin and serves to remind the poem's intended reader of her own identity with Agnes, an identity expressed by the veil with which she has chosen to mark her own head.[26] The angel, meanwhile, functions as a manifestation of the pledge itself; in the angel, the will of Christ and the will of Agnes come together and become inseparable. After prayers sung by Agnes and infused with the power of Christ have struck her unfortunate suitor dead, Agnes is reproached for cruelty by his distraught father. Hrotsvitha emphasizes the reasonable quality of Agnes's answer; her words are sweet (*dulcia*) and she speaks eloquently (*facunde*), in a logical and composed fashion (*bene composita ratione*) (287–88). She explains that it was not she who caused the young man's death but his own impiety, and offers to pray that he may be brought back to life; she does so, weeping and prostrating herself, and the angel appears once again in response to her prayer, restoring the youth to life "by means of the power of the word of God" (304). However little credit Agnes herself seeks for this miracle, it is quite clear to the revived and instantly converted young man that it is the "prayers of the holy virgin Agnes" (328) that have reversed God's decision concerning him. Like the male saints in Aldhelm's *Letter on Virginity*, but unlike her namesake in that text, Agnes has succeeded in raising a man from the dead.

Like his son, Simphronius is converted by the *signum stupendum* (333), which is simultaneously Agnes herself and the miracle she has performed. Other savage pagan priests, however, take over her persecution and condemn her to be burned alive. Agnes's prayer on the pyre evokes the interconnected integrity of her body and heart [*Corpore sed casto, puro cordisque secreto / Carnis spurcitas pertransivi bene cunctas / poenas* (381–83)] and produces another miracle: the flames go out instantly. The judge who presides over her execution is rendered furious by this incident, once again labeled as a *signum stupendum* (399), and orders that she be put to the sword. Here, Hrotsvitha chooses to eschew direct speech for once; where in the versions of both Prudentius and Ambrose, Agnes welcomes her executioner as though he were a lover and imagines her death as an erotic consummation, Hrotsvitha narrates the moment of martyrdom swiftly. The executioner as lover is replaced by the judge's sword, which initially appears to be operating almost independently of human agency, and it pierces Agnes's throat, not her breast, cutting off her words rather than violating her body: *Ense sed inmisso tenerum guttur penetrando / Martyris egregiae iugulum perfodit avare*. . . [With a drawn sword stabbing into her tender neck / He eagerly slit the throat of the excellent martyr (405–06)]. Agnes dies almost gently, falling asleep (*obdormit*) as she gives her last breath.

Once dead, Agnes's bond to Christ is made fully manifest by a shining crown and a martyr's palm. She herself becomes a sign, a pact, and a covenant when she appears to her family, slipping down from the sky accompanied by the Lamb of God and a crowd of virgins, all of whom in this text are female. Her instructions are simple: rejoice with me, she says, "for now in heaven I am joined in the sweet embrace of love with the one to whom I was always devoted with faithful mind here on earth, longing to gaze upon him without end" [*nunc in caelis illi coniungor amoris / Amplexu dulci, quem semper mente fideli / In terris colui, cupiens sine fine tueri* (448–50)]. Agnes's steadfastness of mind has been rewarded, and she herself is the guarantee that it will be rewarded in others. Her parents stop weeping and lift up their voices in song instead: *laudes domino psallebant voce canora* [they sing the praise of god with melodious voice (457)]. The final expression of the sign that Agnes has become is thus expressed through words of praise, through a song or a poem, which is finally indistinguishable from the poem of Hrotsvitha herself. The last vision of the poem returns us to the promise of the beginning, the promise that any virgin who wills it strongly enough may join the heavenly host: *Si velit . . . / sequens agnum carmen cantare sonorum / conservet pure sincero cordis amore / Signum laudabilis, quod portat, virginitatis* [If she wishes to sing the resounding song, following the lamb, let her keep purely with sincere love in her heart the sign which she bears of her praiseworthy virginity (4–9)].

The poem forms a closed circle, beginning and ending in the same place, with the mutual fulfillment of a promise mutually given. This sense of circularity is reinforced by the repetition of key words: *sponsi caelestis in aula* [in the hall of her heavenly spouse] (5) / *regis caelestis in aula* [in the hall of the heavenly king] (449), *cupiens contemnere carnis* [desiring to spurn the flesh] (2) / *cupiens sine fine tueri* [desiring to gaze without end] (453). At the beginning of the poem, the virgin reader was invited to imagine herself following the lamb and singing his song; that song is now made real first through the song of Agnes's family and then through the song, which is the poem itself. The virgin Agnes's heavenly hymns are indistinguishable, finally, from the songs of the virgin Hrostvitha, who has chosen to imitate the martyr by giving forth "a little chime of divine praise" and who invites others to do the same. The circle of song created by the text is transcendant in its perfection. In its expansive motion from Agnes to Hrotsvitha's virgin audience, it is inclusive rather than exclusive, and it mimics the sealed perfection of the virgin's limited and physical body, itself only a manifestation of her limitless and metaphysical soul. This perfection grounds the eloquence of the virgin within the poem, granting her words the power to become miraculous signs, and that of the virgin outside the poem, Hrotsvitha, author of these lines in which the pledge of rhyme confirms the pledge of meter and the end becomes the beginning. The poem itself becomes a *stupendum signum* in its own right, a fully active sign.

The Emperor's New Clothes

If *Agnes* establishes the eloquence of the virgin through a kind of super-charged legal language in which oratory and poetry become one and the same, functioning inevitably to demonstrate the eloquence of author as well as subject, the pair of plays that concern virgin martyrdom in tripli-cate, *Agapes, Chionia and Hirena (ACH)* and *Faith, Hope and Charity (FHC)*, take advantage of other rhetorical weapons, humor and dramatic irony. In the preface to her plays, Hrotsvitha declares that her intention is "to celebrate the praiseworthy chastity of sacred virgins by using the same mode of composition which has been used to celebrate the shameful depravities of lecherous women" (Pref. II: 233). The negative model against whom she writes, she claims, is Terence, although she admits willingly that her work will not be much like his, and opinion is divided as to how well she actually knew the Roman comedian.[27] The only difficulty is that in order to redeem women from the disrepute into which Terence and other male, pagan writers have cast them, she finds herself forced to deal with immodest subjects. Hrotsvitha's disavowal of any prurient interest in her subject matter, like her self-deprecating account of her rustic gatherings in the Gandersheim granary, is a backhanded demonstration of her own skill as an author:

> One thing, however, has not infrequently made me wilt with embarrassment and made me blush, for because of the demands of the genre, I have been compelled to apply my intellect and my pen to representing the despicable madness of unlawful love and the deceptively sweet language of seduction, things which women like us really should not even have heard of. Yet if I had, out of modesty, neglected to treat these subjects, I should not have been able to fulfil my intent, to praise the innocent to the best of my ability. Indeed, the sweeter the honeyed words of seducers, the more sublime the divine help appears, and the more glorious the victory of those who triumph, especially when it is feminine fragility which conquers, and manly strength which is cast into confusion. (Pref. II: 233–34)

Just as Hrotsvitha argued in the introduction to the *Legends* that while she knew perfectly well that she should not really be writing hexameters, she was compelled to do so by divine grace, here she insists that, while she should not really even be reading Terence, she is obliged to revise him by the moral imperative to defend women from his slanders. It is particularly revealing that the seductions she imagines being levied against holy virgins are entirely verbal; sweet words, like the sweet words of Terence himself, constitute the greatest danger, resistance is the resistance to argument, not to shows of force, and victory occurs when the woman's male opponent is cast into confusion. In the two plays with which I am especially concerned, the male persecutors of virgin martyrs will be reduced by the eloquence of their captives into veritable blithering idiots.

Faith, Hope and Charity is not among the best known of Hrotsvitha's plays; that honor probably belongs to *Agapes, Chionia and Hirena*, which is the most frequently anthologized and performed nowadays, or perhaps to *The Conversion of Thais*, which had rather a vogue at the beginning of the twentieth century and was performed in both London and Paris.[28] This neglect is perhaps due to the fact that the first extended confrontation between pagan and Christian in the play consists of a lecture on mathematics, which tends to baffle and bore modern readers as thoroughly as it does the Emperor Hadrian within the play. Nonetheless, as Katharina Wilson notes, the play "summarizes the preceding eight legends and five dramas by glorifying the martyrdom of the allegorical daughters of Wisdom."[29] Like *Agapes, Chionia and Hirena*, with which it shares a familiar plot, *Faith, Hope and Charity* highlights the intelligence of women at the expense of the slow wits and thick tongues of the men who persecute them. In both plays, Hrotsvitha consistently works to shift the emphasis of the narrative from the pathos of the martyrs to the intellectual and argumentative victories of her heroines and the complete humiliation of the villains.

The central figure in *Faith, Hope and Charity* is not actually a virgin at all, but Wisdom, the mother of three little girls aged eight, ten, and twelve, who are cheerfully resolved to die for their faith. The fact that the girls are pre-nubile, even by medieval standards, has a series of effects on the dynamics of persecution. The Emperor Hadrian comments on their beauty, but he does not appear to be motivated by lust like the would-be bridegroom in Agnes. Rather, he continually represents himself as a potential father to the girls, even offering at one point to adopt Faith if she will sacrifice to his gods. Hadrian's unusually paternal impulse toward the girls places him in direct allegorical opposition to their true Father, God, but it also operates dramatically on several different levels. It denies him the potential excuse of being rendered insane by passion, it emphasizes his irrational injustice, and it raises implicit doubt about his temporal authority. What kind of emperor is threatened by little girls, after all?

Hrotsvitha's most substantive alteration to the source of her play, a *passio* that existed in both Greek and Latin, is the virtual invention of the character of Antiochus, the emperor's second in command.[30] The creation of two antagonists permits Hrotsvitha to delineate two forms of behavior, which she identifies as typically masculine. Antiochus is actively anti-Christian, while Hadrian is just deeply stupid:

> Adrianus: Numquid tantillarum / adventus muliercularum / aliquid rei publicae
> adducere poterit detrimentum?
> Antiochus: Permagnum.
> Adrianus: Quod?
> Antiochus: Pacis defectum.
> Adrianus: Quo pacto?
> Antiochus: Et quod maius potest rumpere civilis concordiam pacis, / quam dissonantia observationis? (*FHC* 5: 17)

> Hadrian: What possible harm could the arrival of such little girls do to the state? Antiochus: Great harm. Hadrian: How? Antiochus: By disturbing the peace. Hadrian: But how? Antiochus: And what is more likely to disrupt the harmony of civil peace than religious dissent?

The technique of using swiftly moving dialogue to establish situation and background is one of the elements Hrotsvitha inherited from Terence. Like Terence, too, she uses it to establish character while advancing the plot. Antiochus is represented here and throughout the play as full of anger (he describes himself at one point as "about to burst with rage" [*ego quidem disrumpor prae furore*] (*FHC* 5:18)) and utterly devoted to the persecution of the Christians; Hadrian is strikingly lacking in the rage that generally characterizes pagan persecutors. Instead, he is depicted as little more than a half-wit, unclear on the facts and implications of the situation that confronts him. He turns constantly to Antiochus for advice (*Adrianus: Debeone illam dimittere inpunitam? Antiochus: Nequaquam. Adrianus: Et quid?* [Hadrian: Should I let her go unpunished? Antiochus: Indeed not! Hadrian: What should I do, then?] (*FHC* 5:3)). Only when it comes to torture does Hadrian show the least capacity for independent thought. Sadism and stupidity seem almost causally related in him as he instructs that Faith be flogged, have her nipples cut off, be thrown on a grill, boiled in melted pitch and wax, but cannot come up with a method of actually killing her. Inevitably, it is Antiochus who proposes the practical solution of decapitation. Hadrian tries virtually the same sequence of tortures with Hope (flogging, boiling in a cauldron full of oil) and Charity (flogging, burning in a furnace) without ever learning the lesson of the martyr's impassability, which becomes clear to Antiochus after the death of the second sister.

Our sense of Hadrian's stupidity is confirmed by his response to Wisdom's lecture on numbers, which he describes as a "complicated and perplexing problem" [*scrupulosa et plexilis quaestio* (*FHC* 3:2)] and especially by the attitudes of the women in the play toward him. Both Hadrian and

Antiochus make the mistake of assuming that women are fragile and vulnerable to flattery [*fragilitas sexus feminei / facilius potest blandimentis molliri* (*FHC* 3:8–9)] but in fact it is the men in the play who prove vulnerable to women's words. Wisdom invites her daughters to enjoy the humiliation of the emperor as she defeats him with a mathematical argument; the girls eagerly agree, and Wisdom proceeds to give Hadrian a lecture that he completely fails to understand, admitting at the end of it that he has only been listening out of politeness, hoping to soften up her extreme religious stance.

Hadrian's last lines in the play allude to his combined shame and frustration:

> Adrianus: Erubesco illam ultra videre, / quia nequeo illam laedere.
> Antiochus: Restat ut perimatur gladio.
> Adrianus: Hoc fiat absque mora. (*FHC* 3:3)

> Hadrian: I blush to see her still, for I cannot harm her. Antiochus: She can still be killed with a sword. Hadrian: Let it be done without delay.

The virgins' resistance to torture is also resistance to Hadrian's one and only form of creativity; it is not clear whether he realizes, at the end, that in giving them only death and never pain, he is acceding to their manipulation of him. Death is, after all, all they ever wanted from him. The end of the play, recalling the end of *Agnes*, imagines the three virgin sisters "absorbed into a wider community of women, as an unspecified number of 'Matrons' join Sapientia to mourn the martyred girls,"[31] as Alcuin Blamires puts it.

Like *Faith, Hope and Charity*, the story of *Agapes, Chionia and Hirena* has impeccable hagiographic antecedents, originating in the Greek account of the martyrdom of a number of women in Thessaloniki under Diocletian, which Hrotsvitha appears to have known from a Latin *passio*,[32] although she was also aware of the abbreviated tale told by Aldhelm in the *Poem on Virginity*. Hrotsvitha's transpositions of the *passio* into dramatic form incorporate a series of shifts in emphasis, some subtle and some not so subtle. Thus, the *passio* gives this account of the initial confrontation between the Emperor Diocletian and the three virgins:

> Then Agapes replied: "Most revered [*sacratissime*] emperor, your responsibility is the care of the people, the care of the state and the care of the army; and yet you speak injuriously of the living God, who is your necessary helper, whose mercy spares you." Diocletian said: "This one is mad [*insanit ista*], bring another one." And when Saint Chionia was brought forth, she said, "My sister is not mad [*soror mea non insanit*], but she with proper exercise of judgment finds fault [*reprehendit*] with your unjust threats."[33]

The vocabulary of the play demonstrates indebtedness to the *passio*, but in Hrotsvitha's version, the tone of the exchange is much sharper:

> Agapes: Temere calumpniaris statum Dei omnipotentis: periculum!
> Diocletianus: Cuius?
> Agapes: Tui reique publicae, quam gubernas.
> Diocletianus: Ista insanit! Amoveatur.
> Chionia: Mea germana non insanit, sed tui stultitam iuste reprehendit. (*ACH* 1:3–4)

> Agapes: You dare to insult the dignity of almighty God. This is dangerous!
> Diocletian: To whom? Agapes: To you and to the state, which you govern.
> Diocletian: This one is mad. Take her away. Chione: My sister is not mad, but rightly reproves your stupidity.

Perhaps Agapes' initial address to the emperor as "most reverend" is ironic in the *passio*; nonetheless, she and her sisters remain civil in their exchanges with the emperor. Hrotsvitha's virgins, on the other hand, do not mince words. Agapes' statement concerning the responsibilities of the emperor and his unacknowledged debt to God is transformed in Hrotsvitha's text into something that sounds very much like a threat against the state. This particular transformation serves a dual dramatic purpose; it provides the emperor with at least the suggestion of a political motive for the punishment of the three sisters, but more significantly it alludes to the advent of the empire of Christ, which will inevitably replace the Roman empire. The Terentian anachronism *res publica* may even be intended to convey an extra irony: by 260 C.E., the date of the presumptive martyrdom of the three virgins, the Roman republic had been dead for over two hundred years. The emperor, of course, cannot comprehend the allusion. Chione drives home the dramatic irony and echoes Agapes' aggressive speech when she insists that what her sister is criticizing is not merely the emperor's injustice, but his stupidity; she transforms political incompetence into what he can hardly help but feel as an *ad hominem* attack. The audience of the play, on the other hand, aware of the conventions of the hagiographic genre, knows better; it's nothing personal at all, since the tyrant cannot help but be spiritually foolish, for this is what his role demands.

Hrotsvitha's account of Dulcitius's first encounter with the virgins shows a similar significant redirection of the text, this time influenced by her reading of Aldhelm. The *passio* indicates Dulcitius's infatuation with the girls in an almost perfunctory manner: "When Dulcitius saw them, he was smitten by the sight [*captu oculorum adstrictus*] and stirred in his shameful soul" (*Letter* 50). Aldhelm's version increases the erotic charge of the prefect's response with an injection of vocabulary from the Latin love lyric. He is moved by the *venustas* (charm) of the girls' faces and "as soon as he lays eyes on them [*oculorum. . .captus*] he melts into lust like a candle before a flame" (*Letter* 50). Both the *passio* and Aldhelm's *Letter* emphasize the operation of the male gaze, which here serves an exculpatory function; the allure of the virgins is irresistible, the persecutor is in some sense their captive, their victim. Their own beauty thus becomes, to elaborate Aldhelm's image, the spark that lights the fire which will eventually refuse to consume them.

Hrotsvitha's dramatic format reduces the narratorial evocation of the persecutor's erotic subjectivity. Dulcitius tells us that he's smitten, and in fact Hrotsvitha's vocabulary has clear echoes of both Aldhelm and the *passio*, but the movement from indirect to direct speech means that we are no longer invited to see him as an Ovidian lover, helpless in the grip of passion and metaphor. Instead, Hrotsvitha provides a bit of dialogue in which the markedly unenthusiastic comments of the attending soldiers function to undercut any reading of the virgins' beauty as irresistible. This exchange begins the process of making Dulcitius appear a fool:

> Dulcitius: Papae! Quam pulchrae, quam venustae, quam egregiae puellulae!
> Milites: Perfecte decorae.
> Dulcitius: Captus sum illarum specie.
> Milites: Credibile.
> Dulcitius: Exaestuo illas ad mei amorem trahere.
> Milites: Diffidimus te praevalere. (*ACH* 2:12)

> Dulcitius: Ye gods! What beautiful, charming, gorgeous girls! Soldiers: They're quite pretty. Dulcitius: I'm smitten with their beauty. Soldiers: That's believable. Dulcitius: I'm really hot to make love with them. Soldiers: We doubt you'll succeed.

The responses of the soldiers provide a pragmatic and deflationary counterpoint to Dulcitius's excessive rhetoric with its echoes of erotic lyric, especially when he lays out his plan for getting at the girls later on. When he orders them to put the girls in an inner pantry where the cooking pots are kept, the soldiers ask the question any sane person would: why on earth there? Dulcitius's response, "so that I may visit them as often as I like," does not do much to clarify either the geography of the palace or his state of mind, and the response of the soldiers ("as you command!") suggests only obedience, not understanding or enthusiasm (*ACH* 2:3). The point, of course, is that it is pointless to try to understand the prefect, who has begun to manifest the pathetic madness of lust Hrotsvitha alluded to in her preface.

The scene that follows is justly famous. Dulcitius descends to the kitchens at night, but, deluded by God, enters the wrong door, ending up in the pantry where he makes love to the kitchen utensils under the misapprehension that they are the three virgins, becoming filthy with soot in the process. The incident is briefly described both in the *passio*, which informs us that the governor "begins to embrace the pots and kiss the pans" and eventually emerges all black and sooty, "as though the devil had possessed his body."[34] Aldhelm's account adds an extra layer of metaphor: Dulcitius is "smudged with Ethiopian blackness" (*Letter* 50). The moral message is clear; lust possesses men, blinds them, and makes them the devil's fools.[35] Hrotsvitha's innovation is to position her three protagonists so that they can witness this humiliating process; there is a peephole of some sort between the pantry in which they are imprisoned and the one next door where Dulcitius disports himself among the pots and pans:

> Chionia: Quid sibi uult collisio ollarum, caccaborum et sartaginum?
> Hirena: Lustrabo. Accedite, quaeso, per rimulas perspicite!
> Agapes: Quid est?
> Hirena: Ecce iste stultus mente alienatus aestimat se nostris uti amplexibus.
> Agapes: Quid facit?
> Hirena: Nunc ollas molli fouet gremio, nunc sartagines et caccabos
>   amplectitur mitia libans oscula.
> Chionia: Ridiculum. (*ACH* 4:1–3)

> Chionia: What does this banging together of pots and cooking utensils and pans mean? Hirena: I'll take a look. Do come quick, and look through the crack! Agapes: What is it? Hirena: Look, that idiot, he's out of his mind, he thinks he is enjoying our embraces! Agapes: What's he doing? Hirena: He's fondling the pots with his groin, and now he's hugging the saucepans and other cooking things, and covering them with kisses! Chionia: Absurd!

When the three girls watch the deluded Dulcitius trying to have sex with various kitchen implements, they reverse the normal specular structure of the hagiographical narrative; where Prudentius and Ambrose both invited their audiences to gaze upon the body of the virgin martyr with a compassion that was never entirely separate from the sadistic gaze of the tormentor, Hrotsvitha allows the gaze of the virgins themselves to render their tormentor absurd and sexually powerless. As Alcuin Blamires points out, "Hrotsvitha's probable invention of the sisters' view of this spectacle enables those who were intended victims to engage consciously in unexpected triumph; their commentary magnifies the sense of embarrassment, and situates readers/audience as members of the women's 'team' contemplating the discomfiture of Dulcitius."[36] Not only does Dulcitius fail to rape the girls, it is not even clear whether his attempted sexual congress with the pots and pans is successful. *Molli fovet gremio* literally means something like "caressed in his soft lap"; in its only other occurrences in Hrotsvitha's work (*Gongolfus* 526, *Pafnutius* 13:3), the phrase lacks the sexual connotations it must clearly bear here, but the image itself is always gendered. The most common classical use of the idiom is in the phrase *mollius terrae gremius*, the soft lap or womb of the earth, which receives seeds at planting or bodies at burial, and it is this usage that Hrotsvitha follows in *Pafnutius*, where the eponymous hermit promises the reformed prostitute Thais that once her body has dissolved in the earth, she will rise in the spirit perfected. In Lucretius, the phrase is explicitly feminized, *gremium matris terrae* [the lap of mother earth], while both Catullus and Statius use *gremium* without modification to indicate the female genitalia. Dulcitius's attempted sexual congress with the virgins thus not only humiliates him, it feminizes him at the very moment when he believes himself to be asserting his masculinity.

The rest of the play maintains the themes established in the pantry scene. Dulcitius emerges from the pantry to discover that he has lost his identity along with his masculinity; to the soldiers guarding the door, he looks like the devil himself; to the gatekeeper at the palace, he is a monster whose gender and species are both unclear. Ironically enough, the identity stripped away by his insane attempt at adultery can only be restored by his wife, who recognizes him as her husband, but also as insane. In order to revenge one humiliation with another, Dulcitius commands that the virgins be stripped and publicly shamed, but their clothes cling to their bodies like bark to a tree, and he turns them over in disgust to a higher authority, Count Sisinnius, who will in his turn be humiliated by his captives. The two older girls are thrown into a blazing fire, but it refuses to burn them; instead of suffocating in the flames, they give up the ghost voluntarily, a miracle acclaimed by the soldiers in the same words applied to Agnes in the *Legends: stupendum miraculum* (*FHC* 11:5). The third sister, Hirena, is whisked away by a divine force to the top of a mountain, leaving Sisinnius and his men to chase around its base until they are lost and confused; from her lofty perch, she reiterates his humiliation: *Infelix, erubesce, / Sisinni, erubesce, / teque turpiter victum ingemisce, / quia tenellae infantiam virgunculae / absque armorum apparatu nequivisti superare* [Blush, Sisinnius, you wretch, blush and whimper for you have been shamefully vanquished; without your arms and weapons you couldn't overcome the childlike nature of a tender virgin child (*FHC* 14:3)]. Sisennius can only respond that it matters not to him so long as she dies, and Hirena gets the last word in the play, pointing out that her death will not free him but damn him to hell: *pro tua severitate malignitatis / in tartara dampnaberis; ego autem, martirii palmam / virginitatisque receptura coronam, / intrabo aethereum / aeterni regis thalamum; / cui est honor et gloria / in saecula* [because of your excessive evil temper, you shall be damned to hell, but I, having received the martyr's palm and the crown of virginity, shall enter the heavenly bedroom of the eternal king, to whom is the honor and glory for ever and ever (*FHC* 14:3)]. Significantly, the play does not show her death but leaves only her words hanging in the air; once again, any voyeuristic impulse toward the martyred body of the virgin is forestalled. What we see throughout this drama, as in the legend of Agnes, is not the virgin body but the grotesque and depraved reactions of men in power to that body.

Typically, perhaps, the woodcut by Wolfgang Traut, which illustrates Conrad *Celtis' editio princeps* of Hrotsvitha's works, shows what the text does not. Although the soldiers in the play are incapable of stripping the two older girls at Dulcitius's command, and even the flames of their pyre leave their clothing intact, the illustration represents all three virgins standing naked in a fire whose flames coyly hide their genitals while exposing one plump breast. The attendant soldier threatens them with a sword, which rises phallically from his groin, and Sisinnius (who does not actually attend the immolation in the play) appears dignified rather than frustrated. Two of the three sisters avert their eyes modestly; only in the expression of the third, who should not, according to the narrative, be there at all, is there a shadow of the defiance with which Hrotsvitha invested her protagonists. The girl in the middle looks out of the print at the viewer, and seems as though she might just possibly be winking.

Sophia of Gandersheim

The community at Gandersheim for whom Hrotsvitha wrote would have had little sympathy for Traut's simpering maidens, but the lessons of Hrotsvitha's texts may have been ones they took to heart. Even if we accept that Hrotsvitha's plays were never given full performance in her lifetime, we are probably safe in assuming that they were read and studied by the young women who were educated at Gandersheim under the rule of Gerberga. At least one of the young women who lived at Gandersheim during the period when Hrotsvitha's plays and legends may have formed part of the curriculum is well known to history. Sophia, the daughter of Otto II and the Byzantine Princess Theophano, was sent to be educated at the monastery when she was about five years old, sometime in the early 980s. Perhaps Hrotsvitha, whose last poem, on the foundation of Gandersheim, had been completed in 973, was still alive; even if she was not, her works must have had an irresistible appeal to any young, female member of the Liudolfing dynasty. Not only were the plays and legends full of very young protagonists like Agnes, the two sets of virgin sisters, and Constantina, but Hrotsvitha's epic *Deeds of Otto* recounted the exciting adventures of Sophia's paternal grandmother, Adelheid, including a daring escape across the Alps from a would-be husband who had kidnapped her.[37] Hrotsvitha's vision of women as intelligent and passionate beings with the right to determine their own futures, make their own choices, and resist unjust power wielded by men, finds a close reflection in the career of Sophia.

Sophia took the veil as a canoness at Gandersheim in 987 or 989—she was twelve or fourteen years old, the age of several of Hrotsvitha's protagonists—in an atmosphere of ecclesiastical scandal. She had insisted that the archbishop of Mainz rather than the diocesan bishop of Hildesheim officiate, and although she eventually lost her case, she came close to winning. Had she been successful, the precedent might have altered the course of ecclesiastical history. As it was, Sophia "unleashed over forty years of strife between Mainz and Hildesheim."[38] Her subsequent career was no less extraordinary; she left Gandersheim for two years (995–97) in order to accompany her brother, Otto III, on his progress south into Italy, serving as his consort after the death of their mother. She was condemned and reviled by churchmen, especially those of the Hildesheim party, who found her arrogant and immodest, but she remained one of her brother's closest advisors. After his death she became abbess of Gandersheim and eventually of Essen; both institutions were enormously enriched by her wealth, and empowered by her ambition.[39] Sophia's insistence on making her own choices, particularly with regard to the assumption of that mark of religious vocation, the veil, recall the fierce will of an Agnes; her determined resistance to Bernward of Hildesheim, who tried to assert his authority over her, recalls the behavior of Hrotsvitha's virgin martyrs before prefects and emperors, and embarrassed Bernward mightily. Perhaps her education at Gandersheim had as much influence as her imperial connections upon her notorious career.

The political and temporal power of aristocratic women in Germany waned after Otto's death, however. During the course of the eleventh century, the access of women to control of property steadily diminished, and under Henry II and his heirs, the practice of placing royal daughters in powerful monastic institutions became less and less common; princesses were considered more useful as brides for potential allies.[40] Hrotsvitha's writings may have influenced the careers of Sophia and other Ottonian royal women, even while the existence of powerful women like Gerberga and Sophia made it possible for Hrotsvitha to write as she did. By the time Hildegard of Bingen was born, however, over a century after Hrotsvitha's death, women's access to education and to political power in Germany had been significantly restricted. The self-assurance of Hrotsvitha's virgins reflects the power and influence of the feminine communities in which they were created; for them, virginity is an entirely positive and genuinely powerful condition for women to inhabit, a presumptively authoritative political position from which to speak. Hildegard had no temporal models like Gerberga, princess of the church, no students like Sophia, who challenged the power of a bishop in his own diocese. For her, the image of the virgin martyr will become a medium for creating authority where there was none, of imagining alternative forms of community for women, and indeed of femininity, rather than a representation of any preexistent feminine power.

1. Sainte Reine confronts Olibrius. Two images from the 1999 production of the *Mystère de Sainte-Reine,* performed annually in the Theater of the Rocks at Alise-Sainte Reine.

2. The Martyrdom of Thecla from an 1887 volume in the author's collection. The saint is fully clothed, and has acquired a male companion.

COMEDIA SECVNDA DVLCICVS

3. Wolfgang Traut's illustration for *Agapes, Chionia and Hirena*, from Conrad Celtis's *editio princeps* of Hrotsvitha.

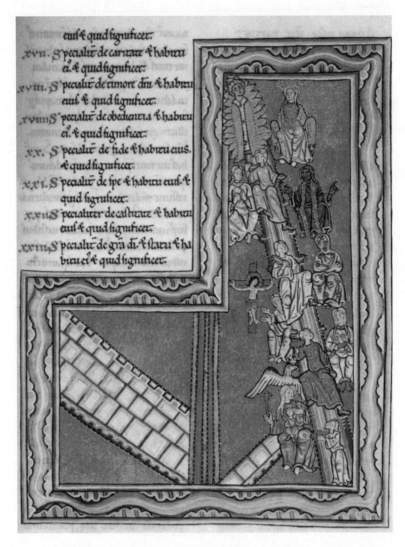

4. The Virtues, from Hildegard's *Scivias*. Fear of God appears as a human figure wrapped in a garment covered with eyes.

5. In this fifteenth-century painting, the artist has cut away the fabric of Saint
Barbara's dress to reveal the multilation of her breasts while leaving her otherwise
fully clothed, thus inviting voyeuristic participation in her torture while simultaneously preserving the saint's modesty.

6. Joan of Arc, accompanied by Catherine and Margaret, in a twentieth-century triumphalist statue by Andre Allar, Domrémy, France (author's photo).

CHAPTER 4

A CHORUS OF VIRGINS: HILDEGARD'S *SYMPHONIA*

Sometime around 1150, Abbess Tengswich of Andernach wrote a letter to a much more celebrated woman of the Church, Hildegard of Bingen. Tengswich professed to be impressed by Hildegard's remarkable prophetic gifts, but she questioned the way in which Hildegard directed her convent on two grounds. For one thing, she had heard that Hildegard only admitted well-born nuns to her sisterhood, a practice that Tengswich considers to be at odds with Christ's choice of fishermen and other members of the lower classes as his disciples; equally disturbing, evidently, was the rumor that Hildegard and her nuns wore elaborate costumes and jewelry on holy days:

> It seems that your virgins on feast days stand up in church singing with unbound hair, and that they wear as ornaments some kind of silk veils long enough to touch the ground and even elegantly wrought crowns on their heads with crosses worked in on either side and in the back; and in the front they have the figure of the Lamb elegantly attached. And on top of this, their fingers are decorated with golden rings; the first shepherd of the Church forbade such things in his letter with this warning: women should comport themselves with modesty, not wearing their hair in curls, or gold, or pearls, or precious clothing. (*Letter* 52: 126)[1]

The "first Shepherd of the Church" was Peter, whose instructions in his first epistle were explicit: "Likewise, you wives should be subordinate to your husbands. . . Your adornment should not be an external one: braiding the hair, wearing gold jewelry, or dressing in fine clothes" (I Peter 3:1–3); Tengswich's allusion includes a reminiscence of a Pauline passage as well: ["Women should adorn themselves with proper conduct, with modesty and self-control, not with braided hairstyles and gold ornaments, or pearls or expensive clothing" (I Tim 2:9)].

Hildegard's response strikes a characteristic declamatory tone, and provides a tantalizing glimpse of the virgin body:

> The form of woman blazed forth and glowed in the first foundation, when that form was formed in which all creatures lay hidden. . . .But the apostle Paul. . .understood this: the woman who lies under the masculine power of her husband, joined to him in the primal Rib, must have great modesty. . . . These things do not apply to the virgin; for she stands forth, beautiful, in the simplicity and integrity of paradise, and shall never appear dry, but shall always remain in the full greenness of the flower of the branch. . . .Virgins are joined to the Holy spirit in holiness and the dawn of virginity. . . .Because of this it is appropriate both according to her privilege and according to the revelation in the mystical breath of the finger of God, that the virgin should wear white clothing, in clear signification of her marriage with Christ, seeing that her will is strengthened by the purity of her clothing. (*Letter* 52r: 127–29)

The letter combines visionary fervor and a remarkable willingness to gloss scripture against the grain. If Tengswich wrote back, her letter has not survived; in any case, it is difficult to imagine what counter-argument she could have made against such inspired rhetoric.

The tone of the exchange between these two women makes it clear that the community headed by Hildegard, where nobly born nuns processed on feast days wearing Apocalyptic costumes, had little in common with other convents. Hildegard herself describes the crowns worn by her nuns more fully in a letter to Guibert of Gembloux; she points out that "virginity has no clear marker except for a black veil and the sign of the cross" and describes the vision that rectified this deficiency by recommending a white veil, which should represent "the shining garment which mankind had and lost in paradise," and a "circlet of three colors joined together to represent the Trinity" with images of angels, cherubs, and the Lamb of God attached (*Letter* 103r: 263). The etiology elaborated by Hildegard in explanation of her praxis is as idiosyncratic as the costumes she designed; it explicitly identifies virginity with original, pre-Lapsarian femininity and, in its absolute essentialism, leaves no space for the virgin to be imagined as other than female, since her special status is defined by her physical integrity, by the fact that she is not "joined to her husband in the primal Rib." Virginity for Hildegard is thus a condition that is not only gendered feminine but actually sexed female. Throughout her work, this emphasis on the corporeality and femininity of virginity runs counter to masculine theological discourse on the subject, creating a virgin body that is both irreducibly and problematically female.

In insisting that the Pauline rules about dress do not apply to virgins, Hildegard takes a position strongly opposed to patristic tradition. Indeed, her argument for the absolute privilege of virginity reads like a direct response to Tertullian's *On the Veiling of Virgins*, although that text was not generally in circulation in the twelfth century. Tertullian's attitude, however, had been transmitted to twelfth century authorities, who were as convinced as the Fathers that virgins must not be allowed to evade the restrictions placed upon the female sex as a whole. Hildegard's contemporary Peter Abelard links the sartorial intimately with the spiritual when he cautions the nuns of the Paraclete against the vanity he assumed to be no less characteristic of holy virgins than of women in general, and even more dangerous in the religious than in the lay. Quoting the First Epistle of Peter, like Tengswich, he adds his own commentary on the apostle's words: "He was right to think it necessary to warn women rather than men away from this vanity, because their weak spirits impel them towards it, since they are more devoted to luxury."[2] Tengswich's letter thus speaks for a familiar and weighty tradition upon the question of virginal rights and privileges. Hildegard's response, on the other hand, creates its own idiosyncratic ground of authority from which to oppose the argument. First, she appeals to scripture in her turn, matching Tengswich's apostolic allusions with one of her own, explaining the symbolism of the crowns by reference to *Revelation*: "They have his name and the name of his Father written upon their foreheads" (Rev. 14:1). In this fashion, Hildegard places her nuns among the heavenly troop of one hundred and forty four thousand chosen virgins seen by John, and manifests her determination to translate the symbolism of the saint's prophetic vision into the daily life of her community.[3] Next, she evokes the authority of her own visionary experience as explanation for the costumes of her sisterhood: the dress of her nuns is authorized by the "revelation in the mystical breath of the finger of God," a revelation vouchsafed to Hildegard herself. For Abelard, as for the Fathers, the virgin's veil is the marker of an inalienably female sexual shame; for Hildegard, it is the marker of freedom from that very shame, and thus an entirely appropriate canvas for symbolic ornamentation.

Hildegard's visions, sketched in the letter to Tengswich and more fully elaborated in the *Scivias* and *Symphonia*, reveal a world where the original greenness (*viriditas*) of Paradise is echoed in the virginity (*virginitas*) of the abbess and her nuns. Dressed as brides of Christ, they became visible and physical manifestations of these two feminine qualities, which were the source of Hildegard's mystical authority, the organizing principles of her life and her poetry, and indeed the fundamental underpinnings of her cosmology.[4] An antiphon and responsory establish the intimate connection between virginity and greenness. "O pulcre facies" (no. 55) explicitly addresses itself to virgins, qualifying them as "builders of the dawn" (3) and "God's sweetest garden" (10). The responsory that follows this, and which,

as Newman notes, "is about Virginity, not virgins,"[5] develops the associations sketched in the antiphon:

O nobilissima viriditas	Most noble green,
que radicas in sole	you take root in the sun
et que in candida serenitate	in luminous serenity,

. . .

Tu rubes ut aurora	You redden like dawn
et ardes ut solis flamma.	and burn like a ray of the sun.
(*Symphonia* 56, 1–3, 10–11)	

Here, as in the letter to Tengswich, virginity and greenness are imagined
as aspects of a radiant paradisiac landscape that exists both at the dawn of
time and in the eternally continuing dawn of divine grace. The force that
Hildegard invokes in "O nobilissima viriditas" as a color, a luminosity, an
intangible, will be experienced in the world of the flesh as a particular kind
of body, characterized by both capacity and integrity. This virgin body is
figured in Hildegard's poems and visionary works as that of Eve, Mary,
Ursula, or Ecclesia, but behind these bodies stands another: that of
Hildegard herself, the "Sibyl of the Rhine." The relationship between the
body of the prophetess and that of the mythic, even cosmic female bodies
her words construct is complex. On the one hand, her body reflects theirs,
imitating their holiness and integrity; on the other, Hildegard's own intact
flesh serves as the guarantee of her prophetic voice, and thus of the visions
it expresses and the legendary bodies it evokes. When Hildegard and her
nuns dress themselves in white gowns, wearing crowns and rings fraught
with significance, they are expressing their holy vows in a way that, rather
than denying their sexuality, highlights it;[6] they are performing their
virginity in a fashion that also performs their identity as a community of
women united in their rejection of the normative, heterosexual, hierarchical order of things as they usually are. For Hildegard and her sisterhood,
I will argue, virginity is a radical femininity, radical in both senses of the
word; it is simultaneously fundamental, the root from which all other fem-
ininities derive, and revolutionary in its rejection of theological tradition.

Eve and Mary

Hildegard's location of virginity in the female body opens the possibility
of a form of sanctity as characteristically and exclusively feminine as the
priesthood was masculine. This scarcely makes Hildegard a feminist; as
Newman reminds us in *Sister of Wisdom*, Hildegard's ideas about gender
and the role of woman were anything but revolutionary in any social or

political sense.[7] Hildegard was simply not very interested in the "empowerment of women," or in reshaping the social fabric of her world. She was strongly opposed to the idea of women as priests, and even disapproved of formal education for them.[8] In her insistence on the separate but equal roles of men and women within the church, she might be more accurately characterized as a radical conservative, hearkening back to the days of independent double monasteries that could be ruled by either men or women. A child of the aristocracy, her social views were elitist; she wrote to Tengswich that just as a farmer would not herd sheep and goats together, neither should a convent contain both noble and peasant women. While unsparing in her criticism of individuals, she was a staunch supporter of the institutions of her time: the Church, which, in idealized form, she celebrated throughout her work; the Papacy, which she maintained against the Emperor Barbarossa; and her own Benedictine order.

Hildegard was, however, profoundly interested in women in both practical and theoretical ways. Her *Causes and Cures* is one of only a handful of medieval European medical texts to treat gynecological problems in detail; in her letters, she counsels women on subjects ranging from the advisability of living the anchoritic life to marital difficulties. Her religious works not only elaborate a "theology of the feminine," rooted in sapiential thinking, as Newman has argued;[9] they also work out, albeit in no very systematic way, a theory of complementary but essential sexual difference that makes woman at least the equal of man before the Fall, and minimizes her post-Lapsarian subjection to him. Furthermore, Hildegard's conceptualization of virginity as a feminine, physical state allows her to imagine the female body in terms that often appear to be deliberately opposed both to the obviously misogynist invective which represented the female body as the grossest kind of flesh, and to the more subtle, Ambrosian rhetoric which transformed virginity into perfect paradox. Hildegard's figuration of the virgin body is important not so much because it establishes any immediately imitable model of empowerment for women but because it reimagines the corporeality of the feminine and the reality of female desire as positive and even redemptive values. This process is especially clear in the songs in which Hildegard links the images of Eve and Mary.

The majority of male medieval writers, following Jerome and Augustine, concurred in regarding woman as a lesser creation of God and in considering Eve primarily responsible for the Fall;[10] Hildegard insists instead on man and woman as beings created separate but equal. Both, according to the *Scivias*, had innocent souls at creation; Hildegard describes Eve before her temptation by the devil as "Eve, who had an innocent soul, for she had been raised up from the innocent Adam carrying in her body the whole multitude of the human race, shining in the predestination of God"

(*Scivias* 1.2.10). Hildegard's Eve, rather than being the origin of all human sin as she was for Tertullian, literally embodies the pre-Lapsarian potential of the human race. Since Hildegard insists even more strongly than most of her contemporaries on regarding the Fall as a *felix culpa*, Eve's sin is the necessary and predestined precursor of the Incarnation. Hildegard, in fact, appears simply to have ignored as completely as possible the entire misogynist tradition concerning the creation. Her personal experience of the divine superseded the official teachings of the church, allowing her to reread authorities she could not afford to dismiss out of hand, such as Saint Paul. In one case at least, this revision is striking: "let them love with pure love, since both man and woman could not exist without having been conceived in such a union, as My friend Paul testifies when he says: 'As the woman is of the man, so is the man for the woman; but all are from God' (I Cor. XII). Which is to say: Woman was created for man, and man was made for woman. As she is from the man, so the man is also from her" (*Scivias* 1.2.12). This is not actually what Paul says; rather, the apostle establishes the dominance of men over women by insisting that "man was not made from woman, but woman from man. Neither was man created for woman, but woman for man" (I Cor. 11:8–9). Although he does go on to equalize the relationship between the sexes ("Woman is not independent of man or man of woman in the Lord," I Cor. 11:11), Paul's primary concern in this passage, as we have seen in chapter 1, was to establish an appropriate hierarchy of sociosexual relationships within the Church at Corinth according to which women would be under the control of men. Hildegard here corrects the written tradition in the name of the voice of God, as though whoever transcribed the apostle's words simply got them wrong.

The *Symphonia* operates differently from Hildegard's prose; the songs do not attempt, as the prophetic writings often do, to explain other texts, or God's operation on earth. Instead, they develop an original poetics with which to delineate a world in which there is little separation between the human and the divine. Hildegard's supersaturated language is at its most potent in the songs that celebrate a vision of the virgin woman at the center of the cosmos; moreover, in the *Symphonia* as it was intended to be experienced, Hildegard's prophetic voice issues forth with particular force not from a single virginal mouth, but from the many mouths of a whole choir of virgins. The *Symphonia* includes sixteen to the Blessed Virgin and thirteen to Saint Ursula and the Eleven Thousand; God the Father, the Holy Ghost, other saints, groups of holy people like widows and patriarchs are all the subject of four or fewer songs. Hildegard shows little interest in the apostles, except for Saint John, the subject of three songs to which I will return in chapter 5. One poem is addressed to Sapientia, a personification of immense importance to Hildegard's theology, and three to

Ecclesia. The absence of any song addressed to the Savior himself is quite striking, especially since Christ is generally the primary subject of medieval hymns.[11] The Virgin and Saint Ursula do not only receive the greatest number of poems, they are also the subject of some of Hildegard's most ambitious and elaborate *sequentiae*. The *sequentia*'s form, asymmetrical and unmetered, allows Hildegard's fluid grammar a great deal of play, so that the minimum of words can express the maximum of meanings;[12] nowhere is this evocative ambiguity put to more effective use than in the poems to Mary.

In reaction against the insistence of nineteenth- and early twentieth-century historians that the increase in devotion to the Virgin in the twelfth century indicated a sort of golden age for women, some feminist scholars have argued that Mary was instead a particularly efficient mechanism for the oppression of women, representing an ideal of femininity without carnality so perfect, and so perfectly separate from the real, that it encouraged medieval women to alienate themselves from their own bodies, and to find themselves, in comparison with Mary's eternal incorruption, both morally and physically corrupt.[13] More recently, Theresa Coletti has argued that such essentializing arguments do not represent very accurately the relationship of medieval people, either men or women, to the Virgin. Instead of being overwhelmed by the vast differences between themselves and Mary, Coletti suggests, they "brought Marian meanings down to earth, overshadowing the ideology of her singular virginity with a social hermeneutics emphasizing her closeness to historical female subjects."[14] Coletti is concerned particularly with the importance of Mary to lay people, and especially married people, who made up the majority of the audience for Middle English drama; Hildegard, however, is similarly interested in the likeness she and her nuns bear to the Blessed Virgin rather than the differences that separate them. The Virgin represents for her the crowning glory of an ideal of bodily purity in which women could participate wholeheartedly, even if they could not reach that unique pinnacle reserved for Mary herself. In spite of Mary's cosmic and impersonal nature, the insistent focus on the most paradoxical moment in her life, the moment when she, as a virgin, conceives a child, forces the image of her physical and very female body to dominate the songs in her honor. In her songs to the Virgin, Hildegard exploits the "complex semiotics of Mary's pure yet dangerous female body"[15] to lay the foundation for a feminine cosmology built upon the concept of the virgin body. In this body, as it is represented by Mary, Eve, Ursula, Ecclesia, and all of those women whose bodies imitate theirs, the metaphysical and the physical will be united, as will the real and ideal.

Hildegard's songs to the Virgin concentrate almost exclusively on the Incarnation, or more accurately on the precise moment of the conception of Christ, a moment whose specificity is contrasted with Mary's timeless preexistence in the mind of God. In the hymn that begins "Ave generosa," Mary is addressed as *intacta puella* and *materia sanctitatis* (*Symphonia* 17.1). The two epithets have a causal relationship, since Mary's virginal integrity makes her the matter or stuff of holiness. The word *materia* is what Rémy de Gourmont called a *mystique calembour*[16] (mystical pun), one of Hildegard's favorite methods of saturating language with meaning. It contains both Mary's name, Maria, and a description of her, *mater*, suggesting an absolute and essential identity between the two terms. Mary, of course, is matter in a biological and even ontological sense. Medieval philosophers had developed Aristotle's scientific model according to which the female contributed the matter of the fetus at conception, the male the spirit, into a symbolic system according to which man represented intellect and spirit, woman sensuality and flesh.[17] In the case of the conception of Christ, the scientific and the moral came together since his flesh, his human body, could only have come to him from his mother's side of the family since his Father was, by definition, bodiless.[18] For Hildegard, motherhood was the greatest gift of God; because of her capacity to bear children, Eve was the most glorious of God's creations at the dawn of the world. This very gift, however, provoked the envy of Satan in Hildegard's idiosyncratic version of the story, inspired him to tempt Eve and bring about the Fall. Motherhood and virginity, which should, according to Hildegard, have remained united in Eve's original, perfect body, were sundered by Satan's envy.[19] It was only in the fallen world that motherhood and virginity became physically incompatible so that for Ambrose, as we have seen, pregnancy was the proof of lost virginity. Hildegard understands this separation as an injury to the primal female body. To be a woman is therefore to suffer throughout one's life the wounds inflicted by Satan on Eve's body, wounds that are simultaneous markers of great power and potential, and great failure.

Women are not alone in experiencing the wounds of original sin; Hildegard represents all passion as a wound, a sort of inflamed and burning ulcer, at least as acute in men as in women. Mary, however, the luminous Mother of holy medicine (*clarissima Mater / sancte medicine* (*Symphonia* 9.1–2)), is unscarred by any of the wounds of original sin, and heals them in others. Her intact body demonstrates fertility as it should have been, as it would have been for Eve had she not succumbed to the serpent, destroying the natural order as originally established by God. In Hildegard's representations of the Incarnation, she eliminates the violence implicitly caused by the wound of passion, which is the wound of Original Sin. In "Ave generosa," she represents Mary's pre-Lapsarian fertility in terms suggesting that both Mary and the Holy Ghost experience a pleasure in the conception of Christ that is intensely sensual, Platonically erotic, in spite of being asexual: *quam valde Deus in te delectebatur / cum amplexionem caloris sui / in te posuit* [how vigorously God took his pleasure in you / when he placed the embrace of his heat / in you (*Symphonia* 17.4)]. Particularly when combined with *valde, delectabatur* (from *delecto,* a word whose meanings include to charm, to delight, and to seduce) cannot help suggesting sexual fulfillment, not simply divine approbation of the Virgin's purity. We are invited to imagine the Holy Ghost reveling quite literally *in* the body of the Virgin, an act that has as a purely natural consequence the production of the milk which will nourish the infant when he is born: *ita quod Filius eius / de te lactatus est* [and so his Son / was fed on your milk (17.4)]. Milk was believed to be menstrual blood transformed by pregnancy; menstruation was the curse of Eve, from which Mary was believed exempt because of her immaculate conception. Yet for Christ to be born of the Virgin, she must at least to this extent function like any other woman, remaining "imperturbably and ineluctably female."[20] The male, on the other hand, is entirely absent from this conception; the Holy Ghost is completely disembodied, just barely masculine, a fact thrown into sharp relief by the intense physicality associated with female sensations here.

Hildegard goes on to mark even more strongly the sensuality of the conception of Christ, this time from Mary's point of view:

Venter enim tuus gaudium habuit,	Your belly rejoiced indeed
cum omnis caelestis symphonia	when the symphony of all the skies
de te sonuit,	rang out from you
. . .	
Viscera tua gaudium habuerunt	Your vitals rejoiced
sicut gramen, super quod ros cadit	like the grass when dew falls on it
cum ei viriditatem infudit.	infusing it with greenness.
(*Symphonia* 17.5–6)	

To take the more traditional of the two images first, Mary's fertility is here linked to the fertility of the earth itself, to the *viriditas* which is the essence of natural fecundity. The universe is imagined as a place of perennial generation, and Mary seems to be both an expression and a conduit for its "greenness." In a more uncommon image, Hildegard once again invokes the Annunciation and exaggerates it; Mary's womb (described in the most physical of terms not only as *viscera,* entrails, the familiar word from the *Ave Maria,* but also *venter,* belly) is not simply full of grace but full of exuberant joy, which expresses itself as music bursting forth from her, just as in the last lines of the poem it bursts forth in celebration from the Church, just as the poem itself bursts forth first from Hildegard's imagination and then from the lips of her choir. This suggests that the pleasure Mary experiences in the Incarnation may be most closely akin to the sensual pleasures of hearing and producing music. As Bruce Wood Holsinger puts it, "music explicitly eroticizes the Virgin's experience, allowing her the sensual pleasures denied her by Christian tradition."[21] Mary's paradoxical virgin body harmonizes intimately with the musical bodies of the allegorical virgin Ecclesia and the real choir of virgins on the Rupertsberg, all of them together expressing a rapture figured as the culmination of and mutual participation in a purely feminine pleasure.

In her most ambitious Marian sequence, "O virga ac diadema," Hildegard sustains much of the same imagery while developing the theme of Mary's restoration of the earthly paradise. The poem grows up around two trees, the Tree of Jesse, of which Mary, the *virgo*, is the loftiest branch, or *virga*, and the Tree of Knowledge. This second Tree is not directly represented but rather suggested by the evocation of Adam and Eve. Mary is given the attributes of spring; she "leafs and blooms" [*tu frondens floruisti* (*Symphonia* 20.1a)], and from her womb comes "a different life from that which Adam stripped from his sons" [*alia vita. . .qua Adam filios suos denudaverat* (*Symphonia* 20.2a)]. Adam operates like winter, tearing the leaves from the family tree that will descend from him. In the seasonal contrast, we may distinguish, as in the "Ave generosa," the opposition between Mary's perfect fertility and the post-Lapsarian and therefore flawed fertility of human beings. While it is commonplace to depict Christ as the New Adam, Mary as the New Eve, in the *Symphonia* Hildegard allows the doubled female figure of Mary/Eve to dominate almost to the point of the exclusion of Adam/Christ. The result is the creation of an overwhelmingly feminine cosmology, and the evocation of a feminine salvation history. Hildegard deflects expectations by pairing Mary with Adam rather than Eve in the first stanzas; Adam thus appears, momentarily at any rate, as the sole agent of the Fall. To further complicate the relationship between Christ and Mary and the First Parents, the verb *producere* (or, in other poems, *educere*) is used consistently of the masculine operation of engendering life. Adam engenders the human race; God brings forth Mary from the line of David [*divina claritas in nobilissima virga / te produxit* (*Symphonia* 20.2b)]. Finally, and paradoxically, the virile power of Adam is proven when he plays the female role of birthgiver in the creation of Eve, who is formed from his body and drawn out through his side by God, just as Christ will be formed from Mary's body:

O quam magnum est	How great in its power is
in viribus suis latus viri	the side of man from which God
de quo Deus formam mulieris	brought forth the form of woman
produxit	
quam fecit speculum	which he made mirror

omnis ornamenti sui   of all his beauties
et amplexionem omnis creaturae suae.   embrace of all creation.
(*Symphonia* 20.4a)

The first woman is here represented as proof of the greatness of the human race, the image of all that is beautiful, and, in an almost Lucretian turn of phrase, the power of love binding all creatures. She also, if we compare this passage to the one from Fragment IV quoted above, has an origin similar to that of Christ, brought forth painlessly from human flesh. The next stanza renders her being indistinguishable from that of the Blessed Virgin: *Inde concinunt caelestia organa / et miratur omnis terra / o laudabilis Maria* [Then heavenly instruments resound / and the earth is amazed / blessed Mary (*Symphonia* 20.4b)]. Nameless in this poem, Eve is described only as *forma mulieris*; the temporal adverb *inde* collapses praise of the form of woman of the Creation with the celebration of the only woman actually named in the poem, Mary. Only context tells us that there are two identities contained within an apparently singular *forma*. The Fall is imagined as the brutal separation of two beings who should have been one: Eve, who embodies the wound inflicted on the cosmos, and Mary, the agent of healing that same wound.

Here as elsewhere, Hildegard emphasizes the role of Satan in the Fall;[22] this results in minimizing the responsibility of Eve, who is represented as far more deserving of sympathy than of blame:

Nam ipsa mulier   That woman, created
quam Deus matrem omnium posuit   by God as the mother of all
viscera sua   tore her own womb
cum vulneribus ignorantiae decerpsit   with the wounds of ignorance
et plenum dolorem   brought forth for her children
generi suo protulit.   the fullness of pain.
(*Symphonia* 20.5a–b)

Eve's wounded womb, graphically evoked, is healed by the superimposition of Mary's radiant womb, which restores creation to its auroral perfection: *de ventre tuo / novus sol processit / qui omnia crimina Evae abstersit* [from your belly / a new sun came forth / to wash away all the crimes of Eve (*Symphonia* 20.6a)]. In the final stanza, Mary becomes an eternal and timeless figure, invoked as Savior of humanity, much larger in Hildegard's imagination than the Son whose limbs she gathers together:

Unde, o Salvatrix, quae novum lumen   So, Savior, who bore new light
humano generi protulisti,   for the human race,
collige membra Filii tui   gather the limbs of your Son
ad caelestem harmonium.   in heavenly harmony.
(*Symphonia* 20.6b)

The image of the Virgin as heavenly conductor of a symphony of holy instruments, instruments that are simultaneously limbs of Christ, members of his Church, voices lifted in his praise, evokes that of Hildegard, the composer and conductor of earthly music of divine praise. In Hildegard's *Symphonia*, in fact, the Virgin is never the silent creature Bernard so admired for her low voice and brevity of speech;[23] she is both the source and the inspiration of celestial music. In "Cum processit factura" the skies praise her, and it is the sound of her voice ringing out in "Cum erubuerint" that raises the fallen human race: . . . *tu clamas clara voce / hoc modo homines elevans / de isto malitioso casu* [Then you call out, clear-voiced / raising humanity in this way / from that vicious Fall (*Symphonia* 14.4–6)].

In the *Symphonia*, Hildegard constructs a pyramid of virginity with Mary at the apex, the virgin martyrs beneath her, and beneath them the sanctified virgins of the Rupertsberg. This hierarchical structure serves an important function, allowing influence and inspiration to flow from the top to the bottom, so that Hildegard and her nuns can be united with the *turba virginum* who imitate the Virgin, and through her, with Christ:

O Fili dilectissime,	Beloved son
quem genui in visceribus meis	whom I carried in my womb
de vi circueuntis rote	by the power of the circling wheel
sancte divinitatis,	of holy divinity
que me creavit	which created me
et omnia membra mea ordinavit	and put in order all my limbs
et in visceribus meis	and invented in my womb
omne genus musicorum	all kinds of music
in omnibus floribus tonorum	in all the flowers of the tones
constituit	
nunc me et te	now you and I
o Fili dulcissime,	my sweetest Son
multa turba virginum sequitur. . .[24]	are followed by a flock of many
	virgins

The words of this song suggest their own inadequacy by indicating that the mystical union of Virgin and virgins can only be expressed in a language beyond words, that of music. The term *membra* suggests, as in "O virga ac diadema," the Pauline description of the Church as the limbs of Christ. Here, however, the *membra* are those of Mary, who is imagined as a sort of meta-Virgin whose body contains a choir of flowers, which Newman suggests may be "self-referential for the chanting nuns."[25] Mary thus no longer appears as the exception that proves the rule of woman's essentially sinful nature, but rather as an image of shimmering potential. The miraculous event that took place inside her body at the Incarnation is mirrored by miracles taking place in other virgin bodies, both legendary and real: they conceive and bring forth beauty without any contact with men. Read in the larger context of the *Symphonia*, the antiphon "O pulcre facies" with which I began my discussion of Hildegard's songs, operates to invest all professed virgins with the qualities that characterize both the Blessed Virgin and the newly created Eve in "O virga ac diadema": like Mary, they are the builders of the dawn, like Eve, the mirrors in which God beholds himself, and the paradigms of all celestial beauties. It is in the series of songs (antiphons, responsories, an irregular sequence, and a hymn, demonstrating Hildegard's mastery of forms) to Saint Ursula and the Eleven Thousand, however, that the value of virginity is most elaborately worked out, and most closely linked to Hildegard and the community of women with which she identified herself.

Eleven Thousand Virgins

According to legend,[26] Ursula undertook a pilgrimage to Rome in order to avoid marriage with an eminently suitable (and even Christian) prince. She was accompanied by eleven thousand other maidens, as well as some priests, bishops, and eventually the pope, who were to act as protectors. On the return journey, the troop of virgins was captured by the Huns, who slaughtered them mercilessly. Ursula's beauty moved the heart of the chief Hun, and he offered to spare her life if she would become his concubine. She refused, and was shot to death with an arrow. The story of Saint Ursula varies in several interesting ways from the paradigmatic tale of the virgin martyr as I have described it in previous chapters. Most obviously, of course, the single protagonist of the exemplary tale is multiplied here by eleven thousand; the story of Saint Ursula thus provides a model not simply for individual virginity but for the institution of communal virginity. The parallel between the martyrs of Cologne and monastic communities of women, with their male confessors and protectors, is strengthened by the presence among Ursula's followers of men, a detail added to the legend in the twelfth century in order to explain the discovery of male as well as female skeletons among the relics at Cologne, and confirmed by the visions of Elisabeth of Schönau. Hildegard acknowledges this refinement of the legend in one of her antiphons for Saint Ursula, explaining that religious men accompanied the women in order to guard their virginity and "minister to them in all things" [*eis in omnibus ministrabant*], presumably by saying Mass (*Symphonia* 63.3). This detail does not merely justify the recent discovery at Cologne; it also allows Hildegard once again to emphasize the interdependence of the two sexes, with separate but absolutely complementary functions in the realm of the spirit as in that of the flesh.

This separation of sexed identities by sacred function, according to which holiness expresses itself most perfectly through the priesthood in men and through virginity in women, allows Hildegard to create a female subject, Ursula, who is both exceptional and imitable, in both body and spirit.

The most significant peculiarity of the Ursula legend in all of its forms, and one which made it particularly apt for Hildegard's purpose, is its absolute identification of virginity and faith. In most versions of the virgin martyr story, such as the tales of Eulalia and Agnes or Hrotsvitha's *Passion of Agapes, Chionia and Hirena*, the assault on the saint's virginity, whether it takes the form of threatened rape or an offer of marriage, is at least explicitly secondary to the demand that she sacrifice to pagan gods or submit in some other way to temporal authority. In the story of Saint Ursula, however, the line between the assault on the virgin's faith and the assault on her chastity is erased. The Hun does not demand that she worship his gods, merely that she become his mistress. Her martyrdom is in the name of virginity at least as much as in the name of faith; the two, in fact, are indistinguishable. The multiplication of a single virgin into many thousands, and the emphasis on virginity as an expression of faith in its own right, make Ursula and the Eleven Thousand both quantitative and qualitative epitomes of the virginal ideal.

The series of songs to Ursula and the Eleven Thousand are written down sequentially in the Dendermonde MS, permitting the shape of the plot to emerge from Hildegard's impressionistic lyrics. Hildegard strips the story of all but the most essential details in order to concentrate on the bones of the narrative and the concepts underlying it. The first poem, the responsory "Spiritui Sancto," emphasizes the formation of a community of virgins whom the Holy Spirit first gathers like doves in Ursula's mind [*qui in mente Ursule virginis. . .velut columbas / collegit (Symphonia* 60.3–6)]. Here as in so many other instances Hildegard takes a conventional, even a tired image, the virgin as dove, and renders it extraordinary by locating the flock of birds inside Ursula's head. There is no indication at all of the translation of the *aureus exercitus* (13), the golden army of virgins, from the realm of the imaginary to that of the real. In one line, the flock of virgins is conceived in Ursula's imagination, and two lines later she is setting out like an Old Testament patriarch, *sicut Abraham* (8). Abraham's descendants, the children of Israel, populated the earth; so will Ursula's descendants, although they will be the children of her inspiration rather than of her body, generation after generation of women imitating her virginal ideal.

Both Newman and Dronke have noted the way in which Hildegard casts the story of Saint Ursula as a reflection of her own life.[27] When she marvels at the great migration of virgins led by Ursula, asking *quis umquam talia / audivit*, her amazement is just a bit disingenuous, since of course anyone who had heard the story of her own removal to the Rupertsberg, against the opposition of the abbot of Saint Disibod, had heard "something like" the story of Ursula's golden army. In the sequence "O Ecclesia," however, the figure of Ursula becomes much more than a simple patron saint or a reflection of the foundress of the Rupertsberg; she is transformed from a human woman into a figure of cosmic significance. The poem, in fact, could be said to be about change and movement, about transformation and the transgression of boundaries, all accomplished upon or within an imagined virgin body. Ecclesia, as she is represented in the first stanza, is a cosmic figure with a female body constructed of Biblical tags and scriptural references: her eyes are like sapphire, her ears like Mount Bethel, her nose like a mountain of myrrh and incense (*Symphonia* 64.1). The allusions to the Song of Songs are both apparent and deliberate, but each one is mutated into something purely Hildegardian. Ecclesia is a powerfully synesthetic creation, appealing to sight, to smell, and to sound, and yet, in spite of the familiarity of the similes that define her—perhaps because of it—she defies the imagination becoming a visionary body whose physical attributes cannot be separated either from their textual origins or from their prophetic ability. This deliberate and surreal confusion of the body itself with what it sees, what it says, and what it means, sets the stage for transformations and transgressions to follow. In the next two stanzas, the focus of the song moves from the mystical and mysterious figure of Ecclesia to the smaller one of the human girl, Ursula.

As Dronke has noted, Ursula imagines a straightforward transition from earth to heaven.[28] She longs, she says, to come to God "as a cloud rushes like sapphire through the purest air" [*velut nubes que in purissimo aere / currit similis saphiro* (*Symphonia* 64.3)], in the same way, perhaps, as the angels who rush up and down Jacob's ladder upon Mount Bethel. Her union with Christ, however, is not so easily accomplished. She becomes an object of mockery first [*ceperunt ludere cum illa*, "they began to tease her" (64.5)] and then the victim of mysterious pain [*ignea sarcina / super ea cecidit*, "a fiery burden fell upon her" (64.5)]. The subject of *ceperunt* is unclear here, and the words *ignea sarcina* have not, to my mind, been fully explained. Dronke understands them to indicate the moment when Ursula confronts martyrdom itself, a "painful experience, as of being weighed down and scorched."[29] This seems an inadequate explanation for two reasons. First, there is nothing in the actual manner of Ursula's death to explain the image of a fiery burden falling upon her; she was, according to most accounts, simply transfixed with an arrow. Even more significantly, the *ignea sarcina* falls upon her well before the moment of her martyrdom, which does not occur until stanza 7, and is strongly marked temporally: "Then (*tunc*) the devil invaded his limbs. . ." It seems a mistake to identify the people who mock Ursula with the Huns who martyr her. The mockery is a reaction to her initial profession of love for Christ, to her desire for unity with him; in the song, it follows immediately upon her representation of herself as a cloud rushing heavenwards: *rumor iste per omnes populos exiit / et dixerunt / innocentia puellaris ignorantie nescit quid dixit* [the rumor of it ran out through the nations and they said "the innocent, in her girlish ignorance, she doesn't know what she's talking about!" (64.4)]. The patronizing and familiar quality of this last remark makes it difficult to ascribe to the demonized, semi-monstrous Huns; it evokes rather the judgment of elders who think they understand what is best for the younger generation. The word *populus*, furthermore, generally refers to the entire population of a country—men, women, and children—and is an improbable term to use of a barbarian horde (which would more usually be called *exercitus*, army). In the plural, *omnes populos* suggests an audience of more than one people, of all the Christian kingdoms, perhaps; this is clearly the meaning of the phrase at the end of "Cum vox sanguinis" (no. 65), where the virgin martyrs become the ornaments of all Christianity: *omnes populi cum illis ornentur* (65.10). The Huns might, at a stretch, be described as *populus*, a people, but never as *populi*, peoples. The operation of rumor, too, is more characteristic of a peaceable population fascinated by the doings of its rulers than of an army drawn up to witness the humiliation or execution of captives of war. I would ascribe these words, therefore, not to the pagans, but to those earlier obstacles in Ursula's path toward sainthood, the compatriots who had dynastic ambitions for her, such as her father and the father of her fiancé.

According to this reading, the *ignea sarcina* becomes the burden Ursula shouldered before that of martyrdom: her vow of virginity. In her exhortation to virginity in the *Scivias*, Hildegard describes the commitment to virginity in terms that make abstinence from sexual activity seem a very fiery burden indeed, given that lust burns in even the best intentioned of human hearts:

> . . .and for His love you will suffer much anguish in yourselves when you overcome that which is sown in the lust of sin by the flavor of the apple; but although you will experience in your seed the streams that flow from the fire of lust, since you cannot be so chaste that the fragility of human weakness will not secretly appear within you, you must in that travail imitate the passion of My Son, and resist within yourselves the burning flames of lust. (*Scivias* 1.2)

Virginity is a fiery burden because it resists the flames of lust, just as the flesh of Eulalia or Agnes resisted the actual flames of her martyrdom.

Imitatio Christi is the essence of martyrdom, and Hildegard therefore imagines the imitation of Christ through virginity as a form of martyrdom in its own right. Ursula, after all, is not the Blessed Virgin conceived without desire, born without original sin. She is rather a member of the "Symphony of Virgins" who implore Christ's help in resisting temptation in "O dulcissime amator," acknowledging the difficulty of their chosen path: *valde durum est contradicere / quod habet gustus pomi* [it is so hard to deny / those things which taste of the apple (*Symphonia* 57.2)]. Ursula herself had evidently forgotten this when she imagined herself rushing through the air toward her Beloved, like a cloud, unencumbered by a body. The body as much as the soul, however, is a gift from God, and outright rejection of it was heresy.[30] Martyrdom would be meaningless without a body to suffer it, just as virginity would be valueless if there were no sexual world to deny in its favor, if the apple had no savor. The *ignea sarcina* that falls upon Ursula serves to remind her of all these things before the final destruction of her body in her martyrdom.

The body exists on an allegorical level as well as a literal level in the song, however. Ursula's vow of virginity is the initial evidence of her *contemptus mundi*, and also the immediate cause of her martyrdom, since it provokes her pagan captors to murder her and her companions. The smell of incense and myrrh once again invades the poem in stanza 6, convincing those who had mocked Ursula of her sanctity, and identifying her with the figure of Ecclesia from the opening of the poem. It also provokes the devil to gather together his "limbs" in a blasphemous parody of the unification of Christ's limbs in the Church, in order to destroy Ursula and her companions. The reference to the devil's *membra*, however, serves more than a simply antithetical purpose; by recalling the Pauline image of the Church as Christ's body, it reminds us that Ursula and her maidens are the very limbs which compose that body. In their martyrdom, Ursula and the Eleven Thousand are transformed from individual virgins into the collective entity which is the virgin Ecclesia. The abstract quality of stanza 7, in which the limbs of the devil, not human men, destroy not a troop of virgins but "the most noble way of life (i.e. virginity) existing in those bodies" [*nobilissimos mores / in corporibus istis* (64.7)] erases the boundary between individual and community while drawing our attention simultaneously to the slaughtered human bodies of Ursula's companions and to the monumental allegorical body of the Church, which is founded upon that slaughter.

In the last stanzas of the song, nothing remains in the cosmic landscape but the composite body of Ecclesia confronting the composite body of Satan, while the elements, as Newman so rightly notes, "give voice to the merely human woe that must speak its grief."[31] The stanza begins with a startling irruption in German, *Wach* [woe]! The moment when the vernacular breaks through into the Latin marks the beginning of a series of textual confusions: *rubicundus sanguis innocentis agni / in desponsatione sua / effusus est* [the crimson blood of the innocent lamb / is spilled / at the wedding feast (64.9)]. In these lines, the distinction between Christ and His martyr is erased; whose blood is being spilled, and at whose wedding feast? The answer, of course, is that the innocent Lamb is both Christ and Ursula/Ecclesia. The wedding feast evokes the Song of Songs again, but bride and bridegroom are no longer distinguishable; their union is total.

In the tenth and last stanza, the mocking earthly symphony is replaced by the glorious heavenly one whose music echoes through so many of Hildegard's songs, and the red blood of Christ flowing together with that of the martyrs brings about a final miraculous change. In one of the antiphons for Saint Ursula, the blood of the slaughtered virgins becomes a flower that can resist the "winter with its serpent blast";[32] here, it takes another form: *guttur serpentis antiqui / in istis margaritas materie Verbi Dei / suffocatum est* [the throat of the ancient serpent / is strangled / by these pears, the stuff of the Word of God (64.10)]. The song that began by representing a female body composed of precious things and of the words of the prophets now ends with a precious thing composed of female bodies who *are* the Word of God, as the Devil is choked by a necklace of virgin-pearls.

In the following hymn, the relationships between blood, jewels, music, and voices are worked out somewhat differently. The song begins with the voice of the blood itself, singing out before the throne of God: *Cum vox sanguinis / Ursule et innocentis turbe eius / ante thronum Dei sonuit / antiqua prophetia venit* . . . [When the voice of the blood / of Ursula and her innocent flock / rang out before the throne of God / an ancient prophecy came forth (*Symphonia* 65.1)]. *Sonuit* is the same word used in the "Ave generosa" to describe the celestial symphony echoing from Mary's womb; the voice of the blood is a musical one, and from the union of blood and music prophecy arises as Hildegard achieves "a daring transposition through which Ursula takes the place of Christ as the antitype of all the Old Testament figures."[33] Newman suggests that *prophetia* (prophecy) may be a scribal error for *propheta* (prophet) and translates accordingly, but it seems to me perfectly in keeping with Hildegard's general willingness to confuse function with agency to imagine a prophecy speaking rather than a prophet, especially since Hildegard's purpose here is to insist upon the truth of prophecy rather than the infallibility of prophets. That truth is revealed by the blood of the virgin martyrs as, in an extraordinary image, Ursula and the eleven thousand are linked to the burning bush:

Turba magna, quam incombustus rubus	This great flock, which the burning
(quem Moyses viderat) significat,	bush (which Moses saw) predicted,
et quam Deus in prima radice plantaverat	planted by God in the primal root,
in homine quem de limo formaverat	in the human he shaped from mud
ut sine commixtione viri viveret	to live unmixed with man,
cum clarissima voce clamavit	in the clearest of voices it cried out
in purissimo auro, thopazio,	in purest gold, in topaz
et saphiro circumamicta in auro.	and in sapphire set in gold.

(Symphonia 65.9)

This stanza is so saturated with images and references that they are not easily disentangled. The burning bush, object of Moses's vision, is here interpreted as signifying the advent not of Mary (a traditional allegory) but of
Ursula and the virgin martyrs. An episode from the Old Testament thus
prefigures not simply one from the New Testament (as Moses's time in the
desert was seen as prefiguring Christ's withdrawal during Lent) but Christian history after the death and resurrection of Christ. In a very curious
maneuver of botanical assimilation, Hildegard imagines the burning bush
as having been planted in the "primal root," which she then identifies with
the gender-neutral first human being from the dawn of creation. The next
line, however, calls into question this very gender-neutrality, and not in the
expected way. The referent of the *ut* clause is not immediately apparent.
Who exactly is to live "unmixed with man" (gender-specific *vir*)? The
answer must be the *turba magna,* the flock of virgins, although the structure
of the sentence offers the first human creature as a more immediate possibility. Virginity, defined as being "unmixed with man," is thus once again
sexed female, established as original, and privileged as an essential part of
God's plan for the human race. The synaesthesia that characterized the
visionary opening of "O Ecclesia" occurs here too as the *vox sanguinis* of
the first stanza becomes a voice calling out not in words or even musical
tones, but in the multicolored precious substances that form the ramparts
of the city of Heaven: gold, topaz, sapphire. Finally, these jewels crystallized
from the voice of the blood of the martyrs become the ornaments of the
citizens of heaven and earth: *Nunc gaudeant omnes celi, et omnes populi cum
illis ornentur.* They function as reminders of the bond between the legendary
virgin martyrs and their successors on the Rupertsberg. Hildegard's sisterhood, like Ursula's followers, is the living fulfillment of ancient prophecy:
in intact bodies and through their voices raised in song, the word of God

is revealed. Their virginity installs them in a tradition of miraculous femininity stretching back from Ursula to Mary to Eve; they are bound together by currents of desire for the disembodied, sexless spouse who is Christ and by shared affection for each other as virgin brides of Christ. While Ursula is the shining, immediate example of independence founded in virginity, however, the prophetic authority that justifies this claim to self-determination is rooted equally deeply in a much more ambivalent figure, that of the Sibyl.

Sibyl of the Rhine

In the *Symphonia* no less than in her visionary works, Hildegard establishes herself as part of a tradition of biblical prophecy. In the songs to Ursula alone, as I have noted, there are allusions to Abraham, Jacob, and Moses, as well as echoes of the Song of Songs, which was read in the Middle Ages as a prophecy of the relationship between Christ and his Church. The only apostle who figures significantly in the *Symphonia* is John, prophet of *Revelation*, the book that had marked Hildegard's prose style so deeply. Kathryn Kerby-Fulton's recent work on Hildegard's visionary texts reminds us that such citations are much more than stylistic, demonstrating as they do the absolute centrality of prophecy to Hildegard's self-image, thought, and political and social relations.[34] Behind all of the biblical male prophets Hildegard invokes, however, hovers the shadowy and unacknowledged figure of a pagan prophetess, the Sibyl. The first explicit description of Hildegard as a Sibyl occurs late, in a letter written by Henry of Langenstein to Bishop Eckard of Worms in 1383. Henry calls Hildegard *theotonicorum sibilla*,[35] the Sibyl of the Germans, staking a particular ethnic claim to her divine inspiration, which would no doubt have irked the woman who saw herself as part of a tradition of prophets with a mission to "reproach the whole world for its present iniquity" (*Letter* 15r:51–52). A German version of the Sibylline prophecy composed in the 1320s, however, links Hildegard to the Sibyl in a rather more oblique manner. The emperor Solomon questions the authority of the Sibyl, who responds with a testy anachronism: "Ask Hildegard of Bingen / by whom the book is written— / I have derived all my words from it."[36] This mildly humorous moment would have no point if Hildegard were not already associated with the Sibyl in the popular mind. Indeed, there is every reason to suppose that Hildegard herself was not only aware of the tradition of Sibylline prophecy, but that her understanding of what it meant to be a virgin and a prophetess was shaped, at least in part, by the image of the pagan Sibyl preserved in Christian texts. While the sophisms of the Fathers had worked hard to reduce virginity into silence and impossibility, their writings nonetheless preserved a pre-Christian image of a different virgin body as the site of prophetic speech. Hildegard recuperates the image of the virgin prophetess from its pagan antecedents without, typically, acknowledging either her sources or the various moves made by patristic writers to prevent Christian women from claiming such oracular authority founded upon virginity.

Early Christian writers expressed conflicting attitudes toward pagan prophetesses. In general, they approved of the Sibyl and disapproved of her Delphic counterpart, the Pythia, a divergence of opinion that appears to have been based at least partially upon different perceptions of their sexual status. The Pythia, according to Diodorus Siculus, writing in the late first century B.C.E., was not a virgin:

> It is said that in ancient times, virgins delivered the oracles because virgins have their natural innocence intact and are in the same case as Artemis; for indeed virgins were alleged to be well suited to guard the secrecy of disclosures made by oracles. In more recent times, however, people say that Echecrates the Thessalian, having arrived at the shrine and beheld the virgin who uttered the oracle, became enamoured of her and violated her. And that the Delphians because of this deplorable event passed a law that in future a virgin should no longer prophesy but that an elderly woman of fifty should declare the oracles, and that she should be dressed as a virgin in the costume of a virgin, as a sort of reminder of the prophetess of ancient times.[37]

Diodorus's account of the Pythia proposes a sort of degenerative chronology in lieu of explanation, leaving the central question open: if the oracle once demanded youthful virgins in order to guard its secrets, why is it now content with chaste old ladies? He both implies a link between the body of the virgin, which is "well suited" to prophecy, and denies this link any real meaning. The virgin of ancient times was an acceptable vehicle for divine speech not only because of her association with Artemis, sister of the God who spoke at Delphi, but because, according to the age-old analogy, one closed "mouth" betokened another, silence and virginity reflected each other. The virgin was also, as demonstrated by the reprehensible behavior of Echecrates, irresistibly appealing precisely because of her virginity, and Apollo was a well-known admirer of virgin beauty who had pursued both Cassandra and Daphne with intentions not much different from those of the Thessalian; Cassandra even received the gift of prophecy in return for promising to sacrifice her virginity to the god (her punishment when she reneged was that her prophecies should never be believed). In the decision that is made to replace the virgin prophetess with an older woman, however, the god himself is curiously absent; evidently he no longer cares about the sexual status of his prophetess, or else he is capable of being deluded by her costume into thinking that she is still a virgin. The antique relationship between divinity and oracle, once apparently both mysterious and erotic, consummated within the intact body of the virgin, has become pragmatic and superficial.

The implied mechanics of oracular speech, in which the god occupied the body of a priestess who spoke in ecstasy, was troubling to Christian writers.[38] In his discussion of the Pythia, Origen represents the female body as inherently unclean: ". . .while the priestess of Apollo is sitting at the mouth of the Castalian cave she receives a spirit through her womb. . . . Consider then whether this does not indicate the impure and foul nature of that spirit in that it enters the prophetess not by open and invisible pores which are far purer than the womb, but through the latter part which it would be wrong for a self-controlled and sensible man to look upon or, I might add, even to touch."[39] For Origen, the nonvirgin status of the Pythia is conclusive proof that the power which occupied her is demonic and not divine; he goes on to say that a real god like the God of the Old Testament would, in any case, have spoken through a man. In one of John Chrysostom's homilies, lack of virginity and ecstatic speech are causally linked; the Pythia prophesies because the god possesses her sexually, behaving like a voodoo priestess in a second-rate Hollywood film:

> This same Pythoness then is said, being a female, to sit at times upon the tripod of Apollo astride, and thus the evil spirit ascending from beneath and entering the lower part of her body, fills the woman with madness and she with dishevelled hair begins to play the bacchanal and to foam at the mouth, and thus being in a frenzy to utter the words of her madness. I know that you are ashamed and blush when you hear these things. . .[40]

The descriptions of Origen and Chrysostom are inevitably biased and may or may not reflect actual practice at Delphi; nonetheless, their extreme reactions to the Pythia serve to highlight the distinctions drawn between Pythia and Sibyl by Christian writers. From a very early period, the Sibyl is imagined as the surprising vehicle of Christian truth, and with one significant exception, to which I shall return, she is never represented as prophesying in the sort of condition that could be confused with either madness or sexual transport. For Lactantius, writing at the beginning of the fourth century and deeply concerned to build bridges between pagan knowledge and Christian belief, the Sibyl was proof of the universal nature of God's truth.[41] The Emperor Constantine, perhaps following Lactantius, credited the Erythraean Sibyl, supposed to have lived at the time of the Trojan War, with prophesying the Incarnation, even though he knew she was a priestess of Apollo.[42] Both Lactantius and Constantine were citing a broadly circulated collection known as the *Sibylline Oracles*, which they believed to be of great antiquity, although we now know them to be, for the most part, products of the Hellenistic period, full of both Jewish and Christian interpolations.[43] Even more influential than the testimony of Lactantius or the emperor himself was that of Augustine, who placed the Sibyl among the citizens of the City of God and provided a Latin translation of the poem attributed to her whose initial letters in Greek spelled out *Iesous Chreistos Theou Uios Soter* (Jesus Christ, Son of God, Savior).[44] Bolstered by such authority, the *Sibylline Oracles* were assured of survival into the Middle Ages, and indeed the "sibyl's song" became practically a genre in its own right.

The Sibyl possessed several characteristics that made her more palatable to Christian writers than the Pythia, and these are curiously interwoven. In his treatise *Against Jovinian*, Jerome gives the Sibyl a prominent place among his pagan virgins, and connects her gift of prophecy explicitly with her virginity: "Varro asserts there were ten whose ornament was virginity, and divination the reward of their virginity. But if in the Aeolian dialect 'Sibyl' is represented by *theobule* we must understand that a knowledge of the 'Counsel of God' is rightly attributed to virginity alone" (1.21).[45] For Jerome, virginity is a more perfect state than chastity, just as the New Testament is more perfect than the Old. Jovinian had cited Deborah, wife of Lappidoth and prophetess and judge of Israel in support of his contention that virginity was not superior to marriage (1.23). Characteristically, Jerome dismisses the example of Deborah by attacking Jovinian's rhetorical ability and especially the way he marshals his arguments; what, he wonders sarcastically, is Deborah doing in a list of military commanders like Joshua and Samson? In any case, it is to him both appropriate and inevitable that the power of prophecy should have passed away from married women like Deborah with the advent of the new era, descending instead on virgins like the four daughters of Philip (Acts 21.9) who were gifted with prophecy (1.39). The Sibyl, unlike the Pythia, fits this new paradigm for prophecy. The purity of her body, furthermore, implicitly accounts for the intelligibility of her speech. Whereas the Pythia is imagined as incoherent, gasping out the words of the god who possesses her in a condition indistinguishable from madness or sexual excitement, the Sibyl is not generally represented in the act of prophesying at all, but rather as having prophesied, and as having already committed the instructions of the God to writing in controlled hexameters, bound up in books. To adopt Parke's distinction, she is a clairvoyant but not a medium;[46] she speaks for but never as the god, and her speech is therefore not tainted by the suspicion of possession, either demonic or sexual.

The only classical authority to represent the Sibyl as speaking ecstatically, like the Pythia, is Vergil:

At Phoebi nondum patiens immanis in antro
bacchatur vates, magnum si pectore possit
excussisse deum; tanto magis ille fatigat
os rabidum, fera corda domans, fingitque premendo.
                                                   (*Aeneid* 6.77–80)

Not yet submissive to Phoebus, the prophetess stormed wildly around the cave, as if she could throw the great god from her breast; all the more he tired her foaming mouth, taming her wild heart and breaking her to his weight.

The editor of the standard school edition of the *Aeneid* notes decorously that the images in this passage derive from taming horses, without acknowledging that the vocabulary of animal training, and particularly horse-breaking, is also always the vocabulary of sexual conquest.[47] Curiously, this passage is never used against the Sibyl as Chrysostom turned similar descriptions against the Pythia. Perhaps it was Vergil's reputation that shielded the Sibyl from the implications of his own words; like the Sibyl herself, Vergil was recognized early as a pagan prophet of Christian truth; Christian readers had discovered in his Fourth Eclogue a prophecy of the birth of Christ issuing from the mouth of the Sibyl of Cumae. As Bernard McGinn notes, "in most of the early references, the Sibyl and Vergil go together as pagan witnesses to the Incarnation."[48] The survival of these two authorities from the past, one the greatest prophetic voice known to the Latin world and the other its greatest poetic voice, permitted a comforting degree of continuity between the old Rome and the new, between the Imperial City and the Eternal City.

The influence of Vergil's lines combined with the patristic emphasis on the Sibyl's virginity to make her a perfectly paradoxical figure, a body sealed and hollow yet open to a divine force which, unlike Origen's demon or Chrysostom's evil spirit, entered her in some unimpeachable way, like a sunbeam through a pane of glass, as the Holy Spirit was supposed to have entered Mary. In his letter to Heloise on communities of women, Abelard evokes the Sibyl and cites Jerome as his authority for insisting that prophecy is the reward of virginity. He then goes on to describe virginity as a particularly feminine state:

Finally, who does not know that women embraced the teachings of Christ and the counsel of the Apostles with such a zeal for chastity that in order to preserve the integrity of flesh and mind alike they offered themselves as a holocaust to God through martyrdom, glorying in the twin crown [of virginity and martyrdom], and "worked to follow the Lamb, bridegroom of virgins, wherever he might go"? For indeed we know perfection in that virtue to be rare in men, frequent in women. We read that not a few of these women had such zeal for this prerogative of the flesh that they did not hesitate to turn their hands against themselves, in order that they should not lose that incorruption they had vowed to God, so that they might come as virgins to the Virgin Bridegroom.[49]

Abelard's letter does not eliminate the erotic from the prophetic; rather, he describes women who are motivated almost exclusively by the erotic, who embrace Christianity quite literally, in the hopes of similarly embracing Christ himself. Their virginity is a sublimation rather than a rejection of desire. What is more, this virginity is a prerogative not simply of the flesh but of female flesh; while he acknowledges virginity as a possibility for men, Abelard clearly perceives it as a primarily and fundamentally feminine phenomenon. For him the virgin body is a female body waiting in a state of perpetual desire to be embraced by her divine lover, very much like the recuperated Sibyl or even the unregenerate Pythia.

That Hildegard was familiar with Abelard's musings on sibyls and virginity is unlikely;[50] nor is it even certain that she knew Vergil. An image of the Sibyl, however, would have been familiar to her from several more popular and accessible sources, for the medieval Sibyl's song was performed across Europe for centuries. One version, composed perhaps as early as the seventh century but well known in the eleventh, resonates especially strongly in Hildegard's work:

> Mundus origo mea est, animam de sidere traxi,
> > Intactum corpus concutit omne deus.
> <Narrabo quodcumque deus mihi spirat in ore,>
> > Si bene devotum senserit ampla fides.
> Multum mea mecum dixerunt carmina carmen;
> > Carmina quae scribo, noverit illa deus. . .

> The universe is my origin, my soul I have drawn from a star,
> My virgin body God has set trembling in every limb.
> <I shall tell whatever God puts in my mouth.>
> if my abundant faith has had true insight into hallowed matter.
> Many a song my own singings have uttered within myself;
> the songs which I write, those God knows. . .[51]

The Sibyl here represents herself as a virgin whose body is sexually intact and whose very integrity invites the divine to invade it, to shake it into speech, to provoke music from it. The Sibyl's body thus resonates with a whole series of hollow and musical female bodies in Hildegard's work: the generic body depicted in *Causes and Cures*, which is "open like a frame of wood in which strings to be strummed are attached, and like windows open to the wind, so that the elements are more forceful [in her] than in men" (105); Mary's symphonic womb in the "Ave generosa"; Hildegard's own weak frame giving forth its "small sound of the trumpet" (*Letter* 201r: 50–51). Nor are these congruences coincidental, for Hildegard was certainly aware of some version of the Sibyl's song.

It is not clear exactly how the Sibyl's song was performed in the early Middle Ages, although some versions were provided with musical notation as early as the ninth century.[52] The most celebrated and influential enactment of the Sibyl's song, however, was undoubtedly that which provided the climax of the *Ordo Prophetarum*, an early liturgical drama that developed out of a *lectio* for Matins frequently used during the Christmas season. By the eleventh century, it had become traditional in many places to base one of the homilies for the Christmas season on what Dronke has described as "an ugly pseudo-Augustinian sermon, *Against Jews, Pagans and Arians*,"[53] which incorporated both the version of the Sibyl's song cited by Augustine and a line from Vergil's Eighth Eclogue in order to combat what was presumed to be the willful blindness of the Jews. By the twelfth century, this homily had taken on the form of a drama in which the various pre-Christian witnesses to the Incarnation spoke or sang *in propria persona*. The list of prophets varies somewhat in different versions, but generally includes Isaiah, Jeremiah, Daniel, Moses, David, Habakuk, Elisabeth and her son John the Baptist, Vergil, and Nebuchadnezzar; the Sibyl comes either last or second last; in some cases, she is followed by Balaam and his ass, whose gift of prophecy presumably has even greater dramatic impact than that of the Roman seer. Thirteenth-century manuscripts from Laon and Rouen both prescribe the Sibyl's costume quite specifically. At Laon, the performer (male, without a doubt) is to be "in women's clothing, with unbound hair, a crown of ivy, behaving madly"; the Rouen *Ordo* describes her more tersely as "crowned and costumed like a woman."[54] In both these texts and in the *Carmina Burana*, the Augustinian prophecy that she sings is indicated by citation of the first line or lines, rather than written out in full; evidently the poem was too well known to be worth the copyist's ink.

In 1151, when Hildegard completed her first book of visionary prose, the *Scivias*, she incorporated several apparently dramatic passages near the end of the work; when the great single-volume manuscript of Hildegard's life work (the "Riesencodex") was produced at the Rupertsberg toward the end her life, it also included a complete dramatic text, prefaced with the brief note *Incipit Ordo Virtutum* (here begins the *Order of the Virtues*). It has been persuasively argued both that this liturgical drama was one of Hildegard's earliest works, and that it was performed in a more or less public setting at least once during her lifetime.[55] The *Ordo Virtutum* is singular in many ways. Its characters are all personifications, like those of the late medieval morality plays, but it predates the earliest morality by two hundred years. It has been called a liturgical drama, but compared with contemporary plays like the Anglo-Norman *Jeu d'Adam*, its connection to the liturgy is so tenuous that the circumstances of its performance remain entirely conjectural; Dronke's suggestion that the *Ordo* was composed for the consecration of the Rupertsberg convent in 1152 is seductive but unprovable.[56] Finally, the play is unique in that it contains seventeen solo parts written for women's voices, as well as a female chorus of Souls. The one major male character, the Devil, shouts; he cannot sing, for music is divine. The only scene in the play that permits singing male voices to be heard is in the opening chorus of Prophets and Patriarchs. This chorus explicitly links Hildegard's play to the *Ordo Prophetarum*. Hildegard's virtues take over from the prophets much as Jerome's Christian virgins took over from the married prophetesses of the Old Testament, transforming prophetic speech into salvific speech through the agency of virginity.

This translation of power is expressed in the first exchange of the play. The Patriarchs and Prophets inquire concerning the identity of a group of figures who seem to them like clouds (*Ordo* 1); the Virtues reply somewhat obliquely: *Verbum dei clarescit in forma hominis / et ideo fulgemus cum illo / edificantes membra sui pulcri corporis* [The Word of God shines forth in human form, and we glow along with Him, building the limbs of his beautiful body (*Ordo* 2–5)]. Given the tradition of the *Ordo Prophetarum*, we should certainly imagine the Sibyl as a member of the chorus of prophets. The form of the Virtues' address, *o antiqui sancti*, does not preclude the presence of a woman (or even, perhaps, of Balaam's ass) in the crowd of Prophets and Patriarchs, because in Latin a group including both sexes is invariably gendered masculine. Only a group consisting entirely of women would be addressed in the feminine. It may also be significant in this context that Hildegard has the Virtues refer to the Patriarchs and Prophets as *antiqui sancti*, ancient holy ones, rather than *antiqui viri* or *viri sancti* (men of old or holy men). The Souls of the play, like the Virtues, are automatically gendered feminine, and Hildegard reinforces this by multiplying references to them as "daughters of the King." Woman rather than man thus becomes in the play the representative human being.[57] Again the contrast with the *Jeu d'Adam*, in which Eve's transgression makes Adam the representative of humanity, is instructive.

The dramatic development of the *Ordo* casts both Anima's fall into sin and her redemption by the Virtues in feminine terms. The Devil tempts her by telling her that, while she must wait for the embrace of God, the world will embrace her now. The response of the Virtues at this point expresses both the sad irony of the situation and a remarkable degree of psychological insight: *Ach, ach, quedam mirabilis victoria / in mirabili desiderio dei surrexit / in qua delectatio carnis se latenter abscondit* [Ah, ah, what an amazing victory rose up in that amazing longing for God—but desire of the flesh was secretly hidden within it (*Ordo* 51–53)]. The lament admits the bitter fact with which Hildegard, leader of a community of women for over a decade at this point in her life, must have been all too familiar: the sublimation of erotic into divine desire is not always complete, and if incomplete is unsuccessful. Balanced against the vulnerability of the desiring soul is the preemptive remedy espoused by the Virtues. Virginity, they sing, is the armor that protects against the assaults of the Devil. Once Anima has turned to the Devil's embrace, the Virtues give voice to the most complex music in the play, the "Flos campi" passage that Davidson describes as "placed within the structure of the drama like a capstone in an arch."[58] The song draws on the ancient tradition of virginity as a flower that dies when it is plucked, and Chastity takes the solo part:

> Castitas: O Virginitas, in regali thalamo stas.
>   O quam dulciter ardes in amplexibus regis,
>   cum sol te perfulget
>   ita quod nobilis flos tuus numquam cadet./
>   O virgo nobilis, te numquam inveniet umbra in cadente flore!
> Virtutes: Flos campi cadit vento, pluvia spargit eum.
>   O Virginitas, tu permanes in symphoniis supernorum civium:
>   unde es suavis flos qui numquam aresces. (*Ordo* 104–11)

Chastity: O Virginity, you stand in the royal bedroom. How sweetly you burn in the king's embraces when the sun shines through you. This is why your noble flower never falls. O noble virgin the shadow of the falling flower shall never find you! Virtues: The flower of the field falls in the wind, the rain spatters it. O Virginity, you remain in the symphony of the citizens of heaven; so you are the sweet blossom who never withers.

The song deploys the same images of transparency and integrity that Hildegard applies to Mary in the *Symphonia*, and imagines the choir of heavenly citizens as a garden of eternal flowers. Many of the Virtues are similarly described in terms of blossoms and light: Charity is the flower of love (76), Obedience is lucent (87), Faith is like a mirror (96), Contempt of the World is the brilliance of life (114), Modesty flowers among white lilies (135). The effect is to recall the errant soul, who penitently admires the clear brilliance of the Virtues (162). Their shining integrity stands in clear opposition to the burning sweetness that has absorbed her into sin [*fervens dulcedo absorbuit me in peccatis* (166)]. She recognizes the loss of her virginity as a wound: "I stink of the wounds with which the ancient serpent has infected me" [. . .*in vulneribus feteo quibus antiquus serpens me contaminavit* (170–71)].

Hildegard is careful to avoid representing virginity as a foolproof shield against the Devil; Chastity has fifteen verses to sing in the *Ordo*, but Humility has twenty-three and is called the Queen of the Virtues, since without her tempering influence any other virtue can lead to sin. It is Humility alone who can provide the "true medicine" (185) that will allow Anima's wounds to be healed. The language of wounds becomes the agent of connection between the Soul and Christ in the final scenes of the play. Humility first appeals to the Virtues to lift Anima up "with all her scars, for the sake of the wounds of Christ" (190), and then makes it clear that these wounds are one and the same: "our great healer has suffered cruel and bitter wounds because of you" (196–97). In the final chorus, however, after the Devil has been bound by the Virtues, these wounds are transformed one final time and linked to the language of flowers. The Virtues and Souls together lift their voices in a hymn to greenness. In the beginning, they sing, all of creation was green and growing and flowers blossomed in the midst of the greenness. As in so many other places in Hildegard's work, the concepts of generative greenness and of virginity, represented by the unplucked blossom, are indistinguishable in the pre-Lapsarian world. "Afterwards," the Virtues sing in a three-word line which is the ultimate distillation of nostalgia, "greenness faded" (254). The wound inflicted upon that original viridity/virginity includes, although it is not limited to, deflo-ration; the only cure for it is the Incarnation of Christ. Figured as a man of battle, Christ is also the paramount healer, who assumes and transforms the wounds incurred by human carnal desires, announcing this redemption to his Heavenly Father:

> Nunc memor esto, quod plenitudo que in primo facta est
> arescere non debuit,
> et tunc in te habuisti
> quod oculus tuus numquam cederet
> usque dum corpus meum videres plenum gemmarum.
> Nam me fatigat quod omnia membra mea in irrisionem vadunt.
> Pater, vide, vulnera mea tibi ostendo. (252–66)

> Now remember, that fullness which was created in the beginning was not intended to wither; at that time, you decided that your gaze would never fal-ter until you saw my body full of jewels. It wearies me that my limbs are exposed to mockery. Father, behold, I show you my wounds.

The phrase *arescere non debuit* recalls the image of the flower of virginity that will never fail from line 111. The "limbs" of Christ are, in the Pauline sense, the members of his church in general, the individual souls that compose all of humanity. In the Ursula cycle, as we have seen, martyrdom provokes mockery and is rewarded by the transformation of words into jewels; the same motifs occur in the *Ordo*, as does the evocation of the members of the community of virgins who sing in Christ's honor. In both cases, this community represents an idealized version of a real group of women: Hildegard's sisterhood of nuns.

The juxtaposition of wounds with greenness, undying flowers, and jewels links the redemptive power of Christ intimately with the protective virtue of virginity, with the special grace that Hildegard would years later insist justified her nuns' assumption of extraordinary costumes on feast days. A parallel to those apocalyptic costumes, which shocked Tengswich and intrigued Guibert of Gembloux, is in fact closely associated with the *Ordo Virtutum*. In the *Scivias*, Hildegard describes a vision of the Virtues; among many, she perceives seven most clearly, and these are the seven who are grouped together in the *Ordo*: Humility, Charity, Fear of God, Obedience, Faith, Hope, and Chastity. The miniature accompanying this part of the *Scivias* is specific enough to have served as a costuming diagram, or perhaps more probably to have been inspired by witnessing a performance of the *Ordo Virtutum*. The representation of Fear of God in particular suggests this; in the text, she is described as larger than the other Virtues and nonhuman in form, covered with eyes that peep out through an enveloping robe. The miniaturist has rendered an obviously human form wrapped in a robe, which appears to have eyes on its surface. This anonymous painter was both talented and accustomed to Hildegard's idiosyncratic iconography, and elsewhere represents with apparent ease beings Hildegard described as nonhuman without anthropomorphizing them (as in the case of the white cloud that represents Eve in the first book of the *Scivias*); her decision to show Fear of God in the form of a human being dressed as something nonhuman strongly suggests that she had actually seen a costume that worked this way.

Did Hildegard's very evident interest in allegorical costume derive from witnessing liturgical dramas like the *Ordo Prophetarum*? Given that she had been a child oblate, such performances seem the most likely occasions during the first half of her life upon which she would have encountered elaborate dress of any sort. The image of the Sibyl, hair unbound and "dressed like a woman" must have touched a chord in Hildegard, also a virgin gifted with prophecy, and may have contributed to the inspiration that produced first a cast of Virtues and then a community of virgins whose dress proclaimed their proud adherence to a code of virginity that freed them unequivocally from masculine control, just as Hildegard had freed herself and the Rupertsberg nuns from the control of the abbot of Saint Disibod. In the *Scivias*, Chastity, wearing a tunic more brilliant than crystal and with an image labeled "Innocence" upon her womb, expresses the concept that lies at the heart of Hildegard's ethos of virginity: *Ego libera sum et non ligata*—"I am free and not bound" (*Scivias* 3.8.7).

This evocation of Apocalyptic costumes brings me back to my point of departure, the rings and crowns Hildegard's nuns wore to celebrate special occasions. The dress and behavior of the Rupertsberg nuns demonstrate the extent to which the power of Hildegard's virginal and explicitly feminine ideal could be enacted through real female bodies. Hildegard's invention or reinvention of the physical female as the ground of sanctity allows her to imagine a female subject existing in a state of separate equality—the term is deliberately loaded, of course. This female subject is, furthermore, defined by the expression of an intensely powerful sensual connection with other women; the voices of the Rupertsberg choir resonate with the cosmic music emanating from Mary's body, they harmonize with the erotic desire of Ursula for her disembodied Spouse, they echo the passion that shook the Sibyl. The presence of God or Christ in much of Hildegard's work is curiously abstract in comparison with the potent evocation of all these musical female bodies; the masculine principle in divinity often seems like little more than a hyphen, a conduit for female desire directed at female objects of desire. Hildegard's utopian vision did not attempt, as many writers before me have noted, the subversion of patriarchal authority. Her visionary rhetoric does, however, permit her to occupy (when it suits her) a strategic position "outside" of the hierarchical structure of the medieval sex–gender system, as a virgin rather than a woman. Whereas most nuns remained bound by the prohibitions directed against women by the Fathers and later authorities, Hildegard effectively freed herself from these by insisting that such prohibitions did not apply, since she, although female, was not a woman, but something more and better: a virgin. In celebrating virginity, Hildegard rejects as perverse the post-Lapsarian world of normative heterosexual commerce; she and her community choose instead a highly eroticized freedom from genital sex. This carefully constructed position undoes the traditional hierarchies according to which medieval authority was usually produced, while it reconfigures the female body as normative and authoritative rather than other and lacking in authority.

CHAPTER 5

PELAGIUS, RUPERT, AND THE PROBLEM OF MALE VIRGINITY IN HROTSVITHA AND HILDEGARD

So deep is the misogyny that informs the philology of courage and cowardice that when a female term is used to praise a man it is really a male term in drag. Take this case: "He is one tough mother." "Mother" is one word for woman that all men hold dear, but not so dear as to make calling a man a mother praiseworthy. For the "tough mother" is not a mother at all but a "motherfucker" who by some small concession to decorum has been euphemized by suppressing the second element of the compound. The honor in being so called is an example of slang's power to make the bad stand in for the good. . . .but even this kind of inversion cannot make a female term pay homage to a male ("He's one tough pussy" just doesn't cut it, whereas "She's got balls" is a compliment). "Bad" can mean "good" but "woman" can't mean "man."

—William Ian Miller, *The Mystery of Courage*, 2000

William Ian Miller's comments[1] on the "philology of courage and cowardice" suggest the realm of discursive difficulty patristic and medieval writers found themselves inhabiting when they addressed the issue of male virginity. As we have seen, the mechanics of male biology made it difficult for writers like Cassian and Augustine to imagine a virgin male if virginity were understood to signify the kind of absolute, physical integrity that could be manifested by a female body. When Tertullian confronted the argument for female integrity, he insisted that it was irrelevant given the ontological spiritual inferiority of women, but still could not represent the male virgin as anything but a castrato for God, an image that grounds the concept of virginity in male imitation of that same denied female integrity. The male virgin body, in fact, is generally imagined not as the mirror image of the female, but as its negative image; where the female is untouched, sealed, a vessel into which nothing enters, the male is imagined in having been touched in the most radical of ways, even, like Origen, surgically altered so that nothing may pour out of him. The language of male virginity is, almost inevitably, the language of emasculation. This is a point ignored by John Bugge in his influential monograph on medieval virginity. "It would be misleading," Bugge writes, "to allow the implication to stand that even at the turn of the twelfth century virginity was only a feminine attribute. . .the historical fact is that for centuries virginity was predicable of both sexes."[2] While chastity, a term that Bugge uses interchangeably with virginity, was certainly predicable of holy people of both sexes, virginity implied a state of bodily integrity imagined, in the age of Abelard no less than in that of Origen, as both normative and definitive for women in ways that were deeply problematic for men. Those medieval writers who, following Tertullian, Augustine, and Jerome, represented virginity as accessible to men at least as easily as to women, had to resist the same kinds of linguistic forces that make calling a man a "tough pussy" impossible.

When making a theological point about perfect continence or chastity, medieval writers like Albertus Magnus and Thomas Aquinas assert that virginity is the same for both sexes; the very language they choose with which to express that similarity, however, inevitably reinscribes the essential difference of gender. Thus Albertus argues that virginity is "an integrity of the flesh which bears witness to the integrity of the mind,"[3] a genderless virtue, only to give as an example of the primacy of mental over physical integrity the instance of a virgin woman who may be injured or wounded in the vagina by a stick or a sword without losing her virginity. Aquinas's discussion of virginity works especially hard to maintain the possibility of virginity equally for male and female bodies. Following Ambrose, he laments the fragility of a *signaculum* that can be destroyed by medical inspection, drawing the conclusion apparently only relevant to women that "virginity does not consist of physical incorruption."[4] He follows this up, however, with a parallel example founded in male biology: neither do nocturnal emissions constitute loss of virginity.[5] Nonetheless, even in Aquinas the word *virgo* itself tends to pull toward the feminine; in his argument, grounded in Cyprian, that virgins participate in a "more sublime glory" than widows or married women, all the pronouns (and indeed the nouns themselves) retain their normative, feminine gender.[6] Moreover, the idea that loss of physical integrity might not incur a concomitant loss of spiritual integrity evidently remained much more troubling in regard to women than to men. Gratian, it is true, argued that the virgin who was raped should not be considered to have lost her virginity, citing as evidence the martyr's declaration from the *passio* of Saint Lucy: "If you have me violated against my will, my chastity will be redoubled into a crown."[7] As I noted in a previous chapter, however, the legendary virgin martyr is never actually raped, so that the question of whether her virginity can be maintained in the case of physical violation needs never be resolved. Not so in real life, governed by canon law; the glosses on the *Decretum* reject Gratian's sympathetic logic and insist that the virgin who has suffered rape has lost her claim to the crown of virginity.[8] In fact, in the medieval period as in the patristic period, discussions concerning loss of virginity continue to center almost obsessively on the female body. Male virgins are not promised crowns, but neither is the loss of their physical integrity imagined in such absolute and damning terms; as Kelly puts it, "to the degree to which female virginity is overdetermined, male virginity is underdetermined."[9]

The hagiographic narrative betrays the asymmetry between male and female virginity again and again, especially in the intimate connection it establishes between virginity and martyrdom. This is a link that is seldom if ever made for men. Compilations of saints' lives like the *Legenda Aurea*, composed by Jacobus de Voragine in the latter half of the thirteenth century, assume that virgins are women, and in fact use the term as an organizational category like "confessor" or "pope." In the *Legenda*, which I shall have occasion to discuss more fully later, all three terms are definitively gendered; there are no male virgins, just as there are no female popes, and virtually every virgin (with the exception of two transvestite saints) is also a martyr. Similarly, Aldhelm's catalogs of virgins established a qualitative difference between the experiences of male and female virgins; male virgins accomplish miraculous things, while female virgins die. Malchus, Aldhelm's solitary male defined exclusively as a virgin, becomes a martyr in the English author's work even though he was not one in the source narrative, Jerome's *Life of Malchus*.[10] In Aldhelm's *Letter*, Malchus's sanctity, like that of female virgins, manifests itself initially and centrally in his rejection of marriage. As though at a loss when confronted with a male virgin who is not also an apostle, a bishop, or an abbot (Aldhelm leaves out most of Jerome's account of Malchus's early life as a monk), Aldhelm makes Malchus at least implicitly a martyr for virginity: "He preferred to die, cruelly pierced by a blade, rather than to save his life by profaning the laws of chastity. He feared no danger to his soul, so long as his virginity was kept intact" (*Letter* 31). Aldhelm's version of the story ends at this point, in spite of the fact that Jerome's first-hand account continued with the tale of Malchus's escape from his cruel, pagan master, his long, chaste marriage to a female companion, and his peaceful demise in a monastery at a very old age. Aldhelm's alterations to Jerome's story suggest that he is working under a strict generic imperative when it comes to telling the tale of a saint whose sanctity is defined exclusively by virginity. The paradigm for such a story is that of the virgin martyr, whose virginity must entail death; therefore, Malchus, imagined as a virgin *tout court* rather than a prophet or apostle who was also coincidentally a virgin, can only be imagined as a martyr for virginity.

In the Middle Ages, the male virgin was not quite so inconceivable as he had been in the patristic period; the male virgin martyr, however, remains virtually unique—queer, in fact, in the most fundamental sense of the word. Significantly, it is two women writers who raise the issue of male virginity most provocatively in the context of martyrdom; in *Pelagius*, Hrotsvitha tells the tale of a creature almost unparalleled in the hagiographic tradition, a martyr who is both virgin and male, while Hildegard's *Life of St Rupert* is the story of a young man who is a near miss on all counts, not quite a virgin, not quite a martyr, and perhaps not even quite male. In the case of *Pelagius*, the narrative of the male virgin is mapped onto the narrative of female virgin martyrdom in a way that produces unusual distortions of the story and reveals with especial force the constitutive quality of the threat of rape. In Hildegard's *Life of St Rupert*, in contrast, the body of the male saint is mapped onto a paradigmatic female body, with equally troubling results. For both Hrotsvitha and Hildegard, the attempt to imagine the male virgin forms a part of the larger project of reimagining the virgin martyr as an inspirational and imitable model for real women.

Pelagius and the Threat of Islam

Hrotsvitha must have heard the story of Pelagius some time during the 950s, a period when the Emperor Otto I and the Umayyad Caliph 'Abd al-Rahman III were involved in an extended exchange of epistolary hostilities. Otto may have initiated contact between the two realms out of concern about piracy in the Mediterranean, but in 951 'Abd al-Rahman sent an embassy led by a Christian bishop to Otto's court, bearing a letter containing insults to the Christian faith. Otto retained the ambassadors for three years, and then sent one of his own, the French monk John of Gorze, to Córdoba bearing a letter, which was, presumably, equally hostile in tone. John, aware that any criticism of Mohammed was a capital crime in Umayyad Spain, seems to have hoped to suffer for his faith in the city that had produced a celebrated martyr movement only a century earlier, but the Christian leaders of Córdoba were having none of it. They had achieved a fragile accord with their Muslim neighbors and had no desire to see it threatened by a volunteer martyr. John was kept outside the city and prevented from seeing the Caliph (who was probably as eager as his Christian subjects to avoid confrontation) for a further three years. Finally, 'Abd al-Rahman decided to put an end to the potentially embarrassing situation and send a second embassy to Otto, asking him to retract the letter carried by John.[11] This embassy was headed by Recemundus, who became a close friend of Liutprand of Cremorna, the Ottonian court historian and in all likelihood one of the readers to whom Hrotsvitha submitted her first book. In the preface to her *Legendae*, Hrotsvitha insists her information about Pelagius comes from someone who had first-hand knowledge of his martyrdom, and Recemundus is the most likely candidate for this role. He may not have been completely honest with Hrotsvitha; either he was describing events he witnessed a quarter of a century earlier, when he was presumably only a very young man, or he was not as immediate a witness as he allowed her to think. The tale he told, however, proved irresistible to someone with Hrotsvitha's interest in the intersection of martyrdom and sexual jeopardy.

The story of Pelagius, as Hrotsvitha tells it, is as follows. A savage Saracen usurper whom she names Abdrahemen is terrorizing Córdoba, having already executed most of its Christian citizens. The tyrant is characterized as "perverse and profane" (*Pelagius* 33).[12] Hrotsvitha declines to expand upon the nature of his perversion at this point in the narrative, but multiplies the vocabulary of corruption surrounding him. His allies are unspeakably wicked (*nefandos*), he "pollutes the ancient home of pure faith" with what is described as a sort of miscegenation, by "mixing the upstanding colonists with pagans in order to persuade them to abandon their hereditary customs and soil themselves with him in profane worship" (*Pelagius* 37–41). Once Córdoba is securely under his thumb, the tyrant turns his attention to Galicia, taking the Christian Duke and twelve other nobles captive. The Duke's son, although only a boy, convinces his father to let him take his place in the tyrant's prison, arguing (ironically, in the light of what is to follow) that he, with his strong young limbs (*validis. . .lacertis*) is better able than his aged parent to submit to a cruel master (*Pelagius* 156–57). Some courtiers discover him in prison; they are moved by his beauty and eloquence and immediately recognize that the tyrant will be too:

> Ipsum felicis certe summum caput urbis
> Corruptum vitiis cognoscebant Sodomitis
> Formosos facie iuvenes ardenter amare
> Hos et amicitiae propriae coniungere velle. (*Pelagius* 204–07)

> They knew for certain that the ruler of the city was corrupted by the vice of Sodom, that he burned with passion for beautiful boys and desired to be joined with them in special friendship.

Pelagius is bathed and dressed and brought before the monarch, who falls in love with him immediately. Now that the precise nature of Abdrahemen's perversion is out of the closet, so to speak, Hrotsvitha spends a surprising amount of time elaborating upon it, treating us to a scene some forty-five lines long in which the king tries to persuade Pelagius to let him embrace him and Pelagius refuses, turning his face away from Abdrahemen's eager kisses. Pelagius, unlike the narrator of the story, does not condemn his captor out of hand for his homosexuality, but rather for his religion. It is not appropriate for a Christian, he insists, to let himself be embraced by a pagan:

> Non decet ergo virum Christi baptismate lotum
> Sobria barbarico complexu subdere colla,
> Sed nec christicolam sacrato crismate tinctum
> Daemonis oscillum spurci captare famelli.
> Ergo corde viros licito complectere stultos,
> Qui tecum fatuos placantur caespite divos;
> Sintque tibi socii, servi qui sunt simulacri. (*Pelagius* 243–49)

> It is not right for a man washed in Christian baptism to submit his righteous neck to barbarian caresses, or for a Christian anointed with sacred oil to take a kiss from the bondsman of a filthy demon. So go with a free heart and embrace those foolish men who worship empty deities with you. Let them be your friends who are enslaved by images.

Once Pelagius has said his piece, he restrains himself no longer; Abdrahemen attempts one more time to kiss him, this time rather more forcefully, and the young man defends himself:

> Callida sed testis confudit ludicra regis
> Osque petit subito pugno regale vibrato
> Intulit et tantum pronis obtutibus ictum,
> Sanguis ut absque mora stillans de vulnere facto
> Barbam foedavit necnon vestes madefecit. (*Pelagius* 271–75)

> But Christ's witness confounded the king's cunning ploy. Suddenly he launched his clenched fist at the royal face and landed such a blow on it as it bent toward him that blood gushing from the wound fouled the king's beard and soaked his clothing.

The imagery could not be more clear: the lecherous pagan who has attempted to soil the virtuous Christian is instead soiled by his own blood, which bursts out like an alternative ejaculation; the verb *foedare* implies not just mess but impurity. Abdrahemen's reaction demonstrates just how completely he has been humiliated; in a mere three lines, he orders that Pelagius be loaded into a catapult and fired over the battlements. Astonishingly, Pelagius's body is not broken in the fall, and the king sends soldiers out to finish him off by beheading him and throwing his remains into the river. The last section of the poem is given over to a rather extended account of the invention of Pelagius's head and body, which are reunited by fishermen and sold to the Christian community for an undisclosed but presumably significant sum of money, and then subjected to a test of authenticity by being baked in an oven.

Pelagius appears to have been a historical martyr; the day of his death is recorded as January 26, 925, and his relics were translated to the cathedral at Léon in 967. The various accounts of his death, however, exist in a somewhat confused temporal relation to Hrotsvitha's text, which is the best-known version. A Mozarabic liturgy in his honor is probably simultaneous with the translation of the relics.[13] This liturgy is probably based upon what claims to be an eyewitness account of Pelagius's death by the Spanish priest Raguel, which may not, however, have been composed until the 960s. Raguel's testimony could thus conceivably be later than Hrotsvitha's poem if *Pelagius* was composed in reaction to the visit of the Mozarabic embassy to Otto in the 950s.[14] Raguel's story, like Hrotsvitha's, represents the Caliph as moved by desire for Pelagius. He attempts to touch the boy *joculariter*, "playfully," a move interpreted by the young saint as a sexual advance and immediately rejected. Pelagius, in a gesture startlingly reminiscent of Thecla in the arena, strips off his clothing and stands forth naked like a late antique martyr, as an athlete for God.[15] It is impossible to establish the degree to which one of these tellings may have influenced the other, and equally impossible to determine how closely the experiences of the actual Pelagius may have been mirrored in those of the hero of Hrotsvitha's poem or Raguel's prose account, but the evidence suggests that the story as it was told and retold and finally institutionalized in the liturgy is motivated by generic concerns at least as much if not more than by historical veracity. These narrative imperatives appear to have been firmly in place both in Mozarabic Spain, where the martyrdom of Pelagius took place, and in Saxony, where Hrotsvitha heard of the beautiful young virgin martyr.

The operation of those mechanics that generate stories about virgin martyrs are especially visible in the representation of the hero, according to Hrotsvitha's source the most beautiful of Christian men, and his antagonist, the demonized and pederastic infidel who attempts to defile him. Pelagius exists only in the hagiographic tradition. References to and representations of 'Abd al-Rahman III, on the other hand, survive in the historical records of both Christians and Muslims. He was fair-haired and blue-eyed and evidently rather embarrassed by his fairness, the legacy of a Basque or Frankish (and almost certainly Christian) mother. The titles he bore, Caliph and Prince of all Believers, were a sort of public announcement that the Ummayad dynasty of Spain no longer recognized the supremacy of the Abbasid caliphs of Baghdad. In order to consolidate his political position and religious reputation, 'Abd al-Rahman launched a series of campaigns against Christians in Northern Spain during the 920s, and he was known to display the severed heads of his enemies as trophies, although such behavior was hardly extreme by tenth-century standards, Christian or Muslim.[16] Historian Mahmoud Makki notes that the conduct of Spanish Christian kings of the period was comparatively less civilized: Ramiro II of Leon "began his reign by gouging out the eyes of his brother Alfonso and those of his paternal cousins, but he proved his courage in opposing al-Nasir ['Abd al-Rahman] although the latter inflicted successive defeats on him."[17] Makki's final assessment of 'Abd al-Rahman is worth quoting: "[he was] mild-tempered, sociable with the populace and possessed of a calm and leisurely manner, though not neglecting affairs of state. His reign is regarded as constituting one of the most brilliant, stable and fruitful periods of the emirate. . .it is no exaggeration to say that he was one of the greatest statesmen to rule Spain in any era."[18]

Might he also have been, in reality, a sexual predator with a taste for young Christian boys? John Boswell argues that there is "no reason to give undue credence to Hrotsvitha's poem"[19] precisely because attempted rape was a hagiographical trope; neither is there any reason to dismiss the evidence of the poem entirely. Medieval Islam had no single and consistent attitude toward homosexuality. Islamic law condemns sodomy much more explicitly and absolutely than either the Old or New Testament, categorizing it as more criminal than lesbianism, bestiality, or necrophilia.[20] But al-Andalusian court society also produced a significant body of homoerotic and indeed pederastic love-poetry in Arabic.[21] If we had 'Abd al-Rahman's side of the story, it might resemble this poem by a Córdoban poet born in 992: "Imperceptibly as a dream, I crept towards him, and, as sweetly as breathing, I drew close to him, / I kissed the whiteness of his neck and sipped the redness of his lips. . ."[22] Or it might not; as Jordan points out, it is impossible "to disentangle the retellings of the passions of Pelagius from the ambivalent reactions of Iberian Christianity to the same-sex love it thought was preached and practiced by Islam."[23]

The Christian hagiographic narrative, in any case, refuses to distinguish between seduction and sexual assault.[24] Of the surviving accounts of the martyrdom of Pelagius, only the *Calendar of Córdoba*, a remarkable document composed in both Arabic and Latin by Recemundus and a Muslim compatriot, is silent concerning the Caliph's advances to the saint, but this is almost certainly because the text itself was a semiofficial production, representing in written form the relatively peaceful cohabitation of Christians and Muslims in the Caliphate.[25] Interestingly, Raguel's *passio*, like Hrostvitha's *Legendae*, seems to have been composed for the edification of a female religious order,[26] which suggests that the subject was understood to be particularly appropriate as inspirational reading material for women, whose interest in the subject of virginity might be assumed to be both emulative and personal. Pelagius, in other words, was a better model for girls than for boys, in spite of his sex. What makes it improbable that Hrotsvitha independently invented the attempted rape of Pelagius is the history of the hagiographic genre in Spain.

The tradition of composing martyrologies for recent victims of persecution had been established in the previous century by Eulogius, a central figure in the "martyr movement," which peaked in Córdoba in the 850s and of which Pelagius's death appears to have been the last gasp. Eulogius and his friend Albar had written anti-Islamist polemics accusing Mohammed of gross promiscuity and establishing the stereotype of Muslims as "proud, luxury-loving, sexually depraved, and violent."[27] Eulogius, furthermore, was deeply concerned to establish the legitimacy of the martyr movement in the face of the objection that the Muslims, unlike the Romans, did not torture their victims, and that the Córdoban martyrs had not been very productive when it came to miracles.[28] Jessica Cope has demonstrated Eulogius's heavy reliance on Prudentius in his account of the nun Pomposa, and argues that Eulogius connects virginity intimately with suitability for martyrdom in the case of women.[29] In fact, Eulogius established a formula for the narration of historical Córdoban martyrdoms that mimicked Prudentius's highly literary creations. Pelagius's identification as a virgin martyr thus demanded the threat of rape, which had become an intrinsic part of such narratives; the attempted rape also substituted for the notoriously lacking torture sequence. It is therefore precisely because Pelagius is imagined as a virgin martyr that the Christian stereotype of 'Abd al-Rahman as a sex-crazed would-be rapist of young boys comes into existence.

Whatever the story Hrotsvitha heard, either at first or second hand from members of the Mozarabic embassy to Otto, it is highly likely that the events of Pelagius's brief life and violent death had already assumed the form dictated by the hagiographical narrative; it was no doubt his function as the exception proving the rule about the gender of the virgin martyr which attracted Hrotsvitha's attention in the first place. Within the context of Hrotsvitha's work, with its strong focus on virginity and its demonstrably protofeminist stance, the story of Pelagius serves two functions. It reminds Hrotsvitha's readers that the only sense in which a male body can emulate the virginity of a female body is with reference to the threat of (homosexual) rape; and it paradoxically serves to reinforce Hrotsvitha's emphasis upon the moral integrity of the female virgin. If boys, like girls, are subject to sexual assault, then the responsibility for rape, and by extension sexual sin in general, cannot be located in some inalienable, irresistible, Eve-derived sensuality lodged in the female body. It must instead be assigned to the irrepressibility of male desire.[30]

Like Virgins: John and Rupert

In Jerome's *Against Jovinian*, the Apostle John is the paradigm of male virginity. "The virgin writer," says Jerome, "expounded mysteries which the married could not, and, briefly to sum up all and show how great was the privilege of John, or rather of the virginity in John, the Virgin Mother was entrusted by the Virgin Lord to the Virgin Disciple."[31] Jerome's use of the word *virgo* to describe men as well as women is adopted by most religious authors of the Middle Ages, as we have seen in the case of Aldhelm, even while it generally retains its primary sense in secular usage.[32] Hildegard, however, avoids the word *virgo* when writing of males, even when dealing with John, whom she made the subject of an antiphon and a responsory in the *Symphonia*. In the first of these, "O speculum columbe," John is described in terms of almost vegetable freshness and fecundity:

O speculum columbe	O mirror of the dove
castissime forme,	most chaste in beauty
qui inspexisti misticam largitatem	who have beheld the mystic largesse
in purissimo fonte:	of the purest spring:
O mira floriditas	O miraculous blossoming
que numquam arescens cecidisti,	who never fell withering
quia altissimus plantator misit te:	for the highest gardener planted you:
O suavissima quies	O sweetest repose
amplexuum solis:	of the sun's embraces
tu es specialis filius Agni	you are the special son of the Lamb
in electa amicicia	in the chosen friendship
nove sobolis.	of a new germination.

(*Symphonia* 35)

John is imagined here not as a flower but rather as the process of flowering, an image that links him to the Virgin Mary, repeatedly described as a lily or a flowering branch in songs like "Ave generosa" or "O frondens virga." The flower is superior to the fruit, because it contains all the potential of fruition without the inevitable decay that must accompany ripeness in the natural world. The last three lines of the song, however, move into a different realm, describing John's relationship to the divine in terms that are strictly masculine. Whereas Saint Ursula is consistently represented as the bride of Christ, John is the son of the Lamb and a member of a chosen group of friends, *electa amicicia*. This image recalls the Germanic *comitatus*, a group of warriors linked by indissoluble bonds of loyalty.

The last word of the poem, *sobolis*, is particularly interesting in this context. It is usually rendered as "generation, race, or lineage," so that the phrase would be understood as "the choice of friendship of a new race." The primary meaning of *soboles* (*suboles* in classical Latin) derives from gardening, however; it means offshoot or sprout, the twig or branch that is grafted from one fruit tree or vine to another. The poem thus ends with a word that returns us to the vegetative and fertile images of the second stanza, although in a less explicitly feminine mode, and suggests that Hildegard's grasp of Latin is much more subtle than is generally thought. Throughout the poem, however, the kind of always potential and therefore always undefiled flourishing, which Hildegard elsewhere associates with *viriditas*, the greenness symbolic of virginity, is never labeled as such. John is indeed *castissime forme*, of most chaste beauty, but this language is much less specific than that which informs a poem like "Ave Generosa" in which Mary is praised as *gloriosa et intacta puella /. . .pupilla castitati* [glorious, intact maiden /. . .pupil of chastity (*Symphonia* 17.1)]. Even the word *castitas*, chastity, is deployed differently. In John's case, he participates in the quality of "chaste beauty"; Mary's chastity, in contrast, is described by a punning bodily metaphor, since *pupilla* can mean either a girl who is under the care of a guardian, or the pupil of the eye, the center of perception. "O virga mediatrix" makes the absolute and absolutely bodily quality of Mary's chastity even more apparent:

. . .sancta viscera tu	. . .your sacred womb
mortem superaverunt	conquered death
et venter tuus	and your belly
omnes creaturas illuminavit	illuminated all creatures
in pulcro flore	in the beautiful blossom
de suavissima integritate	of the sweetest integrity
clausi pudoris tui orto.	born of your sealed modesty.
(*Symphonia* 18)	

Again, Mary's chastity is described in specific and physical terms, in clear distinction from the general, abstract quality of *castissime forme*.

In the responsory "O dulcis electe," the emphasis is once again upon John as the chosen friend of God, conveyed through vegetable imagery reminiscent of "O speculum columbe":

O dulcis electe	Sweet chosen one
qui in ardore ardentis	burning for the burning one
effulsisti, radix,	you shone forth, root,
et qui in splendore Patris	in the glory of the father
elucidasti mistica,	you made mysteries clear

et qui intrasti cubiculum castitatis	and entered the chamber of chastity
in aurea civitate	in the golden city
quam construxit rex. . .	built by the king. . .
Tu enim auxisti pluviam	You increased the rain
cum precessoribus tuis,	you and those who went before
qui miserunt illam	the ones who sent down rain
in viriditate pigmentariorum.	Greening the spice merchants.
(*Symphonia* 36.1–14)	

To see the "root" in this poem as a phallic symbol is probably not simply to betray a post-Freudian mindset; medieval stained glass regularly locates the root of the tree of Jesse in his groin. The action of increasing the rain in order to fertilize the *pigmentarii* (spice merchants, Hildegard's personal symbol for priests[33]) not only recalls the *shoures soote* which inaugurate the *Canterbury Tales*, but also Hildegard's own representation of dew as a fertilizing agent, in songs like "O virga ac diadema" where the falling of dew operates as a shorthand for the natural process of impregnation that the Virgin escaped, or in the *Ordo Virtutum*. Besides being characterized in masculine generative terms, John is once again represented as chaste rather than virginal, and as existing in a less than immediate relationship with chastity; he enters into it like a bridegroom into the marriage chamber rather than expressing it through his own body. John may be perfectly chaste, but he is not a virgin, because in Hildegard's universe, only women are virgins, as the *Scivias* passages that deal with virginity reveal.

In the *Scivias*, Hildegard betrays a double impulse toward the concept of virginity. On the one hand, she emphasizes the value of virginity as a virtue to which all can and should aspire; on the other, she clearly feels that the state of being virgin is inherently feminine. Throughout the *Scivias*, she emphasizes the distinct but complementary paths that are laid out for holy men and women: men should be priests and women should be nuns. Both must live chastely, but in women chastity may take a transfigurative form denied to men, virginity; men have access to their own form of transformation deriving from fleshly forbearance and self-denial in the celebration of the Mass, a transformation that Hildegard represents most clearly in her sequence for Saint Maximin, "Columba aspexit" (*Symphonia* 54). When Hildegard speaks of what may be called universal virginity, the ideal to which all human beings should aspire, she tends to render it in abstract and general terms. Thus when Christ exhorts a crowd of people encouraging them to avoid the sins of the flesh, he addresses them initially with the gender-neutral *homines* (*Scivias* 3.10.1). Once he begins to confront the issue of sexual renunciation specifically, his audience is suddenly divided, according to the heading of part 7: *Admonitio ad virgines et continentes qualiter sanctitatem aggrredi debeant*, which may be rendered as "instructions to virgins and continent ones concerning how they may approach holiness." It is not clear from this whether the terms *virgines* and *continentes* are to be understood as gendered; the only use of the word "virgin" to occur in the body of the chapter, however, certainly is: "Just as a field unploughed bears a flower, so I, the Son of Man, was born of the Virgin without commingling with any man. . . .if you faithfully ask me for this gift, you may receive it in good faith from me: I will grant that you may participate with me in virginity, openly before my Father" (*Scivias* 3.10.10). Frail humankind is here invited to participate in the quality of virginity, while the only virgin in the absolute sense is Mary. Since being a virgin is implicitly connected here with being female, it is tempting to read the chapter heading as referring to consecrated virgin women and continent religious men, both of whom imitate, in their separate ways, the absolute sanctity and integrity of Christ's body.

Hildegard's description of her fifth vision conveys the same ambiguous attitude toward the gendering of virginity. She begins with a general statement about "those who devote themselves to virginity," which almost immediately breaks down into two quite separate categories: "They are beloved imitators of my Son who offer themselves thus to God, not tied by any demand of marriage nor burdened by worldly cares but rejecting fleshly bonds, so that they may not be subject to the anxieties of the flesh, but rather desire to cleave to the glorious innocence of the innocent Lamb" (*Scivias* 2.5.10). Up until this point, although the pronouns are (inevitably) masculine, Hildegard seems to have in mind all of humanity. In the paragraph that follows, however, the divine voice that speaks through her is quite clearly concerned only with the male of the species:

> That man who decides in his soul not to join himself to any rib, but who desires to preserve the modesty of virginity for love of my Son will become His companion if he only perseveres in the work of chastity. . . .But if he later abandons this pact because of a shameful prickling of the flesh and commits adultery, he reduces his liberty to slavery since he corrupts the honor of his head through shameful pleasure when he ought to have imitate the modesty of my Son, and because he has expressed a lie, making a vow to live chaste and not fulfilling it. (*Scivias* 2.5.10)

The man, in this passage, does not aspire to virginity itself but rather to something proximate to virginity: *pudor virginitatis*, the modesty of or associated with virginity. The result of masculine chastity is companionship with Christ, the same kind of relationship we have seen evoked in the songs to Saint John. The consequences of loss of chastity are expressed in an almost chivalric register of lost honor and unfulfilled oaths—a fellowship is here being broken by the behavior of the incontinent man. It appears that as soon as the subject becomes male, the discourse of sexual renunciation configures itself as masculine. This shift is nowhere more obvious than in the final lines of the section, which describe the position of the repentant sexual sinner: "this does not place him back among his companions who flourish in the glory of integrity, for he has deserted their fellowship by casting away the freedom of his oath and has reduced it to the slavery of sin."[34] The idea throughout the passage is that living chastely is something that you do rather than something that you are.

An entirely different kind of integrity is implicit in the parallel passage devoted to sexual renunciation in women: "A maiden who has of her own free will offered herself to my Son in holy betrothal has been taken in by Him in the most seemly fashion, for He wants her to be joined with him as His consort. . .if she breaks her promise, then she will be polluted in the eyes of those who are in celestial joy. . . .As for the man who violates her by seducing her, if he wants to amend his crime, let him mourn as though he had broken open the sky itself" (Scivias 2.5.10). It is clear from this passage that what the man has broken open is the woman's body, sealed by that curiously hypothetical but always fascinating organ, the hymen. The physical damage done is represented as irreparable; the corollary to this absolute loss through sexual intercourse is an equally absolute sense of physical integrity maintained in the woman who escapes intercourse. For Hildegard, loss of physical virginity is not an excuse for speculation on the potential complicity of the virgin in her own rape, as it was for Augustine, who made every rape a seduction. Hildegard instead makes every seduction a rape, and defines rape as a male crime; the woman may be polluted in the quoted passage, but only the man is a criminal. The violation of a virgin is the occasion not of censure and scandal, both attached exclusively to the woman in the case, as it was for Indicia in Ambrose's letter; rather, rape is an occasion for cosmic mourning on account of the catastrophic physical loss inflicted upon the victim by her aggressor, and correspondent spiritual loss willfully inflicted by the aggressor upon himself.

A final pair of passages from the Scivias makes the distinction that Hildegard regularly (if not completely consistently) draws between female virginity and male chastity perfectly apparent: "She who desires My son, and wishes to preserve her virginity for His love. . .does not wish to be dissolved in the furnace of blazing lust but perseveres in chastity, rejecting any husband of the flesh for the sake of spiritual betrothal. She sighs for My Son with her whole desire. . ." (Scivias 2.5.11). Hildegard here represents the virgin not as some improbable creature whose sexuality has been eliminated but as fully female, a woman whose sexual desires have been redirected toward a supernatural object and who is in fact redeemed not in spite of but because of the essential femininity of that desire. The distinction between awareness of the urgings of carnal human nature and giving way to them is one that Hildegard makes repeatedly, and it is characteristic also of the male counterpart of the woman who chooses virginity: "When the strength of a man refuses to take a wife, for love of My Son restraining his own vigorous nature, which would blossom in the engendering of sons, instead controlling his limbs so that they may not carry out the lusts of his flesh, this is pleasing to me, for in this way a man conquers himself" (*Scivias* 2.3.22). The word *virginitas* is conspicuously absent from this passage. Like the virgin, the chaste man chooses Christ over earthly marriage; but he restrains himself from action, from "fulfilling the desires of the flesh," rather than from the more passive sexual pleasure of the woman who is acted upon, "dissolved in the furnace of lust." Male chastity consists of not touching; virginity of not being touched. The two states, like almost every other aspect of gender in Hildegard, are perhaps equal, but they are entirely different; the same vocabulary cannot describe them both. Virginity is clearly conceived as a physical and social characteristic of women: "For virginity unpolluted from the beginning is nobler than widowhood oppressed under the yoke of man, even if the widow, after the grief of losing a husband, should follow the example of virginity" (*Scivias* 2.3.30). A man who chooses chastity, either before or after marriage, can no more be a virgin than a widow can; he can only "follow the example of" virginity. Saint John may be *castissime forme*, but he cannot be *virginea forme*, because male and female are always distinct in Hildegard's visionary world, and virginity is something that pertains to the female.

That virginity in Hildegard's work is a function always gendered as feminine before its association with a character of either sex must inevitably alter the body of the male imagined as virgin, and indeed in the sequence to Saint Rupert called "O Jerusalem," Hildegard reconstructs the saint's male body according to a female model, in order to convey the young man's purity and openness to divine influence. Hildegard is the only source for our knowledge of Saint Rupert; the *Life* that she wrote for him may have served to authorize her removal of her nuns to the Rupertsberg, where her new foundation was consecrated in 1152. The information in the *Life* seems to derive mostly from one of Hildegard's visions, to which she refers in the third stanza of her sequence to Rupert,[35] but it probably also incorporates folk traditions concerning the church on the site that had stood in ruins for three centuries. One suspects, in fact, that had there been no preexisting traditions concerning the occupation of the site, the Living Light might have provided Hildegard with a virgin martyr like Ursula as patron saint for her new foundation, rather than a holy young man like Rupert.

Rupert, according to the *Life*, which gives a narrative account of the events rendered imagistically in the sequence, was a Carolingian aristocrat, born of a pagan father and a Christian mother named Bertha (*Rupert* 1085–86).[36] Hildegard's tale of Rupert's childhood provides a rather upsetting vision of early medieval family life. Bertha's husband Roboldus proves to be both unfaithful and tyrannical, and she consoles herself by praying daily for liberation from him—praying in essence for his death, which occurs when Rupert is about three years old. Rupert, meanwhile, gives early proof of divine inspiration by conceiving a powerful hatred for his father and affirming that the duke is both stupid and idiotic. The child is thus represented from the very beginning as embracing Christianity in its feminine form (it comes to him through his mother, like Christ's humanity) and rejecting paganism in its masculine form when he rejects his lecherous and aggressive father. Rupert's body, meanwhile, is particularly apt to divine inspiration or invasion because of its immaturity, "because God often performs miracles in those who, because of the softness of their sinews and marrow, have not yet attained full knowledge" (*Rupert* 1090). This softness, *mollitia*, is also typical of women; it is one of the words Hildegard uses where other medieval medical theorists use "weakness" to characterize the way in which the female sex is different from the male.[37] For Hildegard, feminine softness and impressionability is exactly what makes the female an appropriate recipient for divine grace. Before he hardens into manhood, a little boy is thus capable of the kind of receptivity that women retain all their lives—as long, that is, as they retain their virginity. Whereas centuries later, Freud would imagine little boys as having to triumph over the earliest, feminine state of being and develop into something better, Hildegard sees the femininity of the boy-child as being the peak of spiritual development, something that can only degenerate in later life.

Indeed, after having a vision of paradise as an orchard tended by the Ancient of Days, making a pilgrimage to Rome, and founding hospices with his mother, Rupert dies of no particular cause at the age of twenty, an age that Hildegard explicitly identifies as premature. God takes his life "lest if he came to full maturity he might follow in the footsteps of his father" (*Rupert* 1090). Masculine maturity is in Hildegard's mind inevitably associated with sexuality; Rupert avoids the whole sticky issue by dying still radiant with innocence [*fulgentem innocentia* (*Rupert* 1090)]. Hildegard's conviction that male maturity necessarily involved a loss of innocence seems related to the widespread medieval anxiety about nocturnal emissions, which had abated only slightly since Cassian wrote his *Conferences*. The debate about whether ejaculation during sleep was sinful and required abstinence from the sacrament was ongoing. A letter that Hildegard seems to have known, ascribed to Gregory the Great and preserved in Bede's

Ecclesiastical History, opined that nocturnal emissions were probably not actually sinful, as long as they had not been preceded by waking lustful thoughts, but that any man who felt that he should refrain from communion after experiencing one was erring on the side of caution.[38] Constantine the African, writing in the late eleventh century, touches upon the subject, while Aquinas in the thirteenth devoted careful thought to it and cited both Augustine and Cassian when concluding that the sinfulness of ejaculation during sleep depended entirely upon the mental state of the sleeper. Hildegard's own discussion of the issue in the *Causes and Cures* is nonjudgmental, but does represent nocturnal sexual arousal as exclusively male, relating it to Adam.[39] For Rupert, therefore, the only escape from the inevitable, eventual biological betrayal of perfect chastity is death.

Like the *Life*, Hildegard's songs to Rupert emphasize his purity and incorruption, characteristics she would surely have described as *virginitas* had they occurred in women. She repeatedly represents his body in feminine terms, using images of viridity and fruitfulness familiar from other contexts. *O tener flos campi / et o dulcis viriditas pomi* [O gentle flower of the field / sweet greenness of the apple], she writes, recalling the song of the Virtues in the *Ordo Virtutum* and the representation of Mary as *viridissima virga*, greenest of branches. "O Jerusalem" imagines Rupert's body as both hollow and intact:

O vas nobile,	O noble vase
quod non est pollutum	neither polluted
nec devoratum	nor devoured
in saltatione antique spelunce	in the leapings of the ancient cave
et quod non est maceratum	unbruised
in vulneribus antiqui perditoris:	by the wounds of the ancient destroyer
In te symphonizat Spiritus sanctus,	In you the Spirit harmonizes
quia angelicis choris associaris	for you are joined to angel choirs
et quoniam in Filio Dei ornaris,	and you adorn the Son of God
cum nullam maculam habes.	for you are without stain.

(*Symphonia* 49.4b-5)

Hildegard represents Rupert as an uncontaminated vessel and aligns that vessel with an ideal of feminine purity by means of a series of images elsewhere associated with the Blessed Virgin. The "dance in the ancient cave" is the same *olde daunce*, presumably, in which the Wife of Bath was so proficient; Rupert's purity is thus identified as sexual innocence. The following stanza confirms this with a deliberately Marian echo (*nullam maculam habes*) and again emphasizes the hollowness of Rupert's body, this time in a musical sense, as though he were the bell of a trumpet or the cavity of a drum; in other poems, as I have argued, Mary was similarly represented as containing the heavenly symphony. Rupert's virginity thus can only express itself through the feminization of his body.

This feminization is obliquely underscored in the *Life*, which not only depicts Rupert according to the images of fruition we have so often seen applied to the Virgin, but which concludes with a curious echo of the creation scene from Genesis. When Rupert reaches the sinister age of twenty and begins to be tempted by his friends *ad voluptatem saeculi*, toward the pleasures of the world (*Rupert* 1089), his mother has a significant dream in which she sees one of the ribs fall from her side, a sight that terrifies her. Shortly afterward, Rupert is stricken with what will prove to be his final illness. It is difficult not to escape the conclusion that Hildegard is deliberately if not satirically revising the creation of Eve here. While Hildegard herself never represents Eve as in any way essentially inferior to Adam, she was certainly aware of the tendency of many other writers to see Eve as secondary, a feeble imitation of the perfection of the pre-Lapsarian Adam; in her account of the life of Rupert, which is full of Edenic echoes and visions, Hildegard redresses the balance, representing her youthful saint as nothing more than a fragment of his mother's body, his holiness deriving entirely from hers. In this context, it is not insignificant that it is Bertha, not Rupert, who builds the church that Hildegard and her sisterhood will reconstruct centuries later.

The sequence to Saint Rupert ends with a cosmic evocation of the city of heaven and its inhabitants:

Et ita turres tue,	And so your towers
o Ierusalem,	O Jerusalem
rutilant et candent per ruborem	burn and glow with the crimson
et per candorem sanctoreum	and the pure white of the saints
et per omnia ornamenta Dei,	and through all the ornaments of God
que tibi non desunt, o Ierusalem	which fail you not, O Jerusalem.
Unde vos, o ornati	And so, O you ornamented ones
et o coronati	you crowned ones
qui habitatis in Ierusalem,	who live in Jerusalem
et o tu Ruperte,	and you, O Rupert
qui es socius eorum	their companion
in hac habitatione,	in that dwelling place
succurrite nobis famulantibus	help us, your servants
et in exilio laborantibus	laboring in exile.
(*Symphonia* 49.9–100)	

This final vision of Rupert betrays some of the same ambiguity that characterizes the relationship of John to the ideal of virginity; Rupert is not directly represented as crowned with either the red of martyrdom or the white of virginity. He is *like* a martyr, although he died in bed, the verse implies, and *like* a virgin, although male.

Only Women Bleed

Remy de Gourmont, writing in the 1890s, in a culture that recognized itself as decadent and even gloried in the name, recommended medieval Latin religious verse as one of the few palliatives to the "immense fatigue" of the *fin-de-siècle*.[40] He was a great admirer of Hildegard, but he found Hrotsvitha shocking, insufficiently "mystical," too clever by half, and dirty-minded into the bargain:

> As for the poem on the death of Saint Pelagius, which comes fourth in the collection, the story of this young martyr to pederasty, victim of the beauty of his face and of his exquisite physique is of a laboriously obscene naïveté which, particularly masquerading as the work of a nun, can only be the bizarre deception of a practical joker who wishes to fool his contemporaries in the most outrageous manner, thus amusing himself at their expense and most of all scorning them.[41]

De Gourmont insists that Hrotsvitha's works were actually a forgery by Conrad Celtis, the German humanist who discovered the Saint Emmeram codex in 1493 and established Hrotsvitha as a sort of Teutonic Sappho.[42] There was perhaps more than a little nationalist sentiment behind de Gourmont's claim, and in any case, Winterfeld's 1902 edition of the codex went a long way toward putting accusations of forgery to rest once and for all.[43] The accusation of obscenity, however, is striking coming from an author who could praise Prudentius's hymn to Eulalia as being in "a positively delicious bad taste, heightened here and there, in the details of the tortures, by a poignant elegance."[44] De Gourmont is also given to raptures on the subject of the breasts of virgin martyrs, which seem less than entirely religious in their enthusiasm:

> Ah, the breasts of virgins, the two breasts of the woman reformed, symbols of the Old and New Testament. . .Has the astonishing sadism of the torturers been sufficiently remarked upon? In women, they inflict torment upon those organs which are most specifically feminine, torturing the breasts with horrible engines, scarring with the iron claws of a horrid beast the secret virginities of these bold virgins! . . .gripping with a ferocious claw the young breasts of the Tyrian Theodosia, crushing them, pressing them, painful pomegranates, clusters of grapes. . .virgin breasts are swollen with milk; they are also swollen with blood. The blood is no less essential: it is baptismal and symbolic.[45]

De Gourmont here remarks upon the sadism of the tormentors described in the works of Ambrose and Damasus not to condemn it but rather to admire it as the impulse that produces the necessary transformation of the female body from a vehicle of worldly desires and worldly hungers to one of spiritual desires and sustenance. His exfoliation of the torments directed at the breasts of Theodosia, and his transformation of them from flesh to metaphorical fruit, implicates his reader in the specular and spectacular mutilation of the human body. The only element in Hrotsvitha's story of Pelagius that could possibly be understood as obscene in contrast to this admirable sadism is the homosexual nature of the threat of rape in her narrative. For de Gourmont, living in a culture in which the "love that dare not speak its name" had just declared itself with terrifying clarity in the trials of Oscar Wilde, the substitution of a breastless boy for a nubile girl was enough to transform sadism from something to be remarked upon, even reveled in, into obscenity in the legal sense of the word.[46]

De Gourmont's reaction, of course, misses Hrotsvitha's point entirely. *Pelagius* is not about homosexuality or sodomy, categories that in any case did not exist in the tenth century, nor even same-sex desire, a vice Hrotsvitha sees as neither more nor less depraved than necrophilia or attempted heterosexual rape. Rather, the story of the male virgin martyr from Spain provides an essential plank in her defense of women and establishes a surprisingly modern vision of sexual abuse, in which victims are not responsible for what happens to them, and in which power rather than sex is really what rape is all about. *Pelagius* also demonstrates another tyranny, the tyranny of genre; in order for a devout young man to be accepted as the exception that proves the rule ("virgin martyrs are always women") he must suffer the constitutive threat of rape, for it is this threat that makes virgins into martyrs. Without the threat of rape, virginity would be invisible, and quite possibly irrelevant, except, of course, to the virgin.

Hildegard is concerned with category in a way that Hrotsvitha is not. Both her mystical and scientific writings are marked by a powerful impulse to separate and organize; thus her visions are divided into parts demarcated in her texts by headings and in the illuminations of the *Scivias* by elaborate internal borders distinguishing registers and incidents, while her zoological treatise, the *Physica*, organizes creatures into categories that are no less strict for being rather unfamiliar to those of us with a post-Linnaean world-view.[47] For Hildegard, biological categories like woman and virgin remain inviolable; Rupert is never allowed to transgress completely the boundaries established by the sex from which, inevitably in Hildegard's world at least, his gender proceeds. As Hildegard understands the sex–gender system, the female sex allows for two gendered categories, *woman* and *virgin*; the male sex only for *man*.

The cases of both Pelagius, male virgin martyr, and Rupert, whose misfortune in being born male prevents him from achieving either virginity or martyrdom, demonstrate the extent to which the definition of virginity in the Middle Ages is located in the female body. Any attempt to take apart and recombine the constitutive components of virgin martyrdom, which include both the gender of the martyr and the sexual nature of the torture inflicted upon the martyr, only makes it clear that virginity is never normative but rather, in some profound sense, abnormal. The narratives of these young men who choose a path to sanctity usually reserved for young women end by taking the idea of virgin martyrdom to inevitable extremes. Pelagius's standing as virgin martyr can only be demonstrated by subjecting him to the "perverse" desires of a male aggressor, but the effect is to reveal all male desire as perverse. The effort it takes to remain in a state approximating virginity actually drives Rupert to an early grave, demonstrating just how radical a choice it is for a man to conform to a female ideal. The stories of both saints, finally, end by confirming that virginity is an avenue to sainthood that is natural, albeit not normative, for the female sex alone.

CHAPTER 6

CATHERINE AND MARGARET: VERNACULAR
VIRGINS AND THE GOLDEN LEGEND

The work of women like Hildegard and Hrotsvitha reflects communities of religious women for whom the virgin body, whether that of Agnes, Ursula, or even Pelagius, served as the guarantee for claims of spiritual autonomy. Such autonomy could, given the right circumstances, be converted into temporal power and influence by certain extraordinary women committed to the virgin life: Sophia of Gandersheim, blessed with both an extraordinary education and imperial connections, was capable of confronting ecclesiastical authority head on, even though in the long run she did not succeed in her challenge; Hildegard, possessed of a much more limited education, nonetheless exploited her role as virgin prophetess to become a central figure in twelfth-century culture. The production of vernacular virgin martyr legends in the interconnected kingdoms of France and England in the twelfth century, however, invites us to inquire about the meaning of these stories to women very different from Hildegard or Sophia. Some of these were princesses, not of the church, but of the royal houses to whose dynastic projects their marriages were central; some were widows; some were religious women whose access to formal education and especially to Latin was increasingly curtailed as the twelfth century progressed. In the Anglo-Norman lives of Saint Margaret, by Wace, and Saint Catherine, by Clemence of Barking, we can perceive reflections of a culture that may initially seem a curious place for the legend of the virgin martyr to flourish, the Angevin courts of Normandy and England. The very different representations of these two saints suggest profoundly conflicted attitudes toward virginity, femininity, and courtly love.

French vernacular literature can fairly be said to begin with a virgin martyr, in the ninth century *Sequence of Saint Eulalia*. This hymn, probably composed to commemorate the discovery of Eulalia's relics in Spain in

878, renders the virgin martyr as pure icon, devoid of any subjectivity. *Buona pulcella fut Eulalia, / Bel auret corps, bellezour anima* [Eulalia was a good girl / she had a beautiful body, a more beautiful soul (1–2)[1]] it begins, establishing in terms that are both absolute and nonspecific the characteristics of its subject. Eulalia is a completely silent figure in the poem; the threats and entreaties of evil counselors swirl around her, but she doesn't listen and in fact seems almost unaware of them. The confrontation between her and Maximian is one-sided:

> Il li enortet, dont lei nonque chielt,
> Qued elle fuiet lo nom christiien.
> Ell'ent adunet lo suon element;
> Melz sostendreiet les empedementz
> Qu'elle perdesse sa virginitét;
> Por os furet morte a grand honestét.
> Enz enl fou lo getterent com arde tost;
> Elle colpes non auret, por o nos coist.
> A czo nos voldret concreidre li rex pagiens;
> Ad une spede li roveret tolir lo chieef.
> La domnizelle celle kose non contredist. . . (*Eulalia* 13–23)

He commands her, though it matters not to her, to deny the name of Christian. She gathers up her strength; she would rather suffer torture than lose her virginity and so she died with great honor. They threw her in the fire to burn her at once. She was without sin and so she did not burn. The pagan king wouldn't tolerate this and he ordered her head to be cut off with a sword. The maiden did not say a word against this. . .

The hymn does not represent the tortures or Eulalia's body in any detail, but neither does it convey any sense of verbal exchange between saint and persecutor. Whatever speech there is is conveyed in indirect discourse, and Eulalia does not participate even in that; the most intimate thing that we are told about her is that nothing matters to her. Eulalia is neither sentimentalized nor eroticized here; her sex is almost irrelevant, the reference to the threat to her virginity perfunctory. She does not, however, seem quite human. Her silence does not derive from that modesty indistinguishable from shame that characterized Ambrose's Virgin of Antioch, but is rather a manifestation of her complete disdain for the world. What appears to be passivity is in fact complete impassivity, evidence of the fact that Eulalia has moved beyond any form of human interaction. She is admirable but in no sense sympathetic, seeming already to have hardened into something other than flesh, gold or silver, perhaps, like the reliquaries containing the bones that had so recently been discovered in Barcelona.

The virgin martyrs who populate twelfth- and thirteenth-century hagiographies tend to share only Eulalia's beauty of body and beauty of spirit; they lack her perfect impassivity, but they make up for this by having more complex personalities, more eventful lives and deaths, and by being memorably verbal. The proliferation of virgin martyrs during this period seems related in provocative ways to the fact that, with the rise of vernacular literature in France and England, hagiography was increasingly produced for and about and consumed by women, even while the access of nuns to education in Latin was being eroded. According to Wogan-Browne's count, out of thirty-six Anglo-Norman saints' lives, sixteen tell the stories of women, and nine of these are virgin martyr narratives.[2] The same period witnessed the beginning of what would be a steady rise in book ownership by laywomen, peaking in the fifteenth century with the extraordinary libraries of such noblewomen as Anne of Brittany.[3] By the thirteenth century, furthermore, narratives of virgin martyrdom had become truly popular; not only were they the subject of rapidly multiplying vernacular lives, destined for a literate aristocratic audience, but they were represented iconographically in spaces that made them fully available even to the illiterate. As Hans Jantzen points out, "in the windows of Chartres, we have a painted *Legenda Aurea* of the most impressive kind, earlier in date than the work of Jacobus de Voragine. These legends in pictures had the merit of being not told but actually seen, and the vivid narrative possibilities of thirteenth century stained glass brought into immediate visual experience a sense of translation to a higher world."[4] The most famous stained glass of the Cathedral at Chartres, the roses, the upper windows of the choir, the incomparable twelfth-century lancets, tell tales derived from the Old and New Testaments. The glass of the clerestory and side aisles, however, narrates the lives of the saints; the stories of Margaret of Antioch and Catherine of Alexandria are told in an early thirteenth-century window in the south chapel of the ambulatory. The life of Saint Margaret occupies four panels. In the first, the saint is represented as a shepherdess, holding a cross; on a hill nearby stand an angel and a monstrous demon. Next, she fights the demon, placing her foot upon its neck. In the last two panels, she is decapitated while a man on a throne looks on, and her soul is carried to heaven. With utter efficiency, the whole story, a paradigmatic martyrdom, is told in a single ring of glass. The story of Saint Catherine follows the paradigm, but expands upon it, taking sixteen panels to tell. The saint stands before a throned and crowned man. She is imprisoned. She debates with five men (representing fifty—space is limited in a stained glass window) while an angel stands behind her. The men are converted (one can tell by their upraised faces) and burnt to death and their souls are taken to heaven. Catherine stands between men with flails in the next panel, and then a queen, identifiable by her crown, visits her in prison. Christ himself, floating in the air, feeds the saint with the Host. She refuses to worship an idol and then stands in the middle of a broken wheel whose spiked parts are crushing people. The queen is seen naked between two men who have pincers attached to her breasts, and then in her tomb. The emperor, with a demon at his side, sentences Catherine and she is beheaded.

I have summarized these two windows in order to demonstrate just how simple the action is, and how easily read. Even the twentieth-century tourist, armed with a diagram indicating the sequence of the panels, can follow the action. It is easy enough to tell that the blonde who is always center stage is the heroine, and that those who oppose her are Bad Guys; even without the occasional angel or devil taking sides, the lines between good and evil are clearly drawn. Nor do we have any doubt of the virtue of our heroine; it is written large, in her face, in her stance, in the peculiar fact, clearly expressed in spite of the inevitable clumsiness of line that characterizes stained glass as a medium, that the hands or instruments of torture laid upon her never seem to touch her. At Chartres, and even more easily in many smaller churches, someone with reasonably good eyes can make out what is going on in the stained glass even in its present dirty and degraded state. When they were new, these legends must have been quite easily legible.

Catherine and Margaret were often linked from the thirteenth century onward. The appear together or in close proximity in the stained glass at Evreux, not far from Chartres, in the Cathedral of Auxerre, and in the smaller Burgundian church of Saint-Julien-du-Sault, to name only a few. That their stories were popular and immediately recognizable is undeniable, but the question of what these stories meant to the medieval people who gazed up at them during a long Mass, or who commissioned them for the good of their souls is less evident. The donor figures in the bottom of the Chartres window are suggestive in this context. In the first of these two panels, placed directly below the ring telling the story of Saint Margaret, Marguerite de Lèves is represented kneeling before the Virgin; in the other panel are her husband and brother-in-law. Marguerite's gift marks the beginning of the cult of Saint Margaret at Chartres, sometime between 1220–27. The prominence given to the story of Saint Catherine, however, suggests that she may have been more important to the donor than her name saint. Certainly, Catherine's cult in Normandy is the older. It was established at St-Trinité-du-Mont in Rouen sometime between 1054 and 1090, when a monk named Symeon is supposed to have brought to France relics from the monastery of Saint Catherine on Mount Sinai.[5] In general, noblewomen in the twelfth and thirteenth centuries had many more opportunities to memorialize a virgin martyr by commissioning a manuscript or a window, or by naming a daughter, than by imitating them even so indirectly as Hildegard did. Nonetheless, virgin martyrs like Catherine and Margaret clearly remained powerfully significant to laywomen like Marguerite de Lèves.

Two texts from the twelfth century help to flesh out the stories of the windows from the thirteenth, and to indicate the rather different cultural functions the images of these two saints could serve. The first, *La Vie de Sainte Marguerite*, is by Wace, and was probably composed between 1130 and 1140, in Normandy. It is relatively short, seven hundred lines, and fairly straightforward, like the story in the window at Chartres. *La Vie de Ste Catherine*, on the other hand, is longer, more elaborate, and more self-consciously didactic. It is the work of Clemence, a nun from the convent of Barking, composed in the last quarter of the twelfth century. The contrast between these two texts demonstrates the way in which the twelfth century continues to inflect the narrative of the virgin martyr along two very different courses. In Wace's story, Margaret's sanctity is located explicitly and emphatically in her virginity. Clemence, on the other hand, emphasizes Catherine's intellect and her eloquence, taking her chastity very much for granted. The sources and intended audiences of these two texts necessarily affect such inclinations, but so, inevitably, do the gender and agenda of the authors. This chapter explores the evolution of the virgin martyr in the world of vernacular hagiography, composed for and read by courtly laywomen as well as professed virgins.

Marguerite of Antioch

Wace's *La Vie de Sainte Marguerite* stands at the beginning of what Brigitte Cazelles calls the "hagiographic romance,"[6] a fact that should not perhaps surprise us since his more famous *Brut* served as inspiration and source for many of the authors of courtly, Arthurian romance. Born in the Channel islands and educated at Caen, Wace implies an association with the court in his *Roman de Rou*, claiming to have known three kings called Henry and been in their time a *clerc lisant*, presumably a cleric part of whose job was to read aloud from devotional works during meals.[7] The most important of these Henrys was Henry II of England, who made Wace Canon of Bayeux, perhaps in recognition for his composition of the *Brut*, a verse "history" of England based upon Geoffrey of Monmouth. Whether or not Henry was ever his patron in a formal sense, Wace clearly wanted him to be, and imagined his audience as an aristocratic and courtly one for whom he could perform the service of translating edifying texts from the Latin. His *Life of St Marguerite*, like his dynastic epics, is designed to provide instruction and give pleasure without giving offence.[8]

Margaret has no claim to be considered a historical saint, and indeed Attwater calls her *vita* a "fictitious romance" and a "farrago."[9] She was declared apocryphal by Pope Gelasius as early as 480, but her cult was established at a very early date both in the East, where she is known as Marina, and in the West. While her name does not appear in the earliest Syrian martyrologies, it is included in Gregory the Great's Roman litanies in the sixth century, and in the Venerable Bede's martyrology in the seventh, which makes Margaret an early arrival in Britain. In the ninth century, Hrabanus Maurus tells her story twice, under the name of Margaret, whose feast day he gives as July 13, and under that of Marina, whose feast he gives as June 18.[10] Both versions include the name Olibrius for the persecutor, an identical list of tortures, and the detail of the devil appearing both as a dragon and *in specie Aethiopis*, in the form of an Ethiopian or black man. She is included in the eleventh-century Sarum Breviary, and her cult appears to have gained impetus after the capture of Constantinople in 1204 at the time of the Fourth Crusade, when the Marina stories returned to Europe to reinforce the Margaret stories.[11] This date at least corresponds closely enough with the donation of the Chartres window by Marguerite de Lèves. Margaret was invoked by women in labor, because she had emerged unscathed from the dragon's mouth, a tradition that I will have more to say about later.

In comparison with Hrotsvitha's virgin saints, or Hildegard's Ursula, Wace's Margaret seems somewhat one-dimensional. In their study of Old French hagiography, *Le Vain Siècle Guerpir*, Phyllis Johnson and Brigitte Cazelles argue for a definitive difference between male and female martyrs: "The male martyr is portrayed as a man of action; the description of the female martyr can bring a more emotive tone to the narrative if the heroine is portrayed as a persecuted woman. The pathetic elements are closely associated with feebleness, rousing the spectators' sympathies and their potential predisposition for sadism and masochism."[12] They are forced to admit that Catherine of Alexandria is an exception to the rule, but it is certainly true that Wace invests Margaret with a high degree of pathos, and makes his account of her significantly more sentimental than that of his primary source, a Latin *passio*.[13] His first description of the saint emphasizes her appearance; she is well born and beautiful (*gente et. . .bele*, 3–4),[14] and he adds that she resembles the gem her name recalls. This resemblance actually explains her holy virginity: *cume ele fu geme preciuse / Ancele Deu fut epuse. . .sa chastée. . .li voa* (18–21). The identification of Margaret with the pearl, *margarita* in the Greek, is traditional, but the effect of the periphrasis is to represent the young saint as a valuable object. Wace insists that her value resides in her life as well as in her *belté*, but he does not demonstrate this. The characteristics that really matter are her beauty and the virginity of which it is the outward manifestation. Like Tertullian's imaginary virgins who seduced the angels of heaven, Margaret has an irresistible bloom about her.

Margaret's charming vulnerability is further emphasized by her family situation. One of Wace's additions to his source is the description of her father as a wicked pagan priest who rejects her because of her religion, a detail that serves to isolate her from the influence of society.[15] Her mother died when she was a child, and she lives with an old nurse whose sheep she keeps, thus forming a perfect picture of pastoral sentimentalism:

> Al champ aleit, berbis gardeit,
> Car sa nurice le vuleit;
> O meschines de son aage
> Meneit berbis en pasturage.
> Olibrius .I. jur la vit
> Berbis gardeit, ce dit l'escrit. (*Marguerite* 81–86)

> She went into the fields and kept sheep, as her nurse desired. In that place, young girls of her age usually took the sheep to pasture. Olibrius saw her one day, keeping her sheep, the text says.

The repetition of *berbis* in this passage, three times in six lines, is quite remarkable. No actual well-born girl of Wace's period would be likely to spend her time herding sheep; as Shulamith Shahar points out, the shepherd's life involved long periods away from home and was thus unsuitable for even peasant women (although they often did participate in dairy husbandry and, in England, in sheepshearing).[16] Instead, Wace's representation of Margaret as a shepherdess evokes two separate literary traditions. On the one hand, she is figured, like Agnes in the homilies of Ambrose, as a lamb to the slaughter, while on the other she evokes an entire tradition of sentimental pastoralism, with roots at least as far back as Longus's *Daphnis and Chloe*, in which Chloe is a shepherdess whose chastity is constantly threatened. Vergil's *Eclogues* transmitted the pastoral poem to the Middle Ages and it would have been familiar to Wace's courtly audience from the *pastourelle*, a poetic genre in which a knight encounters a lovely shepherdess and has sex with her, either with or without her consent.[17] When Olibrius lays eyes upon her and immediately desires her, he is playing precisely the role of the noble aggressor of the *pastourelle*, attracted by the evident innocence, beauty, and (especially?) powerlessness of the peasant shepherdess.[18] Olibrius sends his men to her to ask whether she is slave born or free, and to propose that she become either his wife or his mistress.

Margaret's reaction demonstrates just how conscious she is of her own vulnerability in this situation:

Ele prit mult fort a plurer
E Jhesum Crist a apeler:
"Aies, Sire, merci de mei!
Maintien mei, dist ele, a ta lei,
Ne perde m'ame o les feluns
Qui funt les persecutüuns.
Fai mei, bels Sire, delivrere
Que tuz tens te puisse aorer,
Que ma fei ne seit empiree,
Ne la meie ame cunchïee,
Ma sainteé ne seit müee
Ne la chasteé que t'ai vöee. . ." (*Marguerite* 109–18)

She began to weep aloud and call on Jesus Christ. "Alas, Sire, have mercy upon me! Help me keep true to your law! Do not allow my soul to be lost to these criminals who persecute [the Christians]. Deliver me, beautiful Lord, so that I can continue to worship you, so that my faith may not be diminished, nor my soul soiled, don't let my holiness be changed, or the chastity I've vowed to you."

Margaret herself identifies her holiness with her chastity, or more specifically, the threat to her holiness with the threat to her chastity. Wace, however, does not develop the spiritual dimension of that chastity as Hildegard does in her poems composed at about the same time, providing instead a narrative that focuses entirely upon Margaret as physical being. Olibrius offers her a choice that has to do entirely with the disposition of her body: *Se noz dex ne veus aorer. . . / En fu ardant ton cors metrai. / Le tien Dé guerpis e ta loi, . . .en mon lit te meterai* [If you will not honor our gods. . .I'll put your body in the fire. . .If you abandon your god and your law, I'll put you in my bed (155–62)]. It is no longer a question of marriage here, apparently, but simple concubinage. Margaret's understanding of the situation betrays an exactly parallel exchange of body for soul: *Se mes cors est en peine mis, / M'ame sera en Paradis / Por les peines que out li cors / M'ame sera de peine fors* [If my body is made to suffer / My soul will go to paradise; for the pains suffered by my body / my soul will be released from pain (215–18)]. Olibrius sees Margaret as a body to be dominated and possessed through pain, while the saint sees herself as a body to be transcended through pain, but in both their minds the link between body and suffering is primary and unalterable. It serves to identify Margaret, at least as she exists in this world, along purely Pauline or Jeromian lines: as a woman, she is body, she is flesh, and only through suffering and death can she become other.

The first series of tortures inflicted by Olibrius insists upon this body by stripping it naked, and Wace participates in this insistence by recalling Margaret's nudity to his audience's mind time and time again: *o verges nue batue* ["naked she was beaten with rods" (176)], *le cors li unt tant batu / O les verges tut nu a nu / Qu'a la tere chaeit li sans / Par les costes et les flans* [they beat her body so thoroughly, with rods on her bare flesh that the blood ran onto the ground from her ribs and flanks (189–92)]. The rhyme *batue/nue* is evidently irresistible, while the images of Margaret's blood flowing over her *costes* and *flans* draws our attention to the same parts of the bodies so often praised by writers of erotic courtly poetry. The litany of beatings continues, as does the emphasis on the body: *Sun char li batent li felun* [the wicked men beat her flesh (252)]; *Quant il veient de la char tendre* [When they saw the tender flesh (255)]; *Sa char nurent espessement, / Que l'antraille qui est ou cors / Per le plaiez pendoit defors* [They tormented her flesh so diligently that the entrails inside her body pushed out through the wounds (273–76)].

The exchanges between saint and persecutor, which interrupt this sequence of horrors, are short, shorter in Wace's text than in his source. Significantly, Margaret is not without fear when threatened, a fact that increases our sense of her vulnerability and pathos. Wace conveys her apprehension in several scenes, while establishing that it is assuaged by a courage that comes from outside, from God; during her first torment, when she is beaten with rods, Margaret asks God to preserve her from submitting out of fear [*pur paür* (186)]. The saint's speeches are brief, her theology simple to the point of naïveté: *Bien li tenra ceste promesce, / Je n'en serai ja menteresce* [I will keep this promise, I'll never be a liar (169–70)]. She remarks that Olibrius ought to believe in the Christian God [*En Deu del ciel devez tuit croire* (229)], but takes it for granted that he will not and makes no concerted attempt to convert him. Her eloquence, in fact, owes nothing to that of the martyr as apostle but is rooted in a much more traditionally feminine and deeply ambivalent mode of speech, one that is revealed when she is left alone in her cell. She crosses herself and begins to pray that she may be permitted to see the real author of the torments she is suffering:

Fai que puisse chacier en veie
Mun enemi qui me guerreie,
Qui les crestïens fait pener,
Que ensemble lui puisse aler. (*Marguerite* 293–96)

Let me compel into sight the enemy who makes war on me, who makes Christians suffer, so that I may struggle against him.

Margaret repeats this prayer over and over again, and Wace, following the *passio*, notes that her old nurse visits the prison during this period to bring her bread and wine and is able to overhear the prayer from the window; presumably, this character was the informant of Theotimus, the putative author of the "original" *passio*, who is named both in the end of Wace's poem and in its Latin source as responsible for the interment of Margaret's body. These details indicate a certain anxiety about the scenes that will follow, which may not be due exclusively to the fabulous nature of Margaret's combat with the two demons, but also to the fact that what she actually manages to do is to summon up the devil, hardly an unproblematic achievement, even when accomplished under the sign of the Cross. In fact, the similarity between magical and miraculous acts and between prayer and incantation would drive Thomas Aquinas, in the next century, to expend considerable energy on distinguishing between them.[19]

When the devil finally appears, in the shape of a dragon, Margaret once again demonstrates real fear, not without reason given his terrifying aspect:

> Noirs ert et d'orible façon
> Fu ardant de son nes jetoit
> Fu noir enor son col avoit
> Barbe avoit d'or de fer les dens
> Les ioex ot vairs conm'a serpens
> Puor faisoit entor lui grant
> Glaive avoit en sa main trançant
> Corocha soi et si sifla
> Par la chartre grant fu jeta
> Paor ot la virge et pesance
> Mais en Deu avoit sa fiance. (*Marguerite* 308–18)

He was black and horribly formed, spewing blazing fire through his nose, with black fire around his neck. His beard was gold, his teeth iron, and his eyes green like a snake's. Fear emanated from him. He had a sharp sword in his hand and he raged and hissed, sending out jets of flame through the cell. The virgin was terrified and oppressed with fear, but she put her faith in God.

Margaret's next action, kneeling and beginning to pray, is paradoxically not one of submission, but a way of claiming power, as she invokes God and his protection:

> A la terre s'ajenoilla
> Mains estendues si ora
> Dex dist ele qui pues garder
> Et ciel et terre et air et mer
> Par tot es tu .i. dex meism

Que poesté as en abism
Qu a la mer rive donas
Infer brisas Sathan lias. . . (*Marguerite* 321–30)

She knelt down on the ground with her hands extended and prayed. "God," she said, "who preserves the sky and the earth and the air and the sea, you are the same God in every place, you have power over the deep and you are the one gave the sea its banks, you broke open Hell, you bound Satan. . ."

Although it is the Christian God to whom Margaret prays here, imagined both as the Creator who shaped the sea and as the Saviour who harrowed Hell, her words have odd resonances to a more ancient tradition and a more ancient power:

Tuque triceps Hecate, quae coeptis conscia nostris
Adiutrixque venis cantusque artisque magorum,
Quaeque magos, Tellus, pollentibus instruis herbis,
Auraeque et venti montesque amnesque lacusque
Dique omnes nemorum dique omnes noctis adeste!
Quorum ope, cum volui, ripis mirantibus amnes
In fontes rediere suos. . .[20]

You too, triformed Hecate, who know of my undertakings, come and assist me, and the magical charms and arts with which you, Earth, instructed the Mages with powerful herbs, and the breezes and the winds and the mountains and rivers and lakes and all the gods of the woods and all the gods of night, come! With whose aid, when I wish, I make the streams return through their marvelling banks to their sources. . .

This is the beginning of an incantation pronounced by Medea in Ovid's *Metamorphoses*. In it, as in Margaret's prayer, we find earth, air, fire, and water, and even a reference to having power over those most primal of liminal areas, the banks of bodies of water. I do not mean to imply that there is any direct influence of the Latin text upon Wace or upon his sources, although it is not impossible, given the enormous impact of Ovid upon medieval authors; nor am I suggesting that Margaret is a witch, although the Romans often accused early Christians of witchcraft, an accusation that Hrotsvitha gleefully picks up and places in the mouths of her dim-witted pagan persecutors. The similarity between saint and witch has been noted by modern authors like Cazelles as well as medieval authorities like Aquinas.[21] Still, the language of Margaret's prayer can hardly fail to evoke an ancient tradition of magical eloquence usually associated with feminine practitioners of the occult arts. Similarly, the pose in which Margaret is often represented in painting and sculpture, standing with one foot on the neck of the devil she has conquered, associates her iconographically with

Diana/Artemis whose function as patroness of women in labor Margaret also inherits.[22]

There is a further fascinating point of congruence between Margaret and Medea. After her invocation to the powers of the night, Medea states her own powers, providing a sort of resumé of her experience in the black arts. Chief among these is her ability to make the snakes explode: *Vipereas rumpo verbis et carmine fauces* ["with words and charms I make the throat of snakes explode" (*Metamorphoses* 7.203)]. This is a fairly standard claim by Roman witches, reported also by Vergil and Pliny the Elder.[23] The Latin *carmen* could mean both song or poem, but also "magical spell"; studies of the practice of Roman magic, both in literature and in those actual practices that can be recovered, indicate that a *carmen* was generally composed of both verbal and somatic components, words combined with gestures and also sometimes with the use of herbs, minerals, or animal parts.[24] Margaret provides the verbal component through her prayer, and adds the sign of the Cross, thus creating a Christian *carmen*. The result is immediate: *Li deables . . . / Tote a bien pres le tranglothi / Mais la crois qu'ele ot fait de Crist / Crut el dragon, crever le fist* [The devil nearly swallowed her up completely, but the Cross she had made in Christ's name split the dragon and made him burst (335–38)]. Keller's glossary of the text gives the Modern French *mourir* as translation for *crever*, but the Latin *passio* makes it clear that Wace had in mind something rather more explosive: *vexillo dominice crucis opposito, serpens squalidus continuo crepuit medius* [when she made the lord's sign of the Cross against it, the filthy dragon split immediately in half]. The dragon does not simply die, it splits in half, explodes.[25]

Wace's account of Margaret's encounter with the second devil develops and resolves many of the issues latent in her encounter with the first, explaining what it would have meant for her to be swallowed alive, and also clarifying the distinction between Margaret's prayers and the incantations of a witch. While Wace had suppressed the description of the first devil as resembling a black man, an Ethiopian, he nevertheless represents Rufun as entirely masculine, bearded, and carrying the sword of male authority; the first demon's "brother," Belsabut, clarifies the specific threat posed by this maleness: *Le cors de tei assorbesist / E ta virginité tolsist* [he would have absorbed your body and taken your virginity (71–72)]. Gravdal points out (with reference to the Mombritius *passio*, but the point applies equally to Wace's text) that this curious transformation of penetration into absorption has the effect of dissociating what is clearly to be understood as a form of sexual violence from men and associating it instead with nonhuman males: "The male concupiscence suggested in the first lines is displaced from Olibrius and projected onto a fire-breathing dragon."[26] A parallel displacement occurs when Margaret crosses herself; her gesture reproduces the cruciform sword, sign of the demon's phallic authority. She redraws the weapon that was intended to violate her body upon that very body, which, arms outstretched, becomes the weapon that will destroy the demon instead. The absolute identity between Margaret's faith and Margaret's bodily chastity is never clearer than at this moment.

Margaret replies to the implied threat of the second demon with characteristic straightforwardness and simplicity: *Ne t'entremetes tu jamais / De tolir ma virginité / Je suis espuse Damnedé* [Don't you ever try to take my virginity. I am the bride of Christ (382–84)]. A century later, the author of the Middle English *Seinte Marharete* will use this statement for a long and learned discussion between the saint and the devil on the nature and value of virginity and the various means by which it may be compromised, but Wace's Margaret, as we have seen, is conceived as a simple creature; long debates are not her style. Rather, almost before the words are out of her mouth, they are confirmed by the sudden radiance of the sun itself within the dark cell. This miracle is an addition by Wace to his source, and serves to underline once more the absolute identity of Margaret faith with her bodily integrity. Floating down on the sunbeam, a dove makes the association fully explicit:

> Bone euree virge es tu
> Margerite, qui as vencu
> Le dragon, que crever feis,
> Et cel que soz ton pié as mis.
> Pur ce que ta virginitei
> As confermee a Damledé. (*Marguerite* 391–96)

> You are blessed, Margaret, virgin, who have conquered the dragon you made to explode, and that other upon whom you put your foot. All this is because you have vowed your virginity to God.

Encouraged by this apparition, Margaret turns boldly to the devil and asks him his name and that of his master, for reasons that the texts does not make clear. Is this mere vulgar curiosity, or rather an attempt to gain power over the forces of darkness by discovering their names?[27] In the *passio*, the devil invites Margaret to look him up in the *libris Jamnee et Mambree*.[28] Wace's rendition of this passage is much less specific, and faintly dismissive: *Le lignage savoir porroies / Se tu tuz les libres esgardoies* [you'd know our lineage if you'd read all the books (481–82)]. Keller explains this revision as evidence of Wace's reluctance to include details that he does not fully understand,[29] but this seems insufficient. Because of God's appearance to Abraham among the oaks at Mamre (Gen. 18), the name was associated with prophecy and secret knowledge. The allusion is one that Hildegard, who is generally regarded (although probably wrongly) as less learned than her male contemporaries, would have recognized since she refers to Mamre in *O vox sanguinis* (no. 65). Wace may well have understood the reference and chosen to eliminate it deliberately. Belsabut is stating that if Margaret were a sorceress, she would have known these magical books; the conditional is a way for both the devil and the author to acknowledge that this Margaret is not much of a scholar. If she had been it would have worked against the representation of her as a simple shepherd girl characterized by innocence and faith, whose strength seems to come from outside of her, and whose quasi-magical powers are entirely intelligible in the context of a system that always associates the feminine with the irrational.

Indeed, having received an answer to her question, Margaret dismisses it as something she does not need to know: *Tais toi dist margerite tais / N'ai soing de ta parole mais / N'ai mais cure de ton sermon* [Be silent! I don't care any more about your words, and I'm not interested in your lecture (497–98)]. The whole exchange serves to distinguish Margaret definitively from the kind of person who might have had an interest in books about the devil, and thus from the whole tradition of sorcery. Margaret's intellect remains untouched by any profane knowledge; she chooses to know only that which comes directly from God. Wace thus retains the impression that he has been so concerned to emphasize from the very beginning, by representing his protagonist as a shepherdess and an innocent. Here, as in her confrontation with Olibrius, she eschews the weapons of forensic eloquence, relying instead on her own innate innocence and naïveté.

Finally, while Wace does note that five thousand people (not counting women and children!) are converted when Olibrius tries unsuccessfully to drown Margaret, only to see her instead crowned by the Holy Spirit, he eliminates her final address to the public before her execution. Keller argues that Wace does so in order to make the narrative shapelier, but the result is to weaken Margaret's function as a teacher and apostolic figure. Her martyrdom, rather than becoming an opportunity for her to preach to anyone at all, becomes the singular experience of a young woman who is characterized almost exclusively by a bodily purity, which Wace, like Ambrose before him, takes great pains to separate from the inspirational and potentially inflammatory rhetoric that could characterize the voice of the virgin martyr. Wace's Margaret is clearly represented as more pathetic than the average male martyr, even if not precisely weaker; her words are powerful enough to vanquish the devil, but their power lies in a register that is both associated with women in dubious ways through their association with magical invocation, and clearly dangerous and not to be imitated by the average devout courtly listener.

La Vie de Sainte Marguerite, in fact, reinscribes the Ambrosian narrative in medieval form, particularly through its evocation of the *pastourelle*, without altering any of its essentially repressive features. The passivity of the female martyr, the sadism of the male persecutor, the voyeuristic participation of the audience all remain as intact as the body of the virgin herself. Wace's Margaret embodies a feminine ideal every bit as amenable to patriarchal projects as that crystallized in Ambrose's life of Agnes eight centuries earlier, even if the patriarchal projects of the Plantagenets were generally matrimonial rather than ecclesiastical. It is not, perhaps, easy to imagine Eleanor of Aquitaine, feudal overlord in her own right, notorious crusader and adulteress, dedicatee of Wace's *Brut*, perusing the pages of the same author's hagiographical *oeuvre de jeunesse*; Plantagenet daughters and daughters-in-law, however, whose absolute acquiescence to dynastic projects was an essential element of Angevin diplomacy, may have needed to be encouraged to imitate more conventional role-models. The tale of the innocent and pathetic virgin martyr would have made perfect inspirational reading for princesses like Marguerite of France, daughter of Louis VII and his second wife Constance, Eleanor's successor. Henry II proposed a marriage between his son Henry (later known as the Young King) and this princess in 1157; it was an appealing idea from King Henry's point of view, since if Louis were to die without male issue, it would bring the kingdom of France under the control of the Normans, and he was evidently willing to overlook both the extreme youth of the prince and princess (at the time of their formal betrothal, Henry was three and Marguerite was one) and the fact that the mother of the bridegroom and the father of the bride had once been married. Louis was more squeamish; although the normal custom of the time required that the princess be sent for fosterage to the family of her affianced husband, he refused to have his daughter raised at the court of Eleanor, his ex-wife. Marguerite was instead fostered with a dependent lord of Henry's. The marriage was eventually rushed through, without the immediate consent or presence of the bride's father, when the two children had reached the ripe old ages of three and five.[30] While the date of the composition of *La Vie de Sainte Marguerite* remains unclear (it could be as early as 1135 or as late as 1155), the poet's appeal to an aristocratic audience at the end of the poem makes it perfectly clear that his didactic message, like that of all of his later poems, was more likely to include marriageable maidens like Marguerite than professed virgins.[31]

Catherine of Alexandria and Clemence of Barking

In spite of their frequent cultic and iconographic association, Catherine as imagined by Clemence has little in common with Margaret as imagined by Wace. Her life, like that of any martyr, is a further extension of the example provided by Christ himself, as Clemence notes in the prologue to her poem: . . .*cil ki sul est bon de sei / A nus dunad essample e lei* [he who alone is intrinsically good / has given us both example and law (7–8)].[32] Where the life of Saint Margaret provides an example of how to suffer death for the sake of virginity, however, the life of Saint Catherine teaches a series of more complex lessons. The poem's explicit didactic message echoes several trends in twelfth-century theology, while the image of the virgin martyr it conveys associates the feminine with intellectual and forensic authority in ways that recall Hrotsvitha's virgin protagonists, and even the remote figure of Thecla.

La Vie de Sainte Catherine was composed during the last quarter of the twelfth century at Barking Abbey, where Aldhelm's friend Hildelith had been abbess almost five hundred years earlier. The sisterhood of Barking no longer possessed, as a group, the kind of extraordinary education of Hildelith and her daughters, nor did the convent itself retain the sort of political independence that had characterized the great Anglo-Saxon houses, but Barking remained a center of feminine culture and learning. In at least one respect, Barking in the twelfth century resembled Gandersheim in the tenth.[33] After the Norman conquest, its abbesses were almost without exception women of the royal family or the highest nobility, and as Wogan-Browne has noted, "the exception" in this case "is a rule-proving one."[34] In 1173, as partial reparation for the murder of Thomas à Becket, Henry II appointed Becket's sister Mary as abbess. The abbesses of Barking took precedence over all other abbesses in England, controlled extensive lands, great wealth, and a large population composed not only of professed nuns but of the daughters and mothers of aristocratic houses, who had come to Barking for education or else to retire from the world. They ruled also a population of men, from the laborers who worked the fields to the priests who looked after the souls of the nuns.[35] While a nun like Clemence could not leave Barking for the capital, as Hrotsvitha may have left Gandersheim and as Sophia certainly did, she could count on having the world, or at any rate the worldly, come to her. Nuns from Barking were demonstrably involved in all aspects of the production of hagiographical texts: they were responsible for commissioning, reading, and translating lives of the saints.[36] Since even at Barking nuns were less likely to be Latinate than their male counterparts, Duncan Robertson has argued that "the cultivation of the vernacular was closely related to the 'feminist' mission of the abbey,"[37] an attempt to provide genuinely inspirational female role-models with whom the women of the convent, both religious and lay, might identify.

We know nothing concrete about Clemence except what she tells us in the signature to her poem: *Par nun sui Clemence numée / De Berkinge sui nunain* [I am called Clemence, a nun of Barking (2690–91)]. To this we may add that her Latin was good enough to allow her to translate with ease and fluidity, her confidence great enough to allow her to expand and embroider her source, the so-called Vulgate life,[38] and that her feeling for poetic language was sure and accomplished. Clemence's retelling of the Vulgate does much more than provide a female audience with appropriate devotional reading; it works to engage women's sympathies in complex ways by mounting a direct assault on those contemporary social and political constructions that worked to silence women, from the traditionally exclusionary and masculine educational system to the ideals of courtly love, and demonstrates with skill and confidence just how powerful the voice of the eloquent virgin could be.

In *La Vie de Sainte Catherine*, the weakness that is imagined as an integral aspect of femininity in Wace's *Vie de Sainte Marguerite* scarcely exists. To begin with, Catherine is no rustic orphan like Margaret, but a queen, a feudal overlord in her own right, and an admirable one at that who rules wisely after the death of her father and distributes her wealth among her people, "since god alone was enough for her" [*Kar deu sulement li suffist* (164)]. In distributing her wealth, Catherine performs an *imitatio Christi* of a sort that would be imitated in its turn in the next century by historical saints like Elisabeth of Hungary and her niece Margaret, both of whom outraged their male relatives by giving away money, valuables, and even property to the poor.[39] Catherine's renunciation of the trappings of royalty makes her politically invisible to the usurping Maxence, who has no idea who she is when she first appears before him, but she does not renounce her responsibility to her subjects along with her wealth. When she hears the weeping and wailing of her rightful subjects and fellow Christians forced to choose between death and the denial of their faith, Catherine experiences great pain on their behalf and sets out to confront the tyrant. She is the active pursuivant of martyrdom, not its passive victim.

Clemence's emphasis on Catherine's active faith is matched by an emphasis on her intellectual ability rather than her physical virginity. While there is no question that Catherine is a virgin—she is introduced in the text as *une jofne pulcele. . .noble et bele* [a young maiden. . .noble and beautiful (135–36)], her virginity is not the most interesting thing about her. Whereas Wace rarely refers to Margaret except by words denoting her sexual status such as *virge* (virgin) and *pucele* (maiden), Clemence uses these terms much less frequently, preferring epithets like *Deu amie* (God's lover) or *ancele Deu* (God's servant), both terms that define her according to her relationship to Christ rather than the condition of her body. This contrast is nowhere more evident than in the parallel scenes where divine apparitions appear to the two saints in their prison cells. The dove addresses Margaret as *bone euree virge* [fortunate virgin (*Marguerite* 391)], but the angel who visits Catherine, causing her to feel fear for the only time in the poem, calls her *amie Deu* (*Catherine* 563). The divergent attitudes of Catherine and Margaret are shaped by these divergent definitions. Margaret is represented in a continually defensive posture, defending her virginity against Olibrius and the two devils. Catherine, on the other hand, is the aggressor, and what she fights for is something more complicated and more abstract than the control of her body. She is engaged in a fight for truth, to be waged with intellectual weapons, and especially with the sword of logic. The majority of Clemence's additions to her source come in the form of expansions and refinements of Catherine's arguments. Where Wace made his virgin less argumentative, eliminating or shortening her speeches, Clemence appears to have expended her energy to make Catherine all the more eloquent and persuasive.

Catherine was the recipient of an extraordinary education, even for a legendary princess; as she explains to Maxence, her father had her educated in the liberal arts: *Les arz me fist tutes aprendre / Que des tute sai raisun rendre* [He had me instructed in all the arts / so that I can give a good account of all of them (379–80)].[40] Her training in logic antedates her faith and in fact seems to enable it. Having learned how to reason, she is capable of moving beyond the limited knowledge of her teachers and putting her reason in the service of faith: *Mais puis que jo le sens oi / Del evangelie mun ami, / Presai mult poi lur doctrine. . .* [But once I understood the meaning of the gospel of my Love, I thought very little of their doctrine (385–88)]. In this passage, which is original with Clemence, Catherine separates the methods of thought taught her by her pagan schoolmasters from the content of their teachings. The philosophical training they give her allows her to recognize and understand the perfect logic of the Christian faith and specifically of its most apparently illogical feature, the trinity. Her teachers are logicians, but Catherine builds on logic to become a theologian.

Burgess and Wogan-Browne have demonstrated conclusively Clemence's debt to Anselm, the great English theologian of the previous century whose *Meditation on Human Redemption* resonates through Catherine's debate with the fifty philosophers; indeed, Catherine's account of her education corresponds neatly with Anselm's pedagogical ideal: "With practice and exercise, the student will be made to see through the traps of language, his intellect will no longer be impeded by ambiguities and confusion, and the true structure of things will emerge."[41] The narrator's description of Catherine's education, however, evokes a more combative philosophical training:

> D'escripture la fait aprendre
> Opposer altre e sei defendre.
> El munt n'out dialecticien
> Ki veintre la poust de rien. (*Catherine* 141–44)

> He had her taught to read and write, to argue with others and defend her
> own arguments, and there was no dialectician in the world who could
> overcome her upon any subject.

Dialecticien, as Burgess and Wogan-Browne point out, is an uncommon
word in Anglo-Norman, indeed a highly unusual one to encounter in the
work of a woman writer, since women were formally excluded from the
study of the *trivium* as it was taught in the great schools of the Continent.
Dialectic, moreover, was associated with much more quarrelsome thinkers
than the famously mild Anselm. As a mode of argument, dialectic was supposed to permit the philosopher-theologian to distinguish between truth
and falsehood.[42] In the hands of a truly enthusiastic practitioner, however,
dialectic could become a weapon rather than a simple tool, as Peter Abelard
makes clear in his *History of My Misfortunes*: "I preferred the weapons of
dialectic to all the other teachings of philosophy," he writes, describing his
decision not to become a soldier according to his father's wishes, "and
armed with these I chose the conflicts of disputation instead of the trophies
of war."[43] Throughout his long and chequered career, Abelard could never
resist using his argumentative skill to humiliate someone less eloquent than
he, even when it was perfectly clear that the result of winning a given
confrontation would threaten his career or even his life. For Catherine too,
being right matters more than life itself.

Maxence, confronted with a woman skilled in the art of logic, realizes
that he is out of his league, swiftly decides that he cannot risk public humiliation, and calls in a panel of experts, composed of *rhetorien / Ki parler seivent
e bel e bien* [rhetoricians who really know how to speak (*Catherine* 331–32)].
The task they are to perform is defined as both patriotically and patriar-
chally defensive:

> Que tuit a l'emperur viengent,
> S'onur e sa lei maintiengent,
> Kar une plaideresse ad forte
> Ki de sa lei guerpir l'enorte.
> Si [il] ceste poent cunfundre
> Que ne lur sache mais respundre,
> Que devant tuz seit recreante
> Del desputer dunt tant se vante,

De ses cunseils les frad privez
E sur tuz serrunt honurez. (*Catherine* 329–40)

Let them all come to the emperor in order to uphold his honor and his law,
for a sort of female lawyer is trying to persuade him to abandon that law. If
they can confound this woman, to the point where she doesn't know how
to reply to them, and has to concede the fight, after having boasted of her
argumentative ability, he will make them members of his cabinet and grant
them honor before all others.

Maxence's proclamation demonstrates that he is painfully aware of the
particular danger Catherine poses to his regime—as a usurper, he quite
reasonably fears humiliation more than a legitimate monarch might have.
By calling the saint a *plaideresse*,[44] he both recognizes her unfeminine quasi-
legal training and, disastrously for him, dignifies it; this woman, the word
admits, is not simply mad or misguided. She is someone who has the right
to plead her case before the emperor in open court. When the philosophers
arrive in response to his plea, Maxence elaborates the difficulties of his
position even more explicitly. When Catherine debates, her opponents
are silenced by her eloquence, he explains. A silenced emperor cannot
promulgate laws or maintain his own authority. Paradoxically, silencing
Catherine's voice by physical means will only render her words more
powerful; this is a truism of the martyrological narrative, which Maxence
seems dimly to intuit:

Bien la pusse aver enfrainte
E sa bele parole esteinte,
Mais greindre honur me semblereit
Ki par desputer la veintereit. . . (*Catherine* 437–40)

I could simply have overpowered her and extinguished her fine words, but
it seems to me that it would be more honorable if she were vanquished in
debate.

The emperor's honor can only be salvaged if Catherine falls silent of
her own accord, if she admits herself to be *recreante*; the word implies a self-
recognized defeat or cowardice, and reinforces the combative sense of the
encounter.[45] The contest established here between saint and pagan thus
reverses the terms that characterize it in the *Sequence to Saint Eulalia*; honor
is associated with speech and not silence. Speech, moreover, does not
threaten virginity as it did in Ambrose's homilies; rather, in a roundabout
way, it proceeds from virginity, since virginity permits the virgin's relationship with Christ, and that relationship is both the source and the subject of
her discursive power. Significantly, however, neither Catherine herself nor
the angel who visits her in her cell is particularly concerned about the

preservation of her virginity. Catherine prays for the power to convert her opponents and the angel promises her *sens e raisun e habundance. . . de parler* [good sense and logic and eloquence (567–68)]. Clemence resolutely maintains the focus of her narrative on her heroine's intellectual abilities rather than on her body.

When the debate between Catherine and the fifty philosophers finally begins, however, it is not an example of dialectical disputation as practiced at Paris or Chartres. Catherine addresses one of the central paradoxes of Christianity (and one to which Anselm had dedicated perhaps his most famous treatise, *Cur Deus Homo*): why should God choose to become man and die? The answer she develops is not a proof in any conventional sense; it is, instead, allegorical and poetic, based upon the correspondence of images and the construction of paradoxes: *La mort n'ocist pas Jhesu Crist, / Mais Jhesu en sei mort ocist* [Death did not kill Christ; Christ killed death within himself (873–74)]. The balance of paradoxes like this one is a reflection of the balance established by the great symbols of Christianity. Like Hildegard, and unlike her source, Clemence balances Eve's sin with Mary's sinlessness; the tree of knowledge is reconfigured as the Cross, the forbidden fruit as the body of Christ:

> Par le fruit del fust deveé
> Fud tut le mund a mort livre.
> Jesu fud le fuit accetable
> E a tut le mund feunable. (*Catherine* 977–80)[46]

> By the fruit of the forbidden tree was the whole world given over to death;
> Jesus was the acceptable fruit, and he was fruitful for the whole world.

Catherine cites no Christian authorities beyond her very general paraphrase of scripture; cosmic symmetry is sufficiently evident to make its own case, apparently. She does, however, confront the philosophers with the witness of two pagan authorities, Plato and the Sibyl. In both cases, the testimonies of the ancients are not precisely relevant to the paradox of the Incarnation; instead, they are references to the symbol of the Cross, which Catherine insists that both the philosopher and the prophetess foresaw. The witness of authority itself is thus a testimony to the symbolic method that Catherine's discourse privileges. The Cross does not have a tangible meaning that can be parsed according to grammar or logic; rather, it casts a shadow so long that it revises the very origins of philosophy and prophecy. It is a symbol in the fullest sense, with the symbol's ability to escape the limitations of the rational.

The general outline of Catherine's speech to the philosophers was present already in Clemence's source text, which may help to explain its homiletic rather than dialectical qualities. It is also possible that the author realized that her audience wouldn't sit still for a display of syllogistic logic; perhaps she herself knew of the practice of dialectical argumentation only by vague reputation; or perhaps she was simply too much of a poet to enjoy composing a series of speeches founded in abstraction and opposition. There are, after all, different forms of eloquence, and the poet's need not be identical with that of her subject. In any case, within the text, Catherine's words are fully effective, resulting in the conversion of her opponents, to Maxence's dismay. He begs them once more to defend his honor and his law: *kar tuit en fin huni serrum, se nus victoire n'en avum* [For we will all be humiliated if we do not claim the victory (1071–72)]. Maxence fails to perceive the truly transformative power of Clemence's words; in converting the philosophers, she has not humiliated them but illuminated them. The philosophers' condemnation to death by fire, furthermore, allows Catherine to assert apostolic authority in the mode of Thecla when she assures them that martyrdom is equivalent to baptism; it also begins the process that will leave Maxence, by the end of the poem, not only humiliated but also entirely alone.

Bloody Murder and Courtly Love

Maxence is perhaps the most complicated persecutor in the entire genre of hagiography; some critics, in fact, have found his character rather too complex. For Cazelles and Johnson "the portrayal of the pagan is here both a failure and a success" because, according to them, Catherine seems less realistic than Maxence.[47] This is, perhaps, an excessively post-Romantic attitude, reminiscent of Blake's argument that Milton was of Satan's party without knowing it. For Catherine to be properly exemplary, she must be extraordinary, but Clemence makes her most realistic and most appealing (if not sympathetic in the sense of evoking pathos) in her interactions with Maxence. Furthermore, Clemence's representation of Maxence as a man trying to seduce a younger woman while keeping an eye out for his wife's rights allows her to elaborate a subtle but pointed critique of courtly ideals, courtly literature, and even, perhaps, of court society.

Maxence's abrupt attempt to seduce the saint, following immediately upon his execution of the fifty philosophers, is a transparent example of the substitution of one form of aggression for another: *Angoissus est mult de sa hunte, / Mais quant il veit que rien n'amunte, / Vers la pulcelle se turnad* [He felt an agony of shame, but when he saw that nothing could be done, he turned to the maiden (1240–42)]. Here Clemence takes the threat of rape, which is so much a part of the hagiographical narrative, and uses it to represent with astonishing psychological accuracy the transformation of wounded male self-image into sexual desire and eventually sexual violence.

Maxence proposes to restore his damaged honor by overcoming Catherine's chastity rather than her eloquence, and his appeal is nicely calculated. He begins by praising her eyes, which "always contain a wise smile," and steers away from any prurient comment on her fine figure, pointing out instead how nice she would look in imperial purple (1247–51), thus hinting to Catherine that he may restore her birthright. He promises her a position as a sort of concubine *cum* counselor:

> Secunde en mun palais seras.
> Tu avras aprés la reine
> De tut mun regne la saisine,
> Fors sulement de sun duaire,
> Dunt jo ne li voil pas tort faire.
> Ja destance n'i avrad,
> Firs sul le lit u ele girad. (*Catherine* 1268–74)

> You will be second in my palace, you'll be the next most wealthy person in my realm after the queen; I except only her dowry, for I don't want to wrong her in that area. There will be no difference between you, except for the bed she will lie in.

As Wogan-Browne and Burgess note, the exception of the queen's dowry makes Maxence very much part of Clemence's own world, since the *duaire* "was the gift of bridegroom to bride and, unlike the dowry brought to the husband by the bride, was (at least in theory) property over which Anglo-Norman wives retained control at their husband's death."[48] Maxence concludes with a calculated appeal to Catherine's altruism: he will quite literally put her on a pedestal, in the form of a statue, and whoever bows down to it will be pardoned of crimes. Catherine's response is civil, ironic, and absolutely devastating; she politely overlooks the sexual implications of his proposition, and pokes fun at him, suppressing a laugh and noting *corteisement* (courteously) that statues are vulnerable to both bird droppings and passing dogs (1344–49).

In an expansion upon her source, Clemence insists that in preserving her courtly demeanor, the saint is making one last concerted attempt to convert Maxence; Catherine's genuine desire to save her persecutor sets her apart from the host of virgin martyrs who are only interested in denouncing pagans. Maxence, however, considers himself to be gravely dishonored; the switch has been thrown which will transform desire into violence, and he condemns Catherine to be beaten. In another humanizing moment, Clemence allows Clemence's composure to crack for just one instant under torture; as the blood begins to spurt from her wounds, she exclaims *O chien culvert. . .Fai quanque tun curer fel destine / Tant ne me savras mal faire* [You cowardly dog. . .Do whatever your savage heart desires. You don't know how to hurt me (1471–73)]. This exclamation creates the impression that Catherine does suffer physical pain, but discounts it. Only after this do the divine interventions that preserve her from hunger in her cell and from pain during further tortures begin.

The complications of Maxence's character not only permit the development of Catherine's humanity, but they allow Clemence to condemn the misplaced sense of honor that leads the emperor to act with such cruelty. Nowhere is this clearer than in the episode where Maxence finds himself forced by his own perception of his responsibility to that honor to condemn his queen, converted by Catherine, to death. Her execution is necessary because she has challenged his authority and his honor, reproaching him with needless slaughter and, worse, calling him *chaitif barun* [cowardly baron (2128)]. The insult is doubly cutting; it not only accuses him of cowardice, it strips away his assumed title, rather as though the queen were calling a police chief "officer." It is this confrontation that provokes Maxence's famous lament:

> Reine, fait il, ço que deit,
> Que si paroles encuntre dreit?
> Crestien te unt ensorceree,
> Kar tu es tute enfantomee.
> Tute ma honur ai ore perdue,
> Quan il t'unt si deceue.
> Reine, u averai ge confort
> Apres ta doleruse mort.
> Laisseir ne pois que ne t'ocie;
> Assez m'ert pur mort puis ma vie.
> Coment viveras tu sanz mei,
> Et ge coment viverai sanz tei? (*Catherine* 2165–76)

Queen, he said, what are you doing, speaking out against the right? The Christians have bewitched you, you are enchanted. Now that they have deceived you, I have lost all my honor. O Queen, where will I find comfort after your painful death? I cannot prevent your execution, but my life will not be worth living afterwards. How will you live without me, and how will I live without you?

Maxence here gives voice to a horribly distorted form of courtly rhetoric; his words recall Marie de France's famous lines from *Chievrefoil*, and resonate, as many have noted, even more closely with the *Tristan* romance of Thomas.[49] Robertson argues persuasively that the passage must be read "ironically, as a critical coment on the Tristan romance and on courtly literature in general."[50] This does not mean that we should see Maxence as a simple hypocrite, however; his protestation of love for his queen need not be gainsaid by his determined attempts to seduce Catherine. Rather, he is a man whose passions are tragically confused. He is concerned for his worldly honor rather than his soul, and cannot therefore respond to Catherine's attempts at conversion as the philosophers did; they at least were interested in the truth. He wants both a wife and a mistress, but most of all he wants the women in his life to do what he says, to refrain from challenging his authority under any circumstances. When Catherine's convictions shake the queen out of her conventional role, Maxence is driven to react in the only way he understands, with violence.

Maxence's particular combination of uncontrolled passions can suggest only one historical model. On December 29, 1170, Thomas à Becket died in the Cathedral at Canterbury, on the apparent orders of Henry II. He was immediately revered as a martyr, and his canonization only three years later remains one of the fastest on record. By 1171, Guernes de Pont-Sainte-Maxence was interviewing eyewitnesses for the first account of Becket's life and death, which he composed in England between 1172 and 1174. During that time he visited Barking Abbey, where the abbess was none other than Mary Becket, the murdered archbishop's sister.[51] Henry was not only the murderer of a saint, however; he was a famous adulterer. By 1173 he appears to have become permanently estranged from Eleanor of Aquitaine, and his affair with Rosamond Clifford was celebrated in ballads for centuries. Clemence will have had even more immediate evidence of Henry's infidelity to his queen, however; the abbess who succeeded Mary Becket, in 1174, was the king's illegitimate daughter.[52] MacBain places the composition of *La Vie de Sainte Catherine* anywhere between 1163 and 1189, but the similarities between Maxence and a king whose "self-control could give way to savage bursts of rage and fiendish cruelty"[53] and the close connections of Barking to both Becket and the king strongly suggest a composition date later than 1171. Clemence's text may then be read as an example of virginal eloquence that does more than simply prescribe the imitation of the virgin martyr as appropriate to its aristocratic, feminine audience, or denounce injustice and worldly delusions in general, but which has instead a very specific political point to make. Guernes ended his poem about Thomas à Becket by praying for the conversion of the king; Catherine works hard to convert the emperor, but Clemence implies that there is no hope for such misguided monsters in a Christian world.

The *Golden Legend* and the Law of Conformity

Because me seemeth to be a sovereign weal to incite and exhort men and women to keep them from sloth and idleness, and to let to be understood to such people as be not lettered, the nativities, the lives, the passions, the miracles, and the death of the holy saints. . . .I have submised

myself to translate into English the Legend of the saints which is called Legenda Aurea *in
Latin, that is to say the Golden Legend. For in like wise as gold is most noble above all other
metals, in like wise is this Legend holden most noble above all other works.*

—William Caxton, *The Golden Legend,* 1900

Although the twelfth and thirteenth centuries witnessed an extraordinary
efflorescence of vernacular *vitae* across Western Europe, the most powerful
force in the popularization of hagiography was in fact a Latin text. In about
1260, a Genoese Dominican by the name of Jacobus de Voragine composed
what would prove to be the most popular collection of saints' lives of all
time. It came to be known as the *Legenda Aurea,* the Golden Legend.[54]
Over a thousand manuscripts of the Latin text survive, and as early as 1300
the text had begun to be translated into the various vernaculars. With the
advent of the printing press, editions of the *Golden Legend* multiplied with
near miraculous rapidity. As Ellis notes in his introduction to Caxton's version of the *Legend,* "no other book was more frequently reprinted between
the years 1470 and 1530 than the compilation of Jacobus de Voragine."[55]

The *Legend* tends strongly toward generic representations of its subjects.
Legendary and New Testament saints predominate, and these are divided
into strictly defined categories: apostles, evangelists, repentant prostitutes,
virgins, martyrs, ecclesiastics (mainly popes and bishops), and monastics
(including hermits). These categories, especially among the legendary
saints, tend to be governed by paradigmmatic narratives from which all but
the slightest variations are eliminated.[56] Virgin martyrs compose the single
largest group of female saints in the *Legend,* and they are limited almost
entirely to the category of legendary saints. These combined circumstances
suggest both that the categories of virgin and martyr are as indissolubly
linked for Jacobus in the thirteenth century as they were for Aldhelm in
the seventh, and that their value as pragmatic models is severely limited.
Indeed, there are scarcely any women among the historical or contemporary saints included in the compendium, the exceptions being Helena
the mother of Constantine, who does not rate a chapter of her own, and
Elisabeth of Hungary; the general impression left is that female sanctity
more or less died out with the great persecutions. One would not, perhaps,
expect to find women included in most of the categories that constitute
Jacobus's definitions of post-Constantinian sanctity, since popes, bishops,
doctors of the church, and abbots predominate; there are no saintly abbesses,
however, and few queens, although both classes produced respectable numbers of saints in the early Middle Ages. Some of the omissions are, in fact,
startling; Jacobus devotes several pages to Saint Germain of Auxerre and
includes an anecdote about the invasion of the Huns, but never mentions
Saint Genevieve, patroness of Paris and an important figure in Gregory of

Tours, whom Jacobus cites elsewhere (this is an omission that Caxton's translation rectifies). In his life of another Frankish saint, Rémi, Clothilde appears in passing as an exceptionally good woman, but no mention is made of her veneration as a saint since Merovingian times. The list of Frankish, Anglo-Saxon and German female saints who do not appear in the *Legend* could be multiplied almost *ad infinitum*, but perhaps the omission of Clare of Assisi, canonized in 1255, Italian, like Jacobus, and the sister of Francis, who is the subject of a long chapter, is more surprising. This dearth of female saints betrays the overwhelmingly conservative impulse of the *Legend*.[57] The kind of affective and evaluative difference that separates Wace's Margaret from Clemence's Catherine disappears almost entirely. Details may vary in Jacobus's virgin martyr stories—this one is racked, that one is burnt, a third is boiled in oil—but the representation of the martyr herself varies very little. Catherine and Margaret in the Anglo-Norman lives are connected, in a variety of ways, to the social and literary worlds of Wace and Clemence, as I argued earlier, but Jacobus's virgins are less exemplary than exceptional. In them, virginity and eloquence are so tightly imbricated as to produce a package of pure paradox and contradiction.

The virgins of the *Legend* are the most argumentative of all the martyrs in the collection, by definition an argumentative group since the focus of their tales must be placed upon the confrontation between saint and persecutor. Male martyrs, however, tend to be the strong and silent type, although there are exceptions; soldier saints in particular, like Eustace, Maurice, and Sebastian, are laconic during their passions, while the words of other male martyrs are simply not reported, as though of little interest. Female martyrs, on the other hand, regularly denounce their persecutors in scathing and vituperative terms. Of the twenty virgin martyrs in the *Legend*, a dozen participate in long arguments either with a pagan judge or with the devil himself. Jacobus is especially interested in the miracles performed by saints, and it is almost as though the spectacle of a woman speaking is in and of itself miraculous. The speeches of the virgin martyrs in the *Legend*, however, tend toward the excessive and even the grotesque rather than the inspirational; Saint Lucy goes on lecturing the consul Pascasius even after her throat is cut, while Christina's language and behavior seem like something out of a Jacobean drama. "Christina, my daughter, light of my eyes, have pity on me!" her pagan father implores her. "Why do you call me your daughter," she replies, "when I bear the name of my God?" He orders that she be tortured with iron combs and she flings a bit of her own flesh in his face, crying "Here, tyrant, eat the flesh which you engendered!" In the next phase of her passion, she scares one judge to death and compels a pair of serpents to poison another. Finally, a last judge orders that her tongue be cut out, to arrest her apparently magical power; she flings the severed tongue back in his face, blinding him in one eye, before succumbing to arrows (*Legend* 1.470). The cumulative effect of these examples is to associate the speech of the virgin martyr uncomfortably with that of the other great exemplar of medieval female excessive speech, the riotous, offensive, and emasculating scold.[58]

The threat of rape takes various forms in these narratives, and is often linked directly to a desire to silence the virgin's obstreperous speech. When Lucy insists that the Holy Spirit speaks through her, and inhabits her because she is a virgin, Pascasius orders her to be cast into a brothel: " 'Your body will be violated and you'll lose your holy spirit!' Lucy replied 'The body is soiled only if the soul consents, and if I am violated against my will, my chastity will only be redoubled!' " (*Legend* 1.56). Inevitably, however, the issue of the woman's complicity or noncomplicity in rape is sidestepped; the men who come to carry Lucy off find her too heavy to move, a man who tries to lay a hand on Euphemia is paralyzed, and the first man to look lustfully on Agnes is blinded. In the case of Justina, the devil himself makes an assault upon the saint's virginity, disguised as a girl who proposes to live in chastity with the saint. He tempts Justina by asking whether they are not breaking God's command to increase and multiply, but the saint, although initially tempted, resists and makes the sign of the Cross, which causes the devil to "fade away like a melting candle" (*Legend* 2.224). The temptation of the devil is entirely based upon the proposition that women are inclined to lust. When male martyrs encounter the devil, their temptations are various. Anthony easily overcomes the temptations of fornication, and then encounters devils in other forms, one of whom animates a corpse, which Anthony proceeds to beat savagely; Macharius encounters a devil disguised as a harvester who announces almost without provocation that the saint has vanquished him by his humility, and Satan himself carrying bottles of wine with which to tempt the other monks; Dominic, founder of Jacobus's own order, breaks his vow of silence in order to reprimand a devil who makes faces at him, only to reveal that as master of the chapter house, he has every right to speak. Justina's victory over the devil thus appears as the ultimate condemnation of the female sex; while male saints may oppose the devil with faith or strength or points of procedure, the female is both vulnerable and powerful in her chastity precisely because it is only her body and its purity that matter.

Sherry Reames points out that throughout the *Legend*, Jacobus "goes out of his way to drive home"[59] the lesson of female inferiority. In his analysis of Catherine's exceptional qualities, for instance, he points out that she resisted temptations to which normal women would have succumbed. She had plenty of opportunities to misbehave, after all, because once her father was dead she was surrounded by (presumably male) servants: "She was young, she enjoyed complete liberty because she was alone and free in a palace" (*Legend* 2. 387). In his sermons Jacobus tends to use the chastity of the virgin martyr as an excuse to preach against the immorality of *multae mulieres* (many women).[60] The story of Cecelia, who converted her husband on her wedding night, becomes an excuse in a sermon for "the lesson that women can preserve their chastity only by avoiding dangerous relationships with men."[61] The virgin martyr in Jacobus's compilation thus becomes a deeply ambivalent example. Like Wace's Margaret, she is defined by her body, but she is never either pathetic or sympathetic; like Clemence's Catherine, she is verbally aggressive, but she is also entirely lacking in humor, *courtoisie*, irony, or compassion for her tormentor. Her body becomes the site of and the excuse for ever more inventive tortures, an invitation to sadistic fantasies of the most extreme sorts, as the many illustrations based upon the *Legend* over the centuries demonstrate. She is a woman whose speech is so violent and extreme that it must be silenced at all costs, a maiden who cannot lose her maidenhead, and most of all, she is pathologically eager for death, always already dead. The *Legend* as a whole leaves the powerful impression that the virgin martyr is a figure from the distant past, remote, inimitable, and inhuman, separate both temporally and situationally from both those clerics of the high Middle Ages and the laity, whether common or courtly, to whom they might read it or preach to from it. It is tempting to regard Jacobus's representation of virgin martyrs in such limiting terms, and his elimination of so many potential models for feminine sanctity, as a deliberate reaction against the vernacular hagiographies of his period, which appealed strongly to the laity and especially to women, and which could make space for an ironical Catherine as well as a pathetic Margaret, for a critical Clemence as well as a sycophantic Wace. In spite of his influential and repressive revisionary narrative, however, popular versions of the lives of saints like Catherine and Margaret continued to move and inspire. In the fifteenth century, in France, in fact, they were to inspire the most remarkable of all medieval women: Joan of Arc.

EPILOGUE

JOAN OF ARC

Down the hill from the open-air theater where the *Mystère de Sainte Reine* is performed every autumn stands a monument to another virgin martyr. Wearing a full suit of armor and mounted on a horse caught in mid-stride, Joan of Arc looks past a straggle of houses and over the green valley below. The contrast between the two saints is telling. Despite the local cult devoted to her, Reine seems to belong entirely to legend; Joan's life is the most extensively documented of the medieval period, and her cult is anything but local. Statues of her are ubiquitous in France; Catholic schoolchildren the world over are given prayer cards decorated with appropriately saccharine images to mark her feast day (May 30); she transcends religious affiliation both as a patriotic icon in France and as a pop-culture diva in Europe and North America.[1] This juxtaposition of a local legend and an international heroine may serve to illuminate the degree to which the brief, passionate life of Joan of Arc reflects, refracts, and (perhaps?) finally escapes the paradoxes inherent in the virgin martyr narrative. In the previous chapters, I have argued that the experience of the legendary virgin often informed the lives of medieval women more or less directly, and especially the lives of those rare medieval women who wrote. Hrotsvitha, Hildegard, and Clemence had confronted in various ways the ideological traps inherent in the legend of the virgin martyr; they worked especially hard to undo the connection between virginity, silence, and death by rendering it purely and usefully ironic or metaphorical. Joan, the most visible woman of the Middle Ages, literalized the virgin martyr narrative completely. Paradoxically, Joan, who died for her identification with this role, rather than any of those women who revised and survived such identification, was the one to become a heroine for the ages, even a feminist role-model. The dual impulse I've described as characteristic of virgin martyr stories, toward speech and agency on the one hand and silence and passivity on the other, manifests itself again and again in the telling of Joan's tale, especially in the evocations of her virgin body, the virgin voices that bespoke her, and her martyrdom. No life shows the power latent in the idea of the virgin martyr, both for bliss and for bale, so clearly as that of Joan of Arc.

Joan's story has been told so many times that I will sketch it here only in the briefest terms. Early in the spring of 1429, when the Hundred Years War between France and England was in its last stages, a girl from a village called Domrémy presented herself to the commander of a local garrison. She insisted that she had a divine mission to help the beleaguered Dauphin of France reclaim his kingdom. In the early spring of that year, Joan, who had assumed masculine dress and been given a horse, appeared before Charles VII at Chinon. After being examined by a panel of clergymen at Poitiers, she was granted military equipment. On April 29, she reached the occupied city of Orléans; on May 8, the English forces, which had held the city for more than six months, were routed. Joan was widely credited with this victory and with those that followed during the month of June: Jargeau, Meung-sur-Loire, Beaugency, and Patay.[2] On July 17, she accompanied the Dauphin to Reims and saw him crowned. By autumn, however, Joan's luck seemed to be turning; she tried and failed to take the city of Paris in September, and failed again at La-Charité-sur-Loire in the winter. In the spring of 1430, she was involved in a series of unspectacular engagements; in late May, she rode to the defense of the besieged town of Compiègne, where she was captured by the Burgundians and then sold to the English. She would spend the final year of her short life in prison, where she was extensively interrogated between February and May of 1431. Finally, on May 28, she was condemned as a relapsed heretic; on May 30 she was burned at the stake in Rouen. In 1455–56, a second trial was held, which rescinded the verdict of the first and restored Joan's reputation. She was canonized in 1920.

The transcripts of the two trials, which have come to be known respectively as the condemnation trial and the nullification trial, tell us most of what we know about Joan. They are not unproblematic documents. Each was motivated by a complex tangle of religious and political purposes. Convicting Joan of heresy, for instance, served English interests not only by salving the hurt pride of military commanders defeated by a woman but also by casting doubt upon the moral authority of the king she had crowned at Reims; her conviction also served ecclesiastical agendas by reasserting the function of the church hierarchy as essential mediator between God and humankind, a function Joan had implicitly denied by claiming a mission directly from God. The nullification trial, on the other hand, was a rehabilitation of Charles VII's kingship as well as of Joan's reputation, and some of its testimony reads like purest whitewash. These conflicting agendas have been extensively explored by other scholars, and I intend to take them more or less for granted here. A separate issue is raised by the nature of the surviving documents themselves. The original French minutes of the trial of condemnation survive in two manuscripts, but both are incomplete; the full transcript exists only in a Latin translation produced several years after the trial itself.[3] As Karen Sullivan points out, this makes it problematic, at best, to read the transcripts as "a largely transparent representation of Joan's words and beliefs though which we encounter the heroine herself."[4] The trial records, nonetheless, are utterly irresistible from the point of view of the hagiographer, for here we have, acted out by a real virgin, before real judges, the scene of interrogation and persecution common to every legendary narrative of virgin martyrdom. The ironies, of course, are myriad; the judges in the case are not pagan prefects or emperors, but princes of the Holy Catholic and Apostolic Church, canons, bishops, and doctors of theology. Even more tragically ironic is Joan's apparent inability, to which I shall return, to foresee the inevitable *denouement* of the script as it unfolded around her. A woman, uneducated and alone, she confronted the teams of educated men who interrogated her for months armed only with her considerable intelligence and her faith in God. Her judges, trained in scholastic theology and modes of disputation, turned her own word against her again and again, badgering her about the corporeality of her voices, about her notorious transvestism, about the claims she had made for herself and her mission. Like the legendary confrontations between virgin martyrs and their persecutors, the trial of Joan of Arc revolves obsessively around the two linked issues of the female body and female speech.

Jehanne la Pucelle

For a woman who was probably illiterate, and certainly very busy, Joan was an indefatigable correspondent. Three of her surviving letters bear her signature, "Jehanne," deliberate if somewhat shaky; some, including the famous "Letter to the English," exist in early copies or are cited in other documents. The voice that speaks in Joan's letters is worlds away from the ecstatic poetics of Hildegard or the debonair fictional logic of Catherine of Alexandria as imagined by Clemence. Joan's language is straightforward and enthusiastic in both amity and enmity; the inhabitants of Reims are her "most dear and perfect friends" while the duke of Bedford is the "self-styled regent of the kingdom of France" (Quicherat 5.140). She is more than a little cavalier with regard to syntax, her eloquence that of immediacy rather than of reflection or rhetorical training. One of the most notable features of Joan's letters is her tendency to refer to herself in the third person, and as La Pucelle, which is generally rendered in English as "The Maid." Marina Warner notes that *pucelle* means "virgin, but in a special way, with distinct shades connoting youth, innocence, and, paradoxically, nubility."[5] By Joan's time, the word was no longer the most common term in the language for young girl; other terms, including the more technical *vierge*, were overtaking it; while you might describe an aged nun as *vierge*, however, you would never call her a *pucelle*. *Pucelle*, moreover, was the original word used in French to describe not just a virgin but a virgin saint; the *Sequence to Saint Eulalia*, we may recall, began *buona pulcella fut Eulalia*. By choosing this particular epithet as her title, Joan thus claims an identity that is both founded in bodily integrity and linked to hagiography, an identity that would be fetishized by her supporters and detractors alike.

The compelling quality of this chosen identity is expressed by an anecdote her chaplain, Pasquerel, told at the nullification trial. At Chinon, a man-at-arms who saw Joan entering the king's house called out "Is that the Pucelle?" and went on, "taking the Lord's name in vain, to say that if he could have her for one night, she wouldn't be a virgin when he returned her. Joan said to the man 'In God's name, how can you deny Him, and you so close to your death!' Only an hour later, he fell in the water and was drowned" (3.102). The incident recalls those in the tales of legendary virgin martyrs when a would-be rapist is divinely punished, and it is no doubt influenced by them; it is Pasquerel's recollection of such tales that makes a rather prosaic accidental death by drowning into the equivalent of the blinding by thunderbolt of the young man who looked lustfully at Agnes in Prudentius's poem. Witnesses at the nullification trial constantly evoke the aura of awe that surrounds Joan's virginity. The most celebrated example of this is the testimony of Joan's squire, D'Aulon, who claimed that he had seen her naked breasts and legs in the course of his duties, but had felt no desire at the sight although they were perfectly shapely (3.219). The sacred quality of Joan's virginity repelled desire one way or another, at least according to the hindsight of the second trial.

The fascination with Joan's virginity is also demonstrated by the number of proofs to which it was submitted. Joan's virgin status seems to have been tested twice at Chinon alone; Pasquerel claims to have heard that she was visited by the Dame de Gaucourt and by the Dame de Trèves, who found her to be "a woman, and a virgin, and a maid [*puella*]" (3.102). Significantly, in this case it is her sex itself that is being verified, as well as her chastity. D'Aulon describes an inspection by the King's mother-in-law, Yolanda of Aragon, Queen of Sicily, during which Joan was "examined in the secret parts of her body; but after they had seen and looked at whatever there was to see in such cases, the lady in question informed the king that she and the other ladies were certain that [Joan] was a true and whole virgin in whom might be seen no corruption or violation" (3.204–10). D'Aulon's language here conveys a conventionally masculine sense of bewilderment before the whole question of female virginity; he seems less than certain concerning how such a test would be conducted (what *might* there be to see, "in such cases"?) but entirely willing to believe the testimony of the noble ladies as to Joan's integrity. A skeptical reader might suggest that the ladies in question were not, in any case, fully qualified assessors of physical virginity, and that the French court was willing to be convinced because it wanted to be. It seems likely, however, that a rather more rigorous examination of Joan's body was undertaken when she was a prisoner of the English at Rouen. Various witnesses who had participated in the first trial were called at the second in order to confirm this. Jean Massieu, a minor member of the clergy during the trial at Rouen, testified that Joan was visited by both matrons and midwives [*matronas seu obstetrices*], supervised by the Duchess of Bedford, Anne of Burgundy; he even provides the name of one of the midwives, Anne Bavon. According to Massieu's testimony, it was because Joan was found by these professionals to be virgin that the Duchess of Bedford gave orders that she was not to be molested in any way by her guards (3.155). Boisguillaume, a notary at Rouen, also mentions this test, providing the interesting if dubious detail that the Duke of Bedford spied upon the procedure from some hiding place (3.162). He notes that the results of the test were never entered into the official trial transcript. The comment upon this omission provided by Thomas de Courcelles, an active member of the first trial and the translator of the French minutes into Latin, is utterly convincing: if Joan had *not* been a virgin, he points out, that fact would certainly have found its way into the transcript (3.59). Guillaume de la Chambre, the doctor who examined Joan after a bout of food poisoning, also thought her to be a virgin.[6]

Two points are particularly noteworthy with regard to Joan's corporeal virginity; one is the function of other women in verifying and protecting that virginity. The Duchess of Bedford, who was also the daughter of the Duke of Burgundy, was doubly opposed to Joan on the political plane, and yet took pains to protect her from sexual assault while she was in prison. The aura of fear that surrounds the corporeal integrity of the legendary virgin martyrs, in other words, has its equivalent in the aura of respect accorded Joan's virginity even by her captors, and appears to have created a community of complicity, however tenuous, among the women around her. The second is Joan's clear sense that her virginity is her defining characteristic; it belongs to God and it is what connects her to the saints she would eventually identify with her voices, Catherine of Alexandria and Margaret of Antioch.[7]

Catherine and Margaret

After more than two months of interrogations and investigations, which took place between January and March of 1431, the charges against Joan were condensed into a list consisting of seventy articles known as the "Libelle d'Estivet," for the canon lawyer who composed them. Article 44 states that Joan "had boasted and continued to do so, had claimed publicly and continued to, that saints Catherine and Margaret had promised to take her to paradise and had guarantee that she would be among the blessed if she preserved her virginity; and of this she was certain." When this charge was read to her, according to the transcript, Joan replied "I refer you to Our Lord, and to the answers I've already given" (1.269). These seventy charges were further reduced to twelve (a procedure that came under intense scrutiny during the nullification trial), but the relationship between Joan and her saints remains central. The first article of the twelve empha-sizes the corporeality of Joan's "voices," stating that Joan had often "embraced and kissed" Catherine and Margaret, "touching them physically and corporeally" (1.328), and their appearance, especially their costumes; according to the article, Joan had described her saints as "crowned with beautiful and costly crowns" (1.329). The ninth article reiterates Joan's belief that, if she preserved her virginity as commanded by her voices, she would join them in paradise; the eleventh returns to her physical relation-ship with her saints, to the "embracing and kissing and touching bodily and physically" (1.335).

Joan's voices would become the basis for her condemnation as a heretic and an idolater; neither saints nor angels, according to the canon lawyers who interrogated Joan, could have had bodies to be embraced. Angels are by nature insubstantial, according to authorities unknown to Joan, like Thomas Aquinas, while saints exist in spirit alone until the resurrection.[8] The entities Joan had communicated with must therefore have been demons; in his final pronouncement against her, after her brief recantation and the revocation of that recantation, Pierre Cauchon found her guilty of being a schismatic, idolator, and invoker of demons. Because of her condi-tion as a relapsed heretic, she was turned over to the secular arm and exe-cuted, with what the nullification trial would point out was undue haste.

Joan's identification of her voices with the three saints so often associ-ated with her, Michael the Archangel, Catherine, and Margaret, has often been called into question. Warner points out, "before the trial, Joan did not speak of her voices in the same terms as she used during it."[9] Both she and Sullivan argue that Joan was essentially railroaded by her interrogators into providing incriminatingly detailed and physical descriptions of an experi-ence which it had never previously occurred to her to describe, and which was, in any case, indescribable. Documents other than the trial transcripts rarely mention Joan's voices and never identify them with visions of particular figures. D'Aulon, in his nullification testimony, states that early in their time at Orleans, Joan woke him just as he was falling asleep to tell him that her "counsel" had instructed her that the time had come to attack the English (3.212). At no point, however, does he connect this counsel with a particular saint or angel. Other accounts from the nullification trial are equally indeterminate; it is possible, of course, that these witnesses realized how instrumental the very notion of visitation by embodied saints had been in Joan's condemnation and therefore steered clear of the subject. Accounts of Joan that circulated before the first trial, however, are also consistent in that they describe her simply as divinely inspired. One of the most detailed of these is a letter from Perceval de Boulainvilliers, Charles VII's chamberlain, to the Duke of Milan, written in June of 1429.[10] According to Perceval, Joan's first mystical experience occurred when she was twelve years old. She and some friends who were looking after the sheep in the fields had been racing together, and one of Joan's companions claimed to have seen her running just above the ground. A young man appeared with a summons from Joan's mother, but when she got home, her mother denied having sent for her. Upon her return to the fields, she saw "a shining cloud. . .out of which a voice was formed" (5.117); this voice informed her of her military destiny. In spite of Perceval's rather pretentious language, the whole account has a curiously commonplace quality, which makes it sound authentic. Why that misdirection home to her mother? A detail of this meaningless sort hardly seems to arise from hagiographic or literary convention. The voice from the cloud, however, strikingly recalls the vision Hildegard describes at the beginning of the *Scivias*: "I saw a great splendor, and out of it came a voice from Heaven" (*Protestificatio* 1). Perhaps the essential difference between the two visionaries lies not in their visions but in what they did once they had received them. Hildegard, forty-three years old and a veteran of much negotiation with male ecclesiastical authority in the form of the abbot of Saint Disibod, took the proper steps; she had her vision authenticated by Saint Bernard and Pope Eugenius. Joan was an adolescent, with all of an adolescent's naïveté and enthusiasm; she simply did what the voice told her. At the trial of condemnation, the fact that she did not even discuss her visions with her parish priest was consistently held against her, while the witness of that earlier examining panel at Poitiers, to which Joan appealed again and again, was simply ignored.

Although Joan seems not to have identified her voices with particular angels or saints until pressured by her interrogators to do so, it is significant, as Sullivan notes, that the identification, when it finally does come, is freely made by Joan herself.[11] No one suggested the archangel or the two virgin martyrs to her; they leapt to her lips in the interrogation session on February 27 quite unbidden. That Joan should have had a personal devotion to these saints in particular is hardly surprising; in fact, given their enormous popularity, any other choice would have been rather peculiar. Michael was the French equivalent of Saint George, a national military icon as well as the great warrior archangel of heaven. Catherine and Margaret, as I pointed out in chapter 6, were among the most popular of all saints in the late Middle Ages. The church at Domrémy contains a statue of Saint Margaret that may have been there when Joan was a child, while Saint Catherine was the patron of the neighboring town of Maxey. Catherine and Margaret both appear in the glorious thirteenth-century stained glass at the cathedral at Auxerre, a town Joan helped to liberate on July 2, 1429. It is easy to see how Joan might have apprehended similarities between herself and these two particular virgin martyrs. Margaret, like Joan, had been accustomed to watch the flocks while waiting for a greater destiny to befall her. Catherine was (and still is, in small French towns) the patron saint of all unmarried girls. More importantly, however, Catherine was a young woman who had decided to act on behalf of her people. Like Joan, she stood for resistance against the oppressor; like Joan, she faced down intensive interrogation. At Poitiers, Joan, like Catherine, had convinced the "philosophers" who sat in judgment upon her; at Rouen, she would fail.

In the various interactions between herself and her saints, which Joan eventually described during her questioning at Rouen, Michael quickly fades into the background. Joan claims Catherine and Margaret as her constant companions, and of the two, Catherine is the most forceful. It is Catherine who instructs Joan not to jump from the tower at Beaurevoir, an instruction Joan disobeys; most significantly of all, perhaps, it was Catherine who provided Joan with a sword. On the same day she first named her voices, Joan told her interrogators about the discovery of the sword in the church of Ste-Catherine-de-Fierbois:

> She was asked how she knew the sword was there. . .she knew it was there from her voices and she had never before seen the man who went to get it. She wrote to the churchmen in that place and asked whether she might have the sword, and they sent it to her. . .she loved that sword well, because it was found in the church of Saint Catherine, whom she loved well. (Quicherat 1.76–7)

In her comments upon this episode, Bonnie Wheeler points out that "swords identify, authorize, and authenticate medieval warriors in fact and in legend."[12] Certainly, the sword of Saint Catherine serves an authenticating function for those chroniclers who told Joan's story before the rehabilitation trial, and who were thus in particular need of authenticating details. Jean Chartier, whose account dates from the 1440s, tells the story of the finding of the sword much as Joan herself did; he claims that she knew about it "by divine revelation" (4.55) but does not mention voices.

Chartier also recounts the loss of the sword, which Joan had been rather cagey about during her interrogation. As he tells it, when the army was near Auxerre, Joan flew into a rage at the prostitutes who accompanied the men and beat several of them with the flat of her sword. The blade shattered, and when the king heard of the incident, he was furious, telling Joan that beating whores was the kind of work that demanded nothing more than a good, strong stick (4.71–2). Chartier dates the turn in Joan's luck from this moment; the sword could not be reforged, and he notes, after giving a brief account of her capture and execution, "after the said sword was broken, Joan never prospered in arms again, on behalf of the king or otherwise" (4.93). The Joan of Chartier's account is not yet represented as saintly; rather, she seems to emerge from the world of romance in which it is not uncommon for swords to be revealed divinely, and where the care and keeping of one's sword is equivalent to the keeping of one's honor. Chartier's epilogue suggests, rather oddly, that Joan's sufferings are due to her misuse of her sword, to making a mistake that a properly educated knight would not have made. Interestingly, in the rehabilitation trial, the story of the sword broken on the back of the prostitute resurfaces several times. D'Alençon claims to have seen Joan at Saint Denis, chasing a camp follower and breaking her sword on the woman's back; he tells the story as a proof of Joan's upright nature, linking it to her prohibition on swearing and to his own utter lack of desire for her (3.99). Louis de Contes, Joan's page, tells a bowdlerized version of the same story: Joan did pursue one of the camp followers, "but she didn't hit the woman; instead, she spoke to her gently and lovingly warned her not to get caught again in the company of armed men" (3.73). Here Joan the warchief is being replaced by Joan the saint, who never uses the sword she carries, but brandishes it exclusively as a symbol.

The significance of the sword of Saint Catherine is multiple; it may indeed function, as Wheeler suggests, as a "liminal object" that maps "the juncture of the material and spiritual world."[13] It was certainly perceived as otherworldly by Joan's contemporaries. Even her interrogators had trouble turning the finding of the sword against her, and did so very unconvincingly. The nineteenth article of the Libelle d'Estivet claims first that Joan knew of the location of the sword because she had consulted with demons, and then suggests that the finding of the sword was simply a hoax designed to deceive the king. Joan's response is that she stands by what she has said before, and denies the rest of the charge (1.234). In the Twelve Articles, the accusation concerning the sword is reduced to a single line; like Joan's virginity, the discovery of the sword proved difficult for Cauchon either to deny or to turn to his advantage.[14] More important to my argument, however, is the devotion to Saint Catherine demonstrated by the sword; Joan insists that she loved it for Catherine's sake. Joan's willingness to associate the sword with the saint confirms that the image of the virgin martyr operated for her not as the Church would have liked it to, as an icon of feminine passivity and humility, but rather as a source of strength and the will to resistance. For Joan, the sword borne by so many statues of Saint Catherine is not what it is supposed to be iconographically, that is, a representation of the saint's passion and death; rather, it is a real sword, a practical weapon for the enforcement of justice, a tool with which to drive the English out of France. In reference to another blade, one she took from a Burgundian soldier, Joan made it quite clear what swords were supposed to be used for: giving *de bonnes buffes et de bons torchons* [good blows and good whacks] (1.77). For Joan, the virgin's sword represents the death of others, not the death of the virgin herself. Her reading of the icon of the virgin martyr is, in other words, completely at odds with the official party line of the Church.

Finally, the discovery of the sword of Ste-Catherine-de-Fierbois emphasizes Joan's connection to prophecy. In this incident alone does Joan function unambiguously as someone with access to secret knowledge, someone who can foretell where treasure will be found, someone whose predictions can be proven. The discovery of the sword authenticates not only Joan's role as military leader, as hero, but her access to information of divine origin. It is not at all clear that Joan conceived of herself as a prophet, or even that she knew much about what such a role might entail. As Warner points out, she seems to have been entirely uninterested in, or perhaps unaware of, the apocalyptic tradition that had invested the pronouncements of visionaries like Hildegard with so much authority, and she was deeply skeptical of other visionaries.[15] Joan never claimed to be able to see the future; she simply said that she had been given a special mission, to kick the English out of France. Her contemporaries on the French side, however, had an enormous investment in the notion of a prophecy that would justify the accession of Charles VII. They considered Joan the fulfillment of a whole tangle of oracles. At the rehabilitation trial, several witnesses referred to a tradition that France would be lost by a woman (usually understood to be Isabeau de Bavière, the Dauphin's mother who had allowed her son to be disinherited in favor of Henry VI of England) and regained by a virgin.[16] Joan was represented as the fulfillment of prophecy even during her lifetime; Christine de Pisan, in the poem she wrote during the summer of 1429 celebrating Joan's advent, insists that Merlin, the Sibyl and Bede had all foreseen the coming of a Maid who would liberate France.[17]

From Joan as prophesied by the Sibyl to Joan as a prophet in her own right was a short step, conceptually. A text known as the *Sibylla Francica*, evidently composed by a German cleric during the summer of 1429, insists that Joan should be listed among the Sibyls, whose number he expands to include "moderns" like Hildegard (3.429). He describes Joan-the-Sibyl as "learned in the arts of war, and prescient as to battles" (3.422); something so unnatural as military skill in a woman could only be explained, evidently, as divine inspiration. Evidently, it was Joan's chastity, her status as pure vessel, just like that of Hildegard or the Sibyl herself, which made her an appropriate receptacle for divine inspiration. This point is made with perfect clarity by Martin le Franc, whose defense of the female sex, *Le Champion Des Dames*, appeared in 1440, fifteen years before the rehabilitation trial:

> Aussi je croy en bonne foy
> Que les angles l'accompaignassent
> Car ilz, comme en Jherosme voy,
> Chasteté aiment et embrassent.
> Et tien pour vray qu'ilz lui aidassent
> A gaaigner les fors bolvers
> Et à Patay les yeulx crevassent
> Aux Anglois ruez à l'envers.

> And I believe faithfully that angels accompanied her, for, as we see in Jerome, they love and embrace chastity. And I hold it to be true that they helped her to win the outer barricades and at Patay they smote the eyes of the English as they fled. (Quicherat 5.48)

Martin is one of the very few witnesses outside of the trial at Rouen to even suggest that Joan was accompanied by otherworldly entities; since he was associated with the Burgundian court, he may well have had access to accounts of her testimony at trial, and reinterpreted it in her favor. In any case, his evocation of Joan surrounded by angels permits us to return from the question of her function as prophet to the question of her prophetic voices and her own tragic ending. If Catherine and Margaret were speaking to Joan, what did they tell her about her own future?

The Stake

On the twenty-fourth of May, 1431, a curious scene was acted out in the cemetery of Saint-Ouen at Rouen, one whose meaning still baffles historians. Joan was led up onto a sort of scaffold, with many of her judges present, and made to stand while Guillaume Érard, a theologian and canon of Rouen, preached a hellfire and damnation sermon at her, accusing her of heresy and assorted other abominations. When he had finished,

Joan signed a document of recantation, abjuring her heretical beliefs, the very beliefs she had maintained so steadily throughout the long months of her interrogation, and promised from now on to obey the Church. The signing of this document aroused a storm of speculation as early as the rehabilitation trial, when Jean Massieu insisted that the lengthy version published in the official transcript was not the short confession he read to Joan upon the scaffold and which she signed. Guillaume de Manchon, a notary at the first trial and one of the most voluble witnesses at the second, claimed that Joan smiled as she signed the document, and this putative smile has engendered all sorts of questions. What was it that Joan signed? Was there a switch of documents, a secret mark in the margin of a sort used by Joan in her military dispatches to indicate that she didn't mean what she appeared to be saying? Perhaps there was no smile at all, except in Manchon's revisionist imagination, and Joan signed out of terror and desperation, as a marginal note to the transcript suggests: *Johanna timens ignem dixit se velle obedire Ecclesiae* [Joan, afraid of the fire, said she wished to obey the Church].[18]

Joan's fear, finally, is what separates her from the virgin saints who inspired her. Her recantation is completely intelligible, utterly human, eminently rational in the face of an unimaginably painful and humiliating death. Joan's fear marks the boundary between legend and history with perfect clarity. Many of the legendary virgin martyrs whose stories she must have heard were consigned to the flames, but none of them felt fear or pain; in some cases, indeed, the flames refused the offering of virgin flesh. The impassivity of the legendary virgin martyr, as we have seen, is one of her definitive features. The perfectly virgin body is, within the universe of hagiography, impervious to pain just as the perfectly virgin mind is impervious to fear. Joan, however, had been wounded several times in combat; she knew perfectly well that no matter how sacred her virginity was, it conferred no physical invulnerability. Perhaps she didn't fear death much; she had faced it repeatedly during the year of her military career. Burning alive and choking in heavy smoke, however, is a different matter altogether from a blow received in battle.

What took place after Joan's recantation is as unclear as the circumstances surrounding the signing of the document. From a political perspective, her recantation was a disaster; the English needed Joan dead, not locked up in a prison from which she might be ransomed or rescued, and it has been suggested (most notably by Shaw) that the French may have found it a relief not to be expected to provide either ransom or rescue. Historians have often suggested that Joan was trapped somehow into resuming her male dress, the mark of her heresy, in order to provide the excuse for her execution. This may be true, but in the final analysis, it matters very little, since what Joan said was at least as important as what she did. On the morning of May 28, when challenged as to why she had resumed her men's clothing, she gave a series of answers: she prefers it; she didn't understand that she had undertaken to give it up by signing the document; she is afraid to wear women's clothing when surrounded by men; her judges have not kept their promise to her, that she should be permitted to hear Mass and have her chains removed if she wears a dress; that she would rather die than be in chains all her life. Her final answers, however, are the ones that provoked a clerk to make a famous note in the margin: *responsio mortifera*, fatal answer. She has spoken to her voices, she says, and Catherine and Margaret have informed her that her recantation was treason, an especially loaded word for someone who had defined herself not only by her faith in God but by her loyalty to her king. She recanted, they have told her, to save her life at the expense of her soul (1.455–56). The English were jubilant; Joan was now a relapsed heretic, and nothing could save her from death.

The nature of that death was no less horrible now that Joan had decided, irrevocably, to accept it. Jean Toutmouillé, a Dominican who visited Joan on the morning of her execution, described his encounter with her twice, once for the recorders at Rouen and once for the rehabilitation trial. The two versions differ significantly, but both of them show us a woman struggling with terror. In his first testimony, Toutmouillé describes an almost existential anxiety: "We spoke to her in French, saying, 'Joan, you always said that your voices claimed you would be liberated, and now you see how they have deceived you; tell us the truth.' Joan replied to this by saying, 'Truly, I see that they did deceive me'" (1.481–82). This exchange, which marks perhaps the lowest moment in Joan's whole captivity, refers to the several times during the interrogation when she was asked whether her saints had promised to rescue her. On March 3, Joan insisted that her saints had told her she would be freed, but she didn't know when (1.94); again, on March 14, she insisted that

> Saint Catherine had told her that she would have help, and that she didn't know whether this meant she would be rescued from prison or that perhaps when she was taken to be judged there would be some sort of uproar and she would be delivered then; she thought it would probably be one or the other. And her voices told her that she would be delivered by a great victory; and afterwards they said to her, "do not worry, don't fret about your martyrdom; you'll get to paradise eventually." The voices said this simply and absolutely, that is to say, without any doubt. And by martyrdom, they meant the pain and difficulty she was suffering in prison. She didn't know whether she'd have to suffer even more, but she resigned herself to God. (1.155)

If the trial of Joan of Arc were a literary creation, we would know precisely how to read this response: as an example of rather heavy-handed dramatic irony in which the readers and the voices share a sinister knowledge that is hidden from the protagonist. The words of Joan's voices lend themselves to an obvious interpretation: they promise her deliverance, not from the prison of the English in Rouen, through rescue by her erstwhile companions-at-arms, but from the prison of the flesh, through death. Joan seems incapable of performing such an interpretive act, however. She hopes instead for a literal rescue, perhaps even an uprising in her favor; she had hoped, equally vainly, that the citizens of Paris would rise on her behalf in the autumn of 1429. The term "martyrdom," on the other hand, she refuses to understand literally, glossing it instead as referring to her imprisonment and shying away from considering what it might mean to "suffer even more." Although she knows the ultimate fates of Catherine and Margaret, the "counsel" with whom she has chosen to identify herself, Joan refuses to know her own fate, the end of the story inevitably scripted for the virgin martyr.

Thirty years later, Toutmouillé's testimony about Joan's last morning is much more graphic and pathetic; he had gone with another Dominican, Martin Ladvenu, to offer Joan comfort and to try and move her to penitence and contrition:

> When he told the poor woman about the death she would die that day, which her judges had ordered and intended, and she heard of the hard and cruel death which awaited her, she began to cry out painfully and pitifully, tearing her hear. "Alas! Will they treat me so horribly and cruelly, must my body so whole and clean, which was never corrupted, today be consumed and reduced to ashes? Ah, I'd rather have my head cut off seven times than be burned like that! If only I'd been held in an ecclesiastical prison, as I agreed to be, if I'd been guarded by churchmen and not by my enemies and adversaries, this dreadful thing would never have happened to me." (2.3–4)

The interest of the members of the rehabilitation trial in this testimony particularly concerned the legalities of Joan's imprisonment; she should, indeed, have been kept in a prison administered by the Church, and she should have been attended by women, not by English soldiers. More interesting from the point of view of the hagiographical narrative is Joan's longing for a swift death by the sword. Decapitation was, of course, the conventional fate of the virgin martyr; like virtually every other member of that select sorority, both Catherine and Margaret lost their heads to the executioner's blade, and were often depicted kneeling serenely before their executioners. Joan's desire for a clean death (the exaggeration of her wish is the only part of the speech reported by Toutmouillé that sounds compatible with Joan's usual plain idiom) suggests that in the last hours before her death, she was overwhelmed by the gulf between the martyrdoms she had heard told or seen depicted and the awful reality of what was about to happen to her.

Most of the accounts of Joan's death date from the rehabilitation trial and are therefore suspiciously partisan and full of hagiographical details, which may well have been invented after the fact. Ysambart de la Pierre, another of the Dominicans present at both trials, reported that "one of the English, a man who despised her, was stricken speechless as though in ecstasy when he saw the devout end of her life; and he insisted that when Joan gave up the ghost, he saw a white dove leap forth from the flames" (2.63). This testimony is, however, purest hearsay (Ysambart heard it from another priest who heard it from the Englishman's confessor); in their discussion of it, Pernoud and Clin note that it marks "Joan's fellowship with the martyrs according to the sensibility of medieval Christianity."[19] Establishing such an effect was hardly an accidental effect of testimony from the rehabilitation trial; Ysambert also explicitly compared Joan's sufferings to those of "Ignatius and the other martyrs" (2.7). Politically less partisan, since it was written a decade before the rehabilitation and at the Burgundian court, and consequently more interesting as an indication of authentic attitudes toward Joan's death is a stanza from Martin Le Franc's *Champion des Dames*. The Adversary has suggested that Joan was rightly executed, and that this proves that she was not sent by God, to which the Champion replies:

> De quants saints faisons nous la feste
> Qui moururent honteusement!
> Pense à Jhesus premièrement
> Et puis à ses martirs benois. (Quicherat 5.49)

> How many saints do we celebrate to this day who died shamefully? Think of Jesus first of all, and of his blessed martyrs!

Even the journal of the so-called Bourgeois de Paris (he was actually a clerk associated with the University of Paris, the most anti-Joan of institutions), which contains a contemporary account of the execution, expresses a profound ambivalence concerning her death:

> She was tied to a stake upon the scaffold, which was made of plaster, and the fire was set beneath her. And soon she was dead, and her dressed all burned away, and then the fire was raked back and she was seen by the people, all naked, and all of the secrets which might or could be in a woman were revealed, in order to remove the doubts of the people. And when they had looked long enough at her, dead and tied to the stake, the executioner

rekindled the fire beneath her poor carcass, which was soon burned up and both bone and flesh reduced to ash. There were those present and elsewhere who said she was a martyr for her true lord. And others said no, and that he had done wrong to protect her. So the people said, but whether she had done good or evil, she died that day. (4.471)

It is unclear whether the author witnessed the execution himself, or simply spoke to someone who had, but his account reveals what can only be understood as a failure in the Church's handling of Joan's death. Melzer calls the exposure of Joan's body "the last of a series of violations, but. . .certainly the most heinous,"[20] but what is most significant about the spectacle created by the executioners is how signally it failed to achieve its purpose. While it may have demonstrated conclusively that Joan was indeed a woman (one wonders how many people needed to be convinced of this, by this time?) it in no way foreclosed speculation concerning either her sanctity or her mission. Even the "Bourgeois" uses the language of martyrdom to describe her, although he keeps it resolutely secular; her "true lord" must, from the context, be assumed to be Charles VII. The scene of public torment and humiliation to which Joan was subjected, however, served to ally her inevitably in the popular mind to those ubiquitous representations of the martyrs whom she had chosen to emulate. The effort to disprove Joan's sanctity by exposing her naked body, like that to disprove her virginity by subjecting it to scrutiny produced the opposite effect to that desired. The subsequent disposal of Joan's remains—her ashes were scattered in the Seine—suggests that Cauchon was fully aware of the potential dimension of such a failure; if he had indeed created a martyr, he would at least try to forestall the development of any cult around her relics.

What at least some of those present at Joan's death had witnessed, even on the testimony of a witness as hostile as the "Bourgeois," was the martyrdom of a sacred virgin. It was not a death anaesthetized or aestheticized by either faith or art, like those in stained glass windows or the Golden Legend. Rather, Joan's death broadcast faith by agony itself, as she screamed from the flames the name of her Savior and the names of her saints: Michael, immortal archangel who had never suffered pain, Catherine and Margaret, whose sufferings had preceded hers and which she had, on some level, chosen in choosing them. Joan's life, death, and afterlife in the popular imagination, in fact, recreate in a real body, in a lived life, every aspect of the fictional narrative of virgin martyrdom: the unassailable but constantly assailed virginity, the irrepressible speech, the caustic criticism of corrupt masculine authority. Like those historic women martyrs of the early Church, Joan believed that her commitment to virginity both redeemed and liberated her; with great determination she resisted any argument to the contrary, any suggestion that she was not free to live as her counsel and her conscience demanded: by leaving her family, wearing men's clothes, leading armies, by refusing to capitulate to the tortuous logic of the Inquisition, even by choosing death over lifelong imprisonment and degradation. Joan's life suggests the power for self-determination that remained immanent in the icon of the virgin martyr for women, in spite of all the efforts of patristic writers to enmesh it in ambivalence, to convert a symbol for active and subjective speech into one for passive and objectified silence. In the life of Joan, for the first time since the stories of Thecla, Perpetua, and the martyrs of Palestine, the experience of the virgin martyr, as opposed to the stories told about her, resumes a fully political dimension; Joan was not only a part of the ongoing struggle between France and England, after all. She posed, in her very person, a threat to all the hierarchies of gender, of class, and of religion, which upheld the political systems of the late Middle Ages.

It seems appropriate to end this account of virgin martyrdom not with the image of Joan's death, but with her own words, words that form part of a tradition of virginal eloquence going all the way back to Thecla. These, then are the words of the last of the virgin martyrs:[21]

Jesus-Maria,
King of England, and you duke of Bedford, who call yourself regent of the kingdom of France, William de la Poule, Count of Suffolk, John Lord Talbot, and you, sir Thomas of Scales, who call yourself lieutenant of the duke of Bedford, put yourselves right with the King of Heaven. Surrender to the Maid, who is sent here by God, the King of Heaven, the keys to all of the good towns of France that you have taken and violated. She has come here from God the King of Heaven to restore the royal blood, but she is perfectly ready to make peace, if you are willing to settle accounts with her, provided that you give up France and pay for having occupied her. And all you archers, men-at-arms, gentlemen, and others who are before the city of Orléans, go back to your own countries, for God's sake. And if you do not go, you will hear from the Pucelle who will come see you soon and do you great damage. If you do not do so, King of England, I am chief of the armies, and wherever I find your people in France, I shall make them leave, whether they want to or not; and if they will not obey, I shall have them all killed. I am sent from God, the King of Heaven, to boot you all out of France, body for body. . .If you won't believe this news which comes from God by the Pucelle, then wherever we find you we'll make such a ruckus [ung si gros hahaye] that France won't see the like of it for a thousand years. . .
Signed,
La Pucelle

NOTES

Introduction   Genuine Devotion, Imaginary Bodies

1. Jean-Baptiste Étourneau, *Le martyre de Sainte Reine* (1878) cited in André Godin, "La dramaturgie de sainte Reine" in *Reine au Mont Auxois: Le culte et le pèlerinage de sainte Reine des origines à nos jours*, ed. Philippe Boutry and Dominique Julia (Dijon: Cerf, 1997), p. 234.
2. See Godin, "La dramaturgie de sainte Reine," pp. 217–42.
3. The most significant is a metal plate with a fish upon it, dated to the late fourth or early fifth century. The word REGINA is roughly scratched upon the back. Joël Le Gall, "Un service eucharistique du IVe siècle à Alésia" in *Mélanges Carcopino, Mélanges d'archéologie, d'épigraphie et d'histoire* (Paris: Hachette, 1966), pp. 613–28.
4. Nicole Courtine, "Sainte Reine et la tradition écrite: La *Passio S. Reginae*" in *Reine au Mont Auxois*, pp. 31–35. Also Philippe Boutry, "Sainte Reine et la Critique Savante," pp. 296–99, in the same volume.
5. Boutry, "Sainte Reine et la Critique Savante," pp. 291–94.
6. Saint Lucy is perhaps the only virgin martyr to have survived more successfully; her feast day, December 6, is still celebrated widely in both Sicily and Sweden, and in Sicilian and Swedish communities the world over.
7. As Karen A. Winstead notes in *Virgin Martyrs: Legends of Sainthood in Late Medieval England* (Ithaca: Cornell University Press, 1997) one result of this is "the widespread assumption. . .that virgin martyr legends as a genre express a more or less constant paradigm of sainthood" (p. 4).
8. John Bugge, *Virginitas: An Essay in the History of a Medieval Ideal* (The Hague: Martinus Nijhoff, 1975), p. 4.
9. Bugge, *Virginitas*, p. 110.
10. R. H. Bloch, *Medieval Misogyny and the Invention of Western Romantic Love* (Chicago: University of Chicago Press, 1991). See especially chapter 2, " 'Devil's Gateway' and 'Bride of Christ' " and chapter 3, "The Poetics of Virginity."
11. Bloch, *Medieval Misogyny*, p. 94.
12. For the feminist critique of Bloch's argument as it appeared in abbreviated form in the journal *Representations* 20 (1987), see *Medieval Feminist Newsletter* 7 (1989): 2–16; Bloch's response appeared in the following issue. My own project began with an attempt to recuperate the reactions of late

antique and medieval women to the attempts of patristic and medieval writers to "render virginity impossible" (Bloch, *Medieval Misogyny*, p. 104); Bloch was very helpful in shaping its initial direction.

13. Bloch, *Medieval Misogyny*, p. 4. Christine de Pizan was not, as Bloch claims, the first to mount a "sustained attempt to counter the pernicious effects of misogyny" (p. 3). Hrotsvitha of Gandersheim developed a coherent critique of misogyny five hundred years earlier; see Alcuin Blamires, *The Case for Women in Medieval Culture* (Oxford: Clarendon, 1977).

14. Sigmund Freud, "The Taboo of Virginity," *Standard Edition* 13, p. 193.

15. Simon Gaunt, *Gender and Genre in Medieval French Literature* (Cambridge: Cambridge University Press, 1995), p. 200.

16. See Carolyn Dinshaw's discussion in *Chaucer's Sexual Poetics* (Madison, WI: University of Wisconsin Press, 1989), pp. 15–17.

17. Levi-Strauss, "The Principle of Reciprocity" in *Elementary Structures of Kinship* (Oxford: Beacon, 1969), p. 496.

18. *Hali Meidhad*, ed. and trans. Bella Millett and Jocelyn Wogan Browne, *Medieval English Prose for Women from the Katherine Group and Ancrene Wisse* (Oxford: Oxford University Press, 1992), p. 33.

19. E. Jane Burns, *Bodytalk: When Women Speak in Old French Literature* (Philadelphia: University of Pennsylvania Press, 1993), pp. 7–9.

20. Serge Barret, "La belle Alise fête sa Sainte," *Le Pelerin* 5100, August 31, 1980, quoted in J. P. Clerc, "Le pèlerinage de sainte Reine après 1945" in *Reine au Mont Auxois*, p. 354. Translation is mine.

21. For many critics, this antifeminist and heterosexist impulse remains the defining feature of virgin martyr stories. See e.g. Kathleen Coyne Kelly, *Performing Virginity and Testing Chastity in the Middle Ages* (New York: Routledge, 2000), especially the final chapter; and Brigitte Cazelles, *The Lady As Saint: A Collection of French Hagiographic Romances of the Thirteenth Century* (Philadelphia: University of Pennsylvania Press, 1991), especially "Femininity Circumscribed."

22. Judith Butler, *Bodies that Matter: On the Discursive Limits of Sex* (Routledge: New York, 1993), p. 231. Another point of contact between queer identity and virgin identity lies in the creation of same-sex communities bound together by a shared desire; as Frederick S. Roden notes, "virginal purity, in devotion to the ambigendered body of Christ. . .may be read as a profoundly queer choice for religious"; "Two 'Sisters in Wisdom': Hildegard of Bingen, Christina Rossetti, and Feminist Theology" in *Hildegard of Bingen: A Book of Essays*, ed. Maud Burnett McInerney (New York: Garland Publishing, 1998), p. 235. See also Carolyn Dinshaw, *Getting Medieval: Sexualities and Communities, Pre- and Postmodern* (Durham: Duke University Press, 1999) on queer heterosexuality (pp. 12–13) and on Robert Gluck reading Margery Kempe (pp. 165–72).

23. On reduced opportunities for religious women in the later Middle Ages, see R. W. Southern, *Western Society and the Church in the Middle Ages* (London: Penguin, 1970; rpt. 1988), pp. 312–18; Margaret Wade Labarge, *A Small Sound of the Trumpet: Women in Medieval Life* (Boston: Beacon, 1986),

pp. 208–16; Alexandra Barrett, *Women's Writing in Middle English* (London: Longman, 1992), pp. 2–5.

Chapter 1   Strange Triangle: Tertullian, Perpetua, Thecla

1. References to Tertullian are to these editions, abbreviated as follows. *Against the Jews: Adversus Judaeos, Corpus Christianorum Series Latina* 2 (Turnhout: Brepols, 1954); *On the Soul: De Anima*, ed. and Italian trans. Martino Menghi (Venice: Marsilio, 1988); *On Baptism: Tertullian's Homily on Baptism*, ed. Ernest Evans (London: S.P.C.K., 1964); *Against Heretics: Traité de la prescription contre les hérétiques*, ed. R. F. Refoulé, *Sources Chrétiennes* 46 (Paris: Cerf, 1957); *Veiling of Virgins: Le Voile des Vierges: De virginibus velandis*, ed. Eva Schultz-Flügel, French trans. Paul Mattei, *Sources Chrétiennes* 424 (Paris: Cerf, 1997).

2. On Carthage and its rhetorical culture, see René Braun, "Aux origines de la Chrétienneté d'Afrique: un homme de combat, Tertullien" in *Approches de Tertullien* (Paris: Institut d'Etudes Augustiniennes, 1992), pp. 1–10; Elaine Fantham, *Roman Literary Culture from Cicero to Apuleius* (Baltimore: Johns Hopkins University Press, 1996), pp. 252–63.

3. On gender and late antique rhetoric, see Amy Richlin, "Gender and Rhetoric: Producing Manhood in the Schools" in *Roman Eloquence: Rhetoric in Society and Literature*, ed. William J. Dominik (London: Routledge, 1997), pp. 90–110, and especially Maud W. Gleason, *Making Men: Sophists and Self-Presentation in Ancient Rome* (Princeton: Princeton University Press, 1995). For Tertullian as a product of classic Roman rhetorical training, see Robert Dick Sider, *Ancient Rhetoric and the Art of Tertullian* (Oxford: Oxford University Press, 1971).

4. Bloch, *Medieval Misogyny*, pp. 97–98.

5. Tertullian, *Homily on Baptism*, ed. Ernest Evans (London: S.P.C.K., 1964), 1. This passage has been the subject of a good deal of debate, much of it concerning whether the "writings ascribed to Paul" should be identified with the *Acts of Paul* or some other early and apocryphal Pauline texts; see Stevan L. Davies, "Women, Tertullian and the Acts of Paul" and the "Response" by Thomas W. MacKay in *Semeia 38: The Apocryphal Acts of Apostles* (Decatur, GA: Scholars Press, 1986). Dennis Ronald MacDonald, *The Legend and the Apostle: The Battle for Paul in Story and Canon* (Philadelphia: Westminster Press, 1983) takes it for granted that Tertullian was familiar with some version of the *Acts of Paul* but insists that the people he was writing against may have been citing oral tradition rather than any written text (pp. 17–18). I am less concerned with the question of which text Tertullian may have known than with his reaction to the figure of Thecla in general.

6. Wilhelm Schneemelcher, ed., *Acts of Paul*, trans. R. Wilson (Cambridge: Lutterworth, 1991), p. 393n3.

7. Gillian Clark, *Women in Late Antiquity: Pagan and Christian Lifestyles* (Oxford: Clarendon, 1993), p. 128.

8. Epiphanius describes the Ophites as snake-handlers (*Panarion* 37, 5, 6–8). Irenaeus classifies the Cainites among those heretics who practice all kinds of

immorality as a form of purgation through experience (*Adv. Haer.* XXXI). These anti-heretical witnesses must be taken with a grain of salt. It is not clear what the Cainites actually preached or practiced, or even whether they were related to the Ophites.

9. The *Gospel of Philip*, associated with the Valentinian heresy, maintains "if one go down into the water and come up without having received anything and says 'I am a Christian' he has borrowed the name at interest" (64, 23–24, *Nag Hammadi Library in English*, ed. James M. Robinson, 3rd ed. (Leiden: E. J. Brill, 1988)), thus contrasting the dubious efficacy of such physical rituals with mystical baptism "in the light and the water," which is also conceived as a *hieros gamos* between "free men and virgins" (*Gospel of Philip* 69, 1–3). See also Brown, *Body and Society*, pp. 110–11. The Marcionites allowed women to baptize, to Tertullian's horror; see Walter Bauer, *Orthodoxy and Heresy in Earliest Christianity*, trans. Philadelphia Seminar on Christian Origins, ed. Robert A. Kraft and Gerhard Krodel (Philadelphia: Fortress, 1971), p. 42.

10. "Public disputation between friends on subtle intellectual questions was a pastime of the privileged, highly educated adult males who possessed the requisite leisure to examine proposed topics in the shady groves of the Academy. . ." Richard Lim, *Public Disputation, Power and Social Order in Late Antiquity* (Berkeley: University of California Press, 1995), p. 2.

11. "In one area alone, Tertullian let his imagination run wild. Sexual depravity (though only once, or perhaps never, homosexual vice) he attributed to all without exception. Carpocrates he hailed as a magician and fornicator, the artistic Hermogenes as an unrestrained libertine who seduced women more often than he painted them. . ." Timothy David Barnes, *Tertullian: A Historical and Literary Study* (Oxford: Clarendon, 1971), pp. 216–17. That Tertullian's accusations of sexual misbehavior among heretics were universally heterosexual merely underlines the fact that for him, women were the problem, both within the Catholic church and on its fringes.

12. Evans, ed., *Tertullian's Homily on Baptism*, p. 100n22.

13. The first modern editor of the text believed that Tertullian was the redactor: J. A. Robinson, *The Passion of St. Perpetua* (Cambridge: Cambridge University Press, 1891); Barnes concurs; Anne Jensen, *God's Self-Confident Daughters: Early Christianity and the Liberation of Women*, trans. O. C. Dean Jr. (Louisville, KY: Westminster John Knox Press, 1996) thinks it improbable; Brent Shaw, in "The Passion of Perpetua," *Past and Present* 139 (1993): p. 30 thinks the redactor is as likely as not to have been Tertullian. In any case, it is safe to say that the redactor was someone *like* Tertullian, probably even someone influenced by Tertullian.

14. References are to *Passio Sanctarum Perpetuae et Felicitatis* 2.3, ed. Herbert Musurillo, *The Acts of the Christian Martyrs* (Oxford: Clarendon, 1972).

15. Shaw suggests that Perpetua may have been familiar with the Greek novels (p. 9). Saturus, in his vision, sees Perpetua speaking Greek with others in heaven and shows no surprise, thus implying that she spoke Greek on earth as well (as many Carthaginians did). Peter Dronke argues that she may have

known Vergil; see *Women Writers of the Middle Ages from Perpetua to Marguerite Porete* (Cambridge: Cambridge University Press, 1984) p. 7. If it is reasonable to imagine that she may have been familiar with Greek Romances, surely it is at least as reasonable to suggest that she may also have been familiar with the *Apocryphal Acts of the Apostles*. For the possibility (unlikely, in my opinion) that the original language of Perpetua's text was Greek and not Latin, see G. W. Bowersock, *Martyrdom and Rome* (Cambridge: Cambridge University Press, 1995), pp. 32–34.

16. Joyce E. Salisbury, *Perpetua's Passion: The Death and Memory of a Young Roman Woman* (New York: Routledge, 1997), pp. 89–90.

17. On honor through debasement, and the significance of the term *domina*, see Shaw, "The Passion of Perpetua," pp. 6–7.

18. Compare the speech of Justin Martyr at his interrogation. Justin is as eager as Perpetua to die for his faith, but he can't resist twisting the words of his interrogator here and there. When asked whether "the Christians" meet regularly at his house, he replies "you can't imagine all of us would fit!" His attitude does him no good in any practical sense, but it allows him to score a few points before going down; he proves himself verbally more adept than his opponent. Perpetua is simply not interested in this kind of competition. *Acts of Justin and Companions* II.3, Musurillo, *Acts of the Christian Martyrs*, pp. 42–60.

19. Salisbury, *Perpetua*, p. 91; Dronke, *Women Writers*, p. 5.

20. The representation of Perpetua as a Bride of Christ, stereotypical in later lives of the virgin martyrs, may help to explain the text's complete silence on the subject of her husband. Dronke suggests that any references to Perpetua's husband "may have been excised at a later stage in the textual tradition at any time between 203 and the earliest extant MSS (ca. 900). This could have been, e.g., because a later reviser had in mind an idealized ascetic stereotype of women saints whose only thoughts near death were of God (a stereotype fulfilled par excellence by the virgin martyrs), and hence preferred to eliminate details about Pereptua's relations with her husband" (*Women Writers*, p. 282n3).

21. Salisbury, *Perpetua*, p. 109.

22. Dronke, *Women Writers*, p. 14.

23. Rosemary Rader, "The Martyrdom of Perpetua: A Protest Account of Third Century Christianity," in Patricia Wilson Kastner et al., *A Lost Tradition: Women Writers of the Early Church* (Lanham, MD: University Press of America, 1981), pp. 10–11.

24. Dronke, *Women Writers*, p. 15.

25. Tacitus, *Annals* 15.

26. See René Braun, *Approches de Tertullien: vingt-six éudes sur l'auteur et sur l'oeuvre (1955–1990)* (Paris: Institut d'études augustinennes, 1992), p. 246; Cecil M. Roebuck, *Prophecy in Carthage: Perpetua, Tertullian and Cyprian* (Cleveland: Pilgrim Press, 1992), pp. 15–16

27. I am inclined to accept the dating of Schulz-Flügel here, rather than that of Barnes, who would date the text as much as five years earlier.

28. The literature on I Cor. 11:3–16 is enormous and I cannot pretend to survey it all here. Some of the major points in the debate, however, concern the possibility that the passage may be interpolated (G. W. Trompf, "On Attitudes Towards Women in Paul and Paulinist Literature: I Cor. 11:3–16 and Its Context," *Catholic Biblical Quarterly* 42 (1980)), whether Paul is talking about headdresses or hairstyles (J. Murphy-O'Connor, "Sex and Logic in I Cor. 11:2–16," *Catholic Biblical Quarterly* 50 (1980) and "I Corinthians 11:2–16 Once Again," *Catholic Biblical Quarterly* 50 (1988)), contemporary veiling practices among Jews, Christians, and Pagans, and the nature of religious practice at Corinth (D. R. MacDonald, "Ritual, Sex and Veils at Corinth" in *There is No Male and Female: The Fate of a Dominical Saying in Paul and Gnosticism* (Philadelphia: Fortress, 1987) and "Corinthian Veils and Gnostic Androgynes"). On veils in Paul and Tertullian, see Mary Rose D'Angelo, "Veils, Virgins, and the Tongues of Men and Angels: Women's Heads in Early Christianity" in *Off with Her Head! The Denial of Women's Identity in Myth, Religion and Culture*, ed. Howard Eilberg-Schwartz and Wendy Doniger (Berkeley: University of California Press, 1995), pp. 131–64.

29. See John P. Meier, "On the Veiling of Hermeneutics," *Catholic Biblical Quarterly* 40 (1978) for the argument that Paul may indeed have meant exactly what Tertullian thought he did. J. D. BeDuhn, " 'Because of the Angels': Unveiling Paul's Anthropology in I Corinthians 11," *Journal of Biblical Literature* 118:2 (1999): 295–320 argues, "on account of the angels" refers instead to a gnostic Jewish tradition according to which the angels, and not God, are accountable for the creation of Eve and thus of sexual difference.

30. Meier, "On the Veiling of Hermeneutics," p. 218. On the nonparticipation of Jewish women in cult practice, see also Annie Jaubert, "Le Voile des Femmes," *New Testament Studies* 18 (1971–72): p. 424.

31. Plutarch, *Moralia* 404e, 405c. Ariadne Staples argues that the Vestals functioned as receptacles for a whole complex of political, religious, and social ideologies; while they did not prophesy, their bodies, like those of Christian virgins, could be conceived as containing a highly charged and highly abstract significance. See *From Good Goddess to Vestal Virgins: Sex and Category in Roman Religion* (London: Routledge, 1998), pp. 133–38.

32. Elisabeth Schüssler Fiorenza, *But She Said: Feminist Practices of Biblical Interpretation* (Boston: Beacon, 1992), p. 169.

33. On Montanist traces in *On the Veiling of Virgins*, see Jensen, *God's Self-Confident Daughters*, pp. 144–45.

34. Jensen, *God's Self-Confident Daughters*, p. 162.

35. Cited in Jensen, *God's Self-Confident Daughters*, p. 161.

36. Jensen, *God's Self-Confident Daughters*, p. 146.

37. On this passage, see Kathleen Coyne Kelly, *Performing Virginity and Testing Chastity in the Middle Ages* (New York: Routledge, 2000). Kelly argues, "the consecrated male virgin represents a new ontological category with which Rome had had little previous experience, and for which Latin had no words. By calling his readers' attention to the fact, Tertullian reproduces virginity as a naturalized feminine attribute. . ." (pp. 91–92). This is true

enough, although I would argue that Tertullian ends by denying that virgins of either sex constitute a meaningful ontological category at all. On the unnaturalness of eunuchs, both born and created, see Gleason, pp. 46–48.

38. Susanna Elm, "Montanist Oracles," *Searching the Scriptures v. II: A Feminist Commentary*, ed. Elisabeth Schüssler Fiorenza (New York: Crossroad, 1994), p. 131.

39. Jensen, *God's Self Confident Daughters*, p. 177.

40. See Schneemelcher's introduction to the *Acts of Paul* in *New Testament Apocrypha*, v. 2 for an account of the manuscript tradition. The earliest surviving more or less complete witness to the *Acts of Thecla* is a Coptic MS of the sixth century. There are also fragments preserved in a leaf from a fourth- or fifth-century codex (Papyrus Oxyrhynchus 1602). I follow the practice of Davies and others in referring to the *Acts of Thecla*, although the text is included with the *Acts of Paul*.

41. Stevan L. Davies, *The Revolt of the Widows: The Social World of the Apocryphal Acts* (Carbondale, IL: Southern Illinois University Press, 1980), p. 60.

42. There is no possibility of identifying the author of the text with any security. To begin with, what we call "the text" derives from manuscripts written some three centuries after the text with which Tertullian was familiar, and in a different language. Scheemelcher asserts that "the linguistic form of the text today before us is the work of the author of the AP" (p. 332). This does not mean that the "original" text might not have been the work of a woman, whether literate author or storyteller (see MacDonald for conjecture as to the origin of the Thecla story in women's oral tradition). With these caveats concerning absolute proof in mind, I am more than willing to see the narrative as one composed by women and for women.

43. References to the *Acts of Peter* are to J. K. Elliott, *The Apocryphal New Testament* (Oxford: Clarendon, 1993).

44. Lim, *Public Disputation*, p. 11.

45. James A. Francis, *Subversive Virtue: Asceticism and Authority in the Second Century Pagan World* (University Park: Pennsylvania State University Press, 1995), pp. 6–9.

46. Hypatia was a mathematician, wore a philosopher's cloak, and was supposed to have both pursued and been pursued by her male students. See Maria Dzielska, *Hypatia of Alexandria*, trans. F. Lyra (Cambridge, MA: Harvard University Press, 1995).

47. Cited in Antti Arjava, *Women and Law in Late Antiquity* (Oxford: Clarendon, 1996), p. 245. There were female litigants, but they were represented by men. See Jill Harries, *Law and Empire in Late Antiquity* (Cambridge: Cambridge University Press, 1999), p. 180.

48. Clark, *Women in Late Antiquity*, p. 119.

49. This Paul is not, of course, the "real" Paul of the Epistles. He may not even be the Paul of the *Acta Pauli*, if the *Acta Theclae* is an interpolation with a different author. In fact, he often appears to be the Paul of the deutero-Pauline epistles, manipulated and transformed by the narrator/author to

demonstrate just how completely post-Pauline Christianity is failing women. See Davies, *The Revolt of the Widows*, pp. 50–56 and Ann G. Brock, "Genre of the Acts of Paul: One Tradition Enhancing Another," *Apocrypha* 5 (1994): 19–136.

50. Brock (p. 130) notes that in the *Acts of Paul* generally, 99% of direct discourse is spoken by men; in the *Acts of Thecla*, only 59% is male. She sees these figures as supporting the thesis of feminine authorship.

51. Davies is concerned that these bulls could only be the product of a depraved mind, and works hard to reconcile this pathology with his imagined female author. The truth is that, while it may indeed be depraved to imagine such a torture, the pathology that could do so was cultural, not personal. Audiences in the large cities of the Roman empire were accustomed to witnessing events that combined sex and violence in variations that are nearly unbelievable to us. Perpetua and Felicity were doomed to be gored to death by a heifer as a titillating change from what was apparently the more habitual form of execution. Apuleius' *Metamorphoses* describes the fate reserved for a female poisoner, who was to be raped to death by a wild donkey. On sadistic voyeurism in the Roman arena, see Carlin A. Barton, *The Sorrows of the Ancient Romans: The Gladiator and the Monster* (Princeton: Princeton University Press, 1993).

52. Charlotte Roueché, "Acclamations in the Later Roman Empire: New Evidence from Aphrodisias," *Journal of Roman Studies* 74 (1984): 182.

53. Roueché, "Acclamations," pp. 184–85.

54. Roueché, "Acclamations," p. 188.

55. Roueché, "Acclamations," p. 194. The acclamation of Thecla may be compared with a fifth-century inscription published by Roueché, which was found at Aphrodisias, a city in modern Turkey not far from Pisidian Antioch where the martyrdom of Thecla took place. It begins with the phrase "God is one" goes on to identify the subject of the acclamation, a certain Albinus, builder of various civic monuments, and ends "The whole city, having acclaimed (you) with one voice, says: 'He who forgets you, Albinus clarissimus, does not know God.'"

56. *Vie et Miracles de Sainte Thècle: Texte Grec, Traduction et Commentaire*, Gilbert Dagron, ed. and trans. (Brussels: Bollandists, 1978), 12.1–2.

57. Dagron, *Vie et Miracles*, 13.3.

58. "Dans la Vie Thècle enseigne et baptise...manière de ne pas démentir une tradition, tout en affirmant qu'elle ne fonde pas un droit." Dagron, *Vie et Miracles*, p. 42.

Chapter 2 Androgynous Virgins and the Threat of Rape in the Fourth Century

1. References (as *Martyrs*) are to Eusebius, *Martyrs of Palestine* 8.5, in *Historia Ecclesiastica*, ed. with French trans. Gustave Bardy, 4 vols., *Sources Chretiennes* (Paris: Cerf, 1952–60).

2. G. E. M. de Ste Croix argued that the Great Persecution wasn't so great after all; see "Aspects of the Great Persecution," *HThR* 47 (1954): 75–113. T. D. Barnes, *Constantine and Eusebius* (Cambridge, MA: Harvard University Press, 1981) believes that de Ste Croix underestimates the body count. Certainly Christians in the hundreds died between 303 and 312 in the East as a result of edicts promulgated by Diocletian; many more were tortured and released. See Barnes, *Constantine and Eusebius*, pp. 20–24 and 148–63.

3. On the criteria for establishing historical veracity in accounts of martyrdom, the best is still Hippolyte Delehaye, *Les Passions des Martyrs et les Genres Littéraires* (Brussels: Bollandistes, 1920; rpt. 1966).

4. That Eusebius does not refer to any women who have been raped, but only to those who have been threatened with rape is probably due to a desire to spare their surviving relatives. "Judicial" rape, in the sense of rape sanctioned by authority as an instrument of terror, is a perennial atrocity. See e.g. Tacitus's account of the rape of Sejanus's virgin daughter, *Annals* VI.v.9, and Kelly's discussion, *Performing Virginity*, pp. 48–49. Kelly notes that in hagiographical (as opposed to historical) narratives, "rape is precisely the story that is suppressed" (p. 42).

5. Influential examples of transvestite rhetoric include Jerome's insistence that the woman who leaves her husband for the sake of her Savior "will cease to be a woman and will be called man" (*Adv. Jov.*, PL 23: 533) or Gregory of Nyssa's doubt concerning whether his sister Macrina can still be accurately called a woman, given the degree to which she has surpassed her "nature" (*Life of Macrina*, ed. with French trans. P. Maraval, *Sources chrétiennes* 178 (Paris: Cerf, 1971)). On femaleness as a transcendable defect see, among many others, Elizabeth A. Clarke, *Jerome, Chrysostom and Friends, Studies in Women and Religion* 2 (1979), p. 55; Jane Tibbets Schulenburg, *Forgetful of Their Sex: Female Sanctity and Society ca. 500–1100* (Chicago: University of Chicago Press, 1998), pp. 155–66.

6. For a polemical view of Christians as persecutors, see Ramsay MacMullen, *Christianity and Paganism in the Fourth to Eighth Centuries* (New Haven: Yale University Press, 1997), especially chapter 1.

7. References to Jerome's letters are to *Lettres*, ed. with French trans. Jérome Labourt (Paris: Les Belles Lettres, 1949–63).

8. Ambrose appealed to this law in his attempt to avoid being made bishop of Milan; as governor of Liguria he had presided over judicial torture, Neil B McLynn, *Ambrose of Milan: Church and Court in a Christian Capital* (Berkeley: University of California Press, 1994), p. 45.

9. "Even Euripides' Hippolytus, the most famous sexual abstinent of classical literature, when he says his body is pure of sexual contact. . .boasts his soul is 'a maiden.' His transgressive withdrawal from the life of a citizen finds expression in the extraordinary description of his soul in such perverse gender terms." Simon Goldhill, *Foucault's Virginity: Ancient Erotic Fiction and the History of Sexuality* (Cambridge: Cambridge University Press, 1995), p. 22.

10. Michel Foucault quoting Achilles Tatius in *The Care of the Self: The History of Sexuality*, vol. 3, trans. Robert Hurley (New York: Random House, 1986), p. 231.

11. Is it a deliberate irony on Foucault's part to include the only discussion of female virginity under the general heading of "Boys"? Goldhill suspects not (p. 102) and I am inclined to agree. Foucault's failure to include the female in his *History of Sexuality* is fairly notorious. See Page Du Bois, "The Subject in Antiquity after Foucault" and Amy Richlin, "Foucault's History of Sexuality: A Useful Theory for Women?" in *Rethinking Sexuality: Foucault and Classical Antiquity*, ed. David H. J. Larmour, Paul Allen Miller, and Charles Platter (Princeton: Princeton University Press, 1998).

12. Soranus, *Gunaikeôn Pathôn* A, 5 27–34. trans. Soranos d'Ephese, *Maladies des Femmes* (Paris: Budé, 1988), pp. 14–15. Giulia Sissa uses this passage to argue that the Greeks did not recognize the existence of the hymen at all; see *Greek Virginity*, trans. Arthur Goldhammer (Cambridge, MA: Harvard University Press, 1990), pp. 105–23. See also the first chapter ("Hymenologies," pp. 25–28 and 150n67) of Kelly's *Performing Virgins* on this much disputed passage; Kelly notes that when "Soranus denies that the word *hymena* [*sic*] denotes a specific, discrete part of female anatomy that functions as a seal or a veil. . .he does not identify a structure so much as he describes a site" (p. 26). For Roman writers, the hymen would increasingly become if not structural, at least constitutive of virginity.

13. Aristotle, *Historia Animalium* III.13, ed. and trans. A. L. Peck (Cambridge, MA: Harvard University Press, 1965), pp. 210–12.

14. Aline Rousselle, *Porneia: On Desire and the Body in Antiquity*, trans. Felicia Pheasant (Oxford: Basil Blackwell, 1988), p. 27. Brent D. Shaw, "The Age of Roman Girls at Marriage: Some Reconsiderations," *Journal of Roman Studies* (1987) argues for a higher age for the general (nonaristocratic) population.

15. Doctors were cautioned against asking questions inappropriate to sex: "they also make mistakes by not learning the apparent cause through accurate questioning, but they proceed to heal as though they were dealing with men's diseases." Hippocrates, quoted in Lesley Ann Dean-Jones, *Women's Bodies in Classical Greek Science* (Oxford: Clarendon, 1994), p. 112.

16. Dean-Jones (pp. 31–36) argues that some male physicians had access to some women for some complaints, but also notes that in both Greece and Rome there were female doctors as well as midwives, who presumably specialized in treating women. Soranus identifies modesty as a major concern in his book, which was at least partially intended for the education of female medical practitioners: "the midwife must take care not to stare too fixedly at the genitals of a woman in labor, in case she might out of shame contract her body"; *Gunaikeôn Pathôn* B 1. See also Jackson, *Doctors and Diseases*, p. 99.

17. Soranus, *Gunaikeôn Pathôn* A 9. See also Jody Rubin Pinault, "The Medical Case for Virginity in the Early Second Century C.E.: Soranus of Ephesus, *Gynecology* I.32," *Helios* 19 (1992): 123–39.

18. In entries for *virgo* and *virginitas*, the Oxford Latin Dictionary does not even admit the possibility of these words being applied to men; only *virgineus* is cited as having a possibly masculine meaning, when applied to the husband

(*virgineus vir*) of a very young woman who had never previously been married; even in this case, the quality is obviously transmitted from her to him.

19. On Methodius's extremely sketchy biography, see Musurillo, *St. Methodius: The Symposium, A Treatise on Chastity* (London: Longmans, Green and Co., 1958), pp. 3–5 and T. D. Barnes, "Methodius, Maximian and Valentinus," *Journal of Theological Studies*, n.s. 30 (1979).

20. References are to *Methode d'Olympe, Le Banquet*, ed. Musurillo, French trans. V-H. Debidour (Paris: Cerf, 1963). In Greek, the word for virtue can also function as a feminine proper name, and indeed it does in the *Odyssey*. The English "virtue" derives from the Latin *virtus*, which appears etymologically if not grammatically masculine, containing the word *vir*, man, a fact that Roman and Medieval etymologists never forgot. Debidour's translation uses *Vertu*, thus masculinizing the Greek. Except for occasional differences such as preserving the Greek spelling of Euboulion and other names and using "human" in preference to "man" when Methodius uses a Greek neuter, I follow Musurillo's translation in *St. Methodius*.

21. Epiphanius refers to him as "Methodius, also known as Euboulios." *Adv. Haer* 64, 63, cited in Musurillo, *Methode d'Olympe*. Euboulion and Gregorion are technically Greek neuters operating as feminine diminutives.

22. Musurillo, *St. Methodius*, p. 184n1.

23. Both Musurillo (p. 23) and Brown see the lady of Telmessos as a member or perhaps the founder of a community of virgin women directed by Methodius. Brown conflates characters and author rather misleadingly when he describes the virgins of the *Symposium* "gathered around their spiritual father, a discreet and learned priest" (*Body*, p. 185).

24. Musurillo notes several parallels to Origen in this speech without drawing this conclusion. See p. 199, notes 23, 24, and 26.

25. Gleason, *Making Men*, p. xxii. Musurillo (p. 219n1) gives a more conventional definition of the term, as "the general education given at the ancient Greek universities (Alexandria, Athens, Antioch, etc.) prior to professional studies" without noting that such an education was normally closed to women.

26. The text never represents women in general as temptresses, although it does on one occasion qualify men in general as dangerous to virgins: "Far better would it be for me to die than to betray my marriage bed for you, women mad men, and suffer God's eternal justice in fiery penalties. Save me, O Christ, from these men!" (Methodius, *Symposium*, Hymn 16).

27. Paphnutius, *Histories of the Monks of Upper Egypt and Life of Onnophrius*, trans. Tim Vivian (Kalamazoo, MI: Cistercian Publications, 1993), p. 76.

28. Paphnutius, *Histories of the Monks*, pp. 145–46.

29. John Cassian, *De Institutiones coenobitorum*, ed. J. C. Guy, *Sources chrétiennes* vol. 109 (Paris: Cerf, 1965), preface, p. 2. References to Cassian's *Institutes* are to this edition; references to the *Conferences* are to *Collationes Patrum*, ed. and French trans. E. Pichéry, *Sources Chrétiennes* vols. 42, 54, 64 (Paris: Cerf, 1955).

30. One of Cassian's interlocutors in the *Conferences* seems to imply that Christ was the only man never to have experienced ejaculation. *Coll.* 22,.9.

31. Mary Douglas, *Purity and Danger: An Analysis of Concepts of Pollution and Taboo* (Harmondsworth: Penguin, 1970), p. 126.

32. On interiority and exteriority, see Philip Rousseau, "Cassian, Contemplation and the Coenobitic Life," *Journal of Ecclesiastical History* 26. 2 (1975): 120–22.

33. References to Augustine are to the following editions. *City: De Civitate Dei*, ed. George E. McCracken (Cambridge, MA: Harvard University Press, 1957–72); *Holy Virginity: De Sancta virginitate*, ed. and trans. P. G. Walsh (Oxford: Clarendon, 2001); *Monks, De opera monachorum*, ed. I. Zycha, *Corpus Scriptorum Ecclesiasticorum Latinorum* 41 (1900).

34. Brown, *Body*, p. 271.

35. Brown, *Body*, p. 271. Brown argues that without the movement toward sexual renunciation and corresponding exaltation of virginity, which characterizes the early centuries of Christianity, it would have remained a religion founded upon severe monogamy, absolutely patriarchal like Islam or Judaism. The development of the ascetic ideal created an avenue for women to claim a spiritual authority for themselves and on behalf of others (pp. 207–08). While Brown rightly emphasizes the degree of resistance to this ideal on the part of Late Antique householders, he tends to overlook the profound ambivalence expressed by the Fathers of the Church themselves toward consecrated women.

36. Averil Cameron, "Virginity as Metaphor: Women and the Rhetoric of Early Christianity," *History as Text: The Writing of Ancient History*, ed. A. Cameron (London: Duckworth, 1989), pp. 185–205.

37. J. N. D. Kelly's biography, *Jerome, His Life, Writings and Controversies* (London: Duckworth, 1975) is an engaging introduction, upon which I have relied for the outlines of Jerome's life.

38. Jerome makes the point about heresy as delicately as he can in the letter to Demetrias, an heiress who became famous overnight by professing virginity instead of making a politically advantageous marriage, which would have done much to restore the fortunes of her family after the sack of Rome by Alaric and the Goths. Demetrias had also received a letter of congratulation and instruction from the heretic Pelagius, then at the height of his influence, and Jerome was very much aware of this. In letters to others, he was less reserved.

39. Brown, *Body*, p. 356.

40. References (as *On Virgins*) are to *De Virginibus Libri Tres, Patrologia Latina* 16, pp. 197–244; Letters: *Epistulae, Patrologia Latina* vol. 16.

41. McLynn, *Ambrose of Milan*, p. 56.

42. Paulinus, *Life of Ambrose*, p. 7.

43. McLynn (pp. 53–68) gives a compelling account of the role of the *De Virginibus* in the establishment of Ambrose's episcopate; for the identification of the virgin body with the social body of the church, see Brown, *Body*, pp. 342–65.

44. A hexameter inscription in Agnes's honor by Pope Damasus survives from the wall of her basilica in Rome on the Via Nomentana. For the sources of the legend, see Anne-Marie Palmer, *Prudentius On the Martyrs* (Oxford: Clarendon, 1989) pp. 250–55.

45. It is not clear exactly how Soteris was related to Ambrose and Marcellina. See McLynn, *Ambrose of Milan*, pp. 34–35.

46. References are to Prudentius, *Persistephanon*, ed. H. J. Thomson, 2 vols. (Cambridge, MA: Harvard University Press, 1974).

47. See Vergil, *Aeneid* 4 and perhaps *Propertius* 4.7, in which the poet's recently dead mistress comes to him in a dream, her dress charred from the funeral fire but her hair still untouched. For Prudentius as a poet in the classical tradition, see Palmer, *Prudentius on the Martyrs*, Martha Malamud, *A Poetics of Transformation: Prudentius and Classical Mythology* (Ithaca, NY: Cornell University Press, 1989) and Michael Roberts, *Poetry and the Cult of the Martyrs: The* Liber Peristephanon *of Prudentius* (Ann Arbor, MI: University of Michigan Press, 1993).

48. Bloch, *Medieval Misogyny*, p. 109.

49. Bloch, *Medieval Misogyny*, p. 109.

50. Kelly notes that ". . .the figure of the virgin—female and feminine—often functions as an icon of normative (and compulsory) heterosexual behavior in contemporary culture" (*Performing Virginity*, p. 122); she sees virginity in the Middle Ages as operating almost exclusively as a repressive force. I will argue that the same icon could be turned to operate against both patriarchy and the heterosexual imperative.

51. Bloch, *Medieval Misogyny*, pp. 110–11.

52. See F. Martroye, "L'Affaire Indicia: une sentence de saint Ambroise," *Mélanges Paul Fournier* (Paris: n.p., 1929), pp. 503–10.

53. The phrase is that of William E. Conolly, who sees the double-bind as characteristic of the "Augustinian Imperative," a paradox that, e.g., insists that consecrated virgins must simultaneously pay no heed to their appearance and yet take pains that their hair be neither too fastidiously dressed nor too dishevelled. *The Augustinian Imperative: A Reflection on the Politics of Morality* (London: Sage, 1993), p. 69.

54. Georges Bataille quoting De Sade, *Erotism, Death and Sensuality*, trans. Mary Dalwood (San Francisco: City Lights, 1986), p. 11.

55. Andrea Dworkin, "Sexual Economics: The Terrible Truth," *Letters from a War Zone* (New York: Lawrence Hill, 1993), p. 119.

56. On virginity as an element in the enforcement of compulsory heterosexuality, see Kelly, *Performing Virginity*, p. 13 and especially the final chapter, "Multiple Virgins and Contemporary Virginities."

Chapter 3   From the Sublime to the Ridiculous in the Works of Hrotsvitha

1. Parenthetical references to Hrotsvitha's works will be abbreviated as follows. Pref I: Praefatio I, the preface to the Legends; Pref II: Praefatio II, the

preface to the Dramas; Agnes: *Passio Agnetis*; ACH: *Passio sanctarum virginum Agapis, Chioniae et Hirenae*; FHC: *Passio sanctarum virginum Fidei, Spei et Karitatis*. References are to *Hrotsvithae Opera*, ed. Helene Homeyer (Paderborn: Ferdinand Schöningh, 1970).

2. Quintilian, *De Inst.* 6.3.17, 11.3.30.

3. Gregory of Tours, *Life of St Martin*, trans. Raymond van Dam, *Saints and their Miracles in Late Antique Gaul* (Princeton: Princeton University Press, 1993), p. 201.

4. Dronke, *Women Writers*, pp. 65–66; Katharina M. Wilson, *Hrotsvit of Gandersheim: The Ethics of Authorial Stance* (Leiden: Brill, 1988), pp. 4–8.

5. Jerome, *Letter* 22, 30.

6. Prudentius, *Praefatio* 42.

7. Aldhelm composes a sort of anti-invocation to the Muses early in the *Carmen* (ll. 22–30) in which he cites Vergil in order to declare that he will not ask for inspiration from the same sources as the Roman poet, eschewing the Muses for the inspiration of the Word of God. Parenthetical references to Aldhelm's work are abbreviated as *Letter* (for the *De Virginitate Prosa*) and *Poem* (for the *De Virginitate Carmen*); the edition is Rufus Ehwald, *Aldhelmi Opera Omnia, Monumenta Germaniae Historica, Auctores Antiquissimi* 15 (Berlin: 1919). My translations of Aldhelm are much influenced by Lapidge and Rosier, *Aldhelm: The Poetic Works* (Cambridge: D. S. Brewer, 1985), and by Lapidge and Michael Herren, *Aldhelm, The Prose Works* (Cambridge: D. S. Brewer, 1979).

8. Bede, *Historia Ecclesiastica* 5.18.

9. The earliest manuscript is Wirceburgensis M.th.f.21. See Lapidge and Rosier, introduction to *Aldhelm: The Poetic Works*, p. 2.

10. The association of bees with both asexual reproduction (and thus chastity) and poetry derives from Vergil's Fourth *Georgic*, in which the beekeeper Aristaeus regains his bees by doing penance for the deaths of Orpheus and Eurydice.

11. Aldhelm's catalog of male virgins is not unique, in spite of Kelly's claim to the contrary (". . .without precedent. . .Aldhelm includes a catalogue of male virgins," *Performing Virginity*, p. 95). In fact, Aldhelm's catalog is derived from Jerome's *Against Jovinian*, which includes most of the same Biblical examples (Elijah, Elisha, Daniel, Joshua, Jeremiah, John the Baptist, and John the Evangelist (*Adv. Jov.* I, 16–26)). Aldhelm continues this list into his own period.

12. Bloch, *Medieval Misogyny*, p. 62.

13. See Ovid, *Metamorphoses* 5, pp. 395–401.

14. Malchus is one of the rare *exempla* who is dropped in the poetic recension of the text, which in other ways mirrors the proportions of virgins and martyrs I have described above quite closely. The *Poem* also replaces the lecture on feminine clothing with an allegorical struggle between the virtues and the vices.

15. The same close association of virginity and martyrdom in the case of women is evident in the *Martyrologium* of Hrabanus Maurus, the Carolingian Abbot

of Fulda (Migne, *Patrologia Latina* v. 110). Hrabanus's text is somewhat resistant to counting games since he often lists a martyr several times, giving birthdays as well as death days in some cases (Thecla, for reasons that escape me, occurs three times) and because he often lists anonymous groups. Should the seven holy virgins of Syrmio "who earned the crown together" (April) be identified with the six holy virgins of Syrmio mentioned in May? Did one get lost between the months? Even the most conservative of calculations, counting as virgin only those whom Hrabanus explicitly identifies as such, suggests that slightly more than 50% of the women mentioned in the *Martyrologium* were virgins. My strong suspicion is that many others, about whom Hrabanus gives no details, should also be included in this figure, which would then be closer to 60% or 70%.

16. On the distinction, often not absolute, between the kind of institution characterized as canonical and that conceived of as Benedictine, see Suzanne Fonay Wemple, "Monastic Life of Women from the Merovingians to the Ottonians," in *Hrotsvit of Gandersheim: Rara Avis in Saxonia? A Collection of Essays*, ed. Katharina M. Wilson (Ann Arbor: MARC, 1987), pp. 39–42.

17. Wemple, "Monastic Life," p. 42.

18. Feruccio Bertini, *Il "Teatro" di Rosvita con un saggio di traduzione e di interpretazione del Callimaco* (Genoa: Tilgher, 1979), pp. 9–10.

19. Bertini, *Rosvita*, p. 10.

20. He may have chosen her over his Burgundian mother, Adelheid, and his Greek wife, Theophano, because she was German. See Jo Ann McNamara and Suzanne Wemple, "The Power of Women through the Family in Medieval Europe 500–1100," Erler and Kolaleski, *Women and Power in the Middle Ages*, p. 94.

21. Edmond-René Labande, "Mirabilia mundi: Essai sur la personnalité d'Otton III," *Cahiers de Civilization Mediévale* 6:3 (1963): 302–03. Translation is mine.

22. Theophano was not the only person at the Ottonian court who could speak and read Greek, although her husband never learned the language; Liutprand served as an ambassador to Constantinople and drops Greek tags into his *Antapodosis* for effect; Gerberga knew Greek, her son Otto III had a Greek tutor, and it is not unreasonable to suppose that Theophano's daughter, Sophia, who was educated at Gandersheim in the 980s, did too. See Bertini, *Rosvita*, p. 15.

23. See Homeyer's apparatus for an extensive comparison. It is worth noting that the fragments from the *Peristephanon* do not necessarily derive from *Per.* 14, the legend of Agnes; some of the closest correspondences are recollected from other poems. *Hrotsvitha's omniparens verbi genitor mundique creator* (*Agnes* 373) e.g., reprises a line from *Peristephanon* 13 (Cyprian): *omnipotens genitor. . .et creator orbis*. This suggests a broad familiarity with Prudentius rather than a straightforward recapitulation of his version of the story.

24. Pseudo-Ambrose, Epistle I, *Patrologia Latina* 3: 735–42. While I tend to agree with the conclusions Elizabeth Petroff's draws concerning the value of heroic virginity in the *Legends*, she seems to me to overstate the alterations

Hrotsvitha makes to her source. Rather, it is Hrotsvitha's choice of this particular source in preference to others with which she was familiar that is particularly significant. See Petroff "Eloquence and Heroic Virginity in Hrotsvit's Verse Legends," *Body and Soul: Essays on Medieval Women and Mysticism* (Oxford: Oxford University Press, 1994), pp. 91–93.

25. Pseudo-Ambrose, *Epistle* 1:3.

26. The inhabitants of mixed institutions like Gandersheim might choose to live as *virgines velatae,* "veiled virgins," following the stricter Benedictine rule, or *virgines non velatae,* "unveiled virgins" according to the Canonical rule (Bertini, *Rosvita* 10).

27. Wilson argues convincingly for Hrotsvitha's very medieval understanding of Terence, which differs enormously from the understanding of twentieth-century classical scholars. See *Ethics of Authorial Stance,* especially chapters 4 and 5. Homeyer's apparatus points out many echoes of Terence, some of which, however, are less than convincing.

28. I follow the practice of Dronke and Wilson, giving the plays their original titles rather than the more familiar ones; thus, *Agapes, Chionia and Hirena* rather than *Dulcitius. Faith, Hope and Charity* is usually called *Sapientia,* after the mother in the play.

29. Katharina Wilson, trans., *The Dramas of Hrotsvit of Gandersheim* (Saskatoon, SA: Peregrina, 1985), p. 7.

30. On the sources, see Homeyer, *Opera,* pp. 350–52, and Adele Simonetti, "Le fonti agiografiche di due drammi di Rosvita," *Studia Medievale* 30.2 (1989): 661–95. Simonetti notes the invention of Antiochus, who is mentioned only in passing in the source (p. 669).

31. Alcuin Blamires, *The Case for Women in Medieval Culture* (Oxford: Clarendon, 1977), p. 158.

32. *Passio SS Agapes, Chioniae et Irenes,* AASS April, v. 10 (Paris/Rome, 1866), 244–50. Musurillo considers the account to be based in fact. See his introduction to *Acts of the Christian Martyrs,* pp. xii, xlii–xliii.

33. *Passio SS Agapes, Chioniae et Irenes,* p. 248.

34. *Passio SS Agapes, Chioniae et Irenes,* p. 248.

35. On the Satanic imagery and the motif of the kitchen as Hell, see Sandro Sticca, "Hrotsvitha's Dulcitius and Christian Symbolism," *Mediaeval Studies* 32 (1970): 108–27. The kitchen is also the location of much foolery and plotting by slaves in Roman Comedy.

36. Blamires, *Case for Women,* p. 155n9.

37. For the adventures of Adelheid, see *Gesta Ottonis,* ll. 467–665 and Wilson, *Ethics,* pp. 21–22.

38. K. J. Leyser, *Rule and Conflict in Early Medieval Society: Ottonian Saxony* (Bloomington: Indiana University Press, 1979), p. 50.

39. On Sophia, see Thangmar, *Vita Bernwardi,* ed. Georg Pertz, *Monumenta Germaniae Historiae* 4 for a hostile contemporary view; Labande, "Mirabilia mundi," pp. 303–04, 455–56; John W. Bernhardt, *Itinerant Kingship and Royal Monasteries in Early Medieval Germany* (Cambridge: Cambridge University Press, 1993) pp. 150–55; and Joseph S. Tunison, *Dramatic Traditions of the Dark*

Ages (Chicago: University of Chicago Press), pp. 156–62. Tunison argues that Hrotsvitha and Sophia were "contemporary as nuns" (p. 162) although this is by no means certain and there was in any case at least thirty-five years between them.

40. Jo Ann McNamara and Suzanne Wemple, "The Power of Women through the Family in Medieval Europe 500–1100," ed. Erler and Kowaleski, *Women and Power in the Middle Ages*, pp. 96–97.

Chapter 4   A Chorus of Virgins: Hildegard's *Symphonia*

1. References to Hildegard's works are abbreviated as follows, and are to the editions cited here. *Letter*: Epistolarium Hildegardis, ed. L.Van Acker, *Corpus Christianorum Continuatio Medievalis* 91–91a (Turnhout: Brepols, 1991, 1993). *Scivias: Hildegardis Scivias*, ed. Adelgund Fuhrkotter and Angela Carlevaris, *Corpus Christianorum Continuatio Medievalis* 43, 43a (Turnhout: Brepols, 1978). *Symphonia: Symphonia armonie celestium*, ed. and trans. Barbara Newman (Ithaca, NY: Cornell University Press, 1988); I have used Newman's numbering of the songs but translations are my own. *Life: Vita Sanctae Hildegardis*, PL 197. *Causes and Cures: Causae et Curae*, ed. P. Kaiser (Lipsia:Teubner, 1903). *Ordo: Ordo Virtutum*, ed. Peter Dronke, *Nine Medieval Latin Plays* (Cambridge: Cambridge University Press, 1994).

2. Abelard, Letter 8 to Heloise, *Lettres Complètes d'Abélard et d'Héloise*, ed. M Gréard (Paris: Garnier, 1904), p. 261.

3. On this kind of translation see Barbara Newman, *Sister of Wisdom: St Hildegard's Theology of the Feminine* (Berkeley: University of California Press, 1987), p. 222. There appears to be no distinction, for Hildegard, between the magical operation of symbolic language, its devotional function, and its literary function.

4. On *viriditas* as the energy of nature, linked to female fertility, see Heinrich Schipperges, *Hildegard of Bingen: Healing and the Nature of the Cosmos*, trans. John A. Broadwin (Princeton: Markus Wiener, 1998), pp. 66–68. For *viriditas* as a "transcendental attribute of being" see Helen J. John, "Hildegard of Bingen: A New Medieval Philosopher?" in Cecile J. Tougas and Sara Ebenreck, *Presenting Women Philosophers* (Philadelphia: Temple University Press, 2000), p. 34.

5. Newman, *Symphonia*, p. 304.

6. See Michela Pereira, "Maternità e sessualità in Ildegarda di Bingen: Proposte di lettura," *Quaderni Storici* 44 *Parto e Maternità, momenti della biografia femminile* (Ancona: Rome, 1980), p. 565.

7. Newman, *Sister of Wisdom*, p. 254.

8. The *Acta Inquisitionis*, prepared for the never completed canonization procedure, tells the story of Hildegard's encounter with a young woman who had "turned herself into a scholar" [*in scholarem se transmutaverat*], presumably by wearing the clothes of a clerk. Hildegard instructs her to "return to the better state" [*convertere ad statum meliorem*] since her days are numbered.

The girl confesses her deception and dies (with a clear conscience, one hopes) within the year. *Acta* III, PL 197:133. Anna Silvas points out (*Jutta and Hildegard: The Biographical Sources* (University Park, PA: Pennsylvania State University Press, 1999), p. 262n23) that Hildegard's disapproval is directed at scholasticism as much as it is at cross-dressing. For her, the contemplative, monastic life was the better part, especially for women, whose natural gifts lay in this area. See Flanagan, *Hildegard of Bingen: A Visionary Life* (Routledge: London, 1989), p. 217n8.

9. In *Sister of Wisdom*, especially chapter 2, "The Feminine Divine."

10. See d'Alverny, "Comment les théologiens. . .," pp. 105–29 for a survey.

11. According to Patrick Diehl in *The Medieval European Religious Lyric: An Ars Poetica* (Berkeley: University of California Press, 1985), by the twelfth century, the Virgin "threatens to eclipse her son" (p. 59) as a subject. In Hildegard's poetry the eclipse is complete, except for two of the miscellaneous compositions Newman edits as "songs without music" at the end of the *Symphonia*; one of these, "O fili dilectissime," is in the voice of the Virgin addressing her Son.

12. Hildegard's poetic voice, with its often idiosyncratic combinations of the sentimental and the surreal, the naïve and the contrived, unnerved many of her twentieth-century readers. F. J. E. Raby is dismissive of "Hildegarde, the famous mystic, whose sequences are in prose," in his *History of Christian-Latin Poetry from the Beginnings to the Close of the Middle Ages* (Oxford: Clarendon, 1953), p. 294; according to Joseph Szövérffy, *A Concise History of Medieval Latin Hymnody* (Leiden: Classical Folia, 1985) "her strange songs set to music are often suspected [by whom, one wonders?] of being first drafts" (p. 86). Hildegard's contemporaries embraced her as an innovator; as early as 1149, Odo of Soissons had been impressed by what he called her "songs in a new style" [*modos novi carminis*]. Letter 40, 22.

13. See e.g., Julia Kristeva, "Stabat Mater," *The Kristeva Reader*, ed. Toril Moi (New York: Columbia University Press, 1986), pp. 160–86; Penny Schine Gold, *The Lady and the Virgin: Image, Attitude and Experience in Twelfth Century France* (Chicago: University of Chicago Press, 1985), pp. 68–75.

14. Theresa Coletti, "Purity and Danger: The Paradox of Mary's Body and the Engendering of the Infancy Narrative in the English Mystery Cycles," in *Feminist Approaches to the Body in Medieval Literature*, ed. Linda Lomperis and Sarah Stanbury (Philadelphia: University of Pennsylvania Press, 1993), p. 85.

15. Coletti, "Purity and Danger," pp. 83–84.

16. Rémy de Gourmont, *Le Latin Mystique: les poètes de l'antiphonaire et la symbolique au moyen âge* (Paris: Mercure de France, 1895; rpt. 1981), p. 276. De Gourmont is one of Hildegard's few unabashed admirers between the Renaissance and the revival of interest in her work, which began in the 1970s.

17. Ernaud de Bonneval, Alain de Lille, and Adam de Courlandon all developed aspects of this symbolic system in the twelfth and thirteenth centuries; see d'Alverny, "Comment les Philosophes. . ." Abelard's *In Hexaemeron* uses a more elaborate logic, based on the distinction between *imago* and *similitudo*,

to establish a hierarchical relationship between man and woman (*Patrologia Latina* 128). The point of such symbolic paradigms was not so much to define men and women (or male and female) as to use the terms "man" and "woman" to express different functions. Distinctions between the symbolic and the literal, however, are not always clearly maintained, so that the rhetorical identification of "woman" with sensuality slides easily into the definition of women as sexually depraved.

18. See Thomas Aquinas, *Summa Contra Gentiles*, trans. the English Dominican Fathers (London: Burns, Oates and Washbourne, 1929) 4.14: ". . .there will be no unlikeness through difference of material between Christ's body which was formed by God's power from material taken from his mother only, and our bodies, which are formed by nature's power, although the material from which they are fashioned is taken from both parents."

19. In Fragment 4, Hildegard imagines Eve both conceiving and giving birth by a sort of osmosis, which would not involve any breach of bodily integrity or loss of virginity; Augustine suggests something similar (*De peccato originali* 40). See Newman, *Sister of Wisdom*, pp. 111–14.

20. Charles T. Wood, "The Doctors' Dilemma: Sin, Salvation and the Menstrual Cycle in Medieval Thought," *Speculum* 56 (1981): 726.

21. Bruce W. Holsinger, "The Flesh of the Voice: Embodiment and the Homoerotics of Devotion in the Music of Hildegard of Bingen," *Signs* 19:I (1993): 101. See also Holsinger, "Sine tactu viri: The Musical Somatics of Hildegard of Bingen," *Music, Body and Desire in Medieval Culture: Hildegard of Bingen to Chaucer* (Stanford, CA: Stanford University Press, 2001), pp. 87–136.

22. *Liber Vitae Meritorum* 2.40; *Scivias* 1.2.9–10. See Newman, *Sister of Wisdom*, pp. 112–13.

23. Bernard of Clairvaux, "On Humility and Pride" 22.53, *Selected Works*, trans. G. R. Evans (New York: Paulist Press, 1987), p. 140.

24. Hildegard, "O Fili dilectissime," *Symphonia*, p. 260. This song is included in Newman's edition as one of four "songs with out music," and is unnumbered.

25. Newman, *Symphonia*, p. 318.

26. The legend of Saint Ursula first appears in a tenth-century *passio*; it was retold in the eleventh century, and then in Geoffrey of Monmouth's *History of the Kings of Britain* (Ursula was supposed to have been a British princess). Hildegard need not have been familiar with any of these, since the discovery in 1106 of a large number of bones next to the cathedral at Cologne, presumed to be those of the virgin martyrs eulogized in a terse fourth-century inscription, had aroused great local interest in Ursula and her companions. Hildegard's younger contemporary and protegée, Elisabeth of Schönau, received a series of visions about them, which may or may not have influenced Hildegard. See Dronke, *Poetic Individuality in the Middle Ages* (Oxford: Clarendon, 1970), p. 161n2; Newman, *Sister of Wisdom*, pp. 245–48; *Symphonia*, p. 308. I am grateful to Sabina Flanagan for allowing me to read an unpublished paper on the subject.

27. Newman, *Symphonia*, p. 310; Dronke, *Poetic Individuality*, p. 152. See also Kathryn L. Bumpass, "A Musical Reading of Hildegard's Responsory

'Spiritui Sancto,' " *Hildegard of Bingen: A Book of Essays*, ed. Maud Burnett McInerney (New York: Garland Publishing, 1998), pp. 155–73.

28. Dronke, *Poetic Individuality*, p. 164.

29. Dronke, *Poetic Individuality*, p. 164.

30. This is a point Hildegard made forcefully in her sermons against the Cathar heresy. See Letter 15R.

31. Newman, *Symphonia*, p. 312.

32. "O rubor sanguinis" (no. 61), discussed in Dronke, *Poetic Individuality*, pp. 153–54. The translation is his.

33. Newman, *Symphonia*, p. 312.

34. Kathryn Kerby-Fulton, "Prophet and Reformer: Smoke in the Vineyard," in *Voice of the Living Light: Hildegard of Bingen and Her Word*, ed. Barbara Newman (Berkeley: University of California Press, 1998), pp. 70–90. See also chapter 2 of Kerby-Fulton's *Reformist Apocalypticism and Piers Plowman* (Cambridge: Cambridge University Press, 1990), which argues for a much more extended *nachsleben* for Hildegard's prophecies than has generally been acknowledged.

35. Gustav Sommerfeldt, "Die Prophetien der hl. Hildegard von Bingen in einem Schrieben des Magisters Heinrich v. Langenstein (1383)," *Historische Jahrbuch* 30 (1909): 47.

36. From a strophic German poem cited by Dronke, "Medieval Sibyls: Their Character and their 'Auctoritas,' " *Studi Medievali* (1994): 608–09.

37. Diodorus Siculus 16, 26, trans. Charles L. Sherman, Loeb Classical Library (Cambridge, MA: Harvard University Press, 1952).

38. It remains troubling to some modern writers as well. In an influential book, Joseph Fontenrose insists that the Pythia's "madness" is a construct of late antique and especially Christian writers, not attested in classical sources, and that she did not prophesy in ecstasy. His account of the Delphic oracle limits the participation of the Pythia and argues that the oracles were actually composed by priests. See *The Delphic Oracle: Its Responses and Operations* (Berkeley: University of California Press, 1978), p. 196. This assumption, widespread among classical scholars, has recently been challenged by Lisa Maurizio: "The Pythia's male interpreters believed that they could close off that space, circumvent the female and linguistic ambiguity, interpret and speak directly to Apollo. Most modern scholars have done the same insofar as they read Delphic ambiguity as a manipulative that served the shrine or treat ambiguity as a product of the male imaginary. I have tried to recognize the functional uses of ambiguity at Delphi and the effects of male imagination and male dominance on the Pythias, but to not concede that either influence determined or erased the Pythias" ("The Voice at the Center of the World: The Pythia's Ambiguity and Authority," in André Lardinois and Laura McClure, *Making Silence Speak: Women's Voices in Greek Literature and Society* (Princeton: Princeton University Press, 2001), p. 54). See also Maurizio, "Anthropology and Spirit Possession: A Reconsideration of the Pythia's Role at Delphi," *Journal of Hellenic Studies* 115 (1995): 69–86.

NOTES 233

39. Origen, *Contra Celsum* 7.3, trans. Henry Chadwick (Oxford: Oxford University Press, 1953).

40. John Chrysostom, *Homily 29.2 on First Corinthians*, in *A Select Library of the Nicene and Post Nicene Fathers*, ser. 2, ed. Philip Schaff and Henry Wace (Grand Rapids, MI: Eerdmans, 1952), v. 12.

41. Lactantius *Div. Inst.* Epitome 73. Properly speaking, one should say Sibyls and not Sibyl. Lactantius, following Varro, lists ten of them. They were all felt, however, to be in some sense essentially the same.

42. Constantine, *Ad Sanctum Coetum* 19. See H. W. Parke, *Sibyls and Sibylline Prophecy in Classical Antiquity* (New York: Routledge, 1988), pp. 164–66.

43. On the Jewish elements in the *Oracula Sibyllina*, see Parke, *Sybilline Prophecy*, pp. 5–9; David Flusser, "An Early Jewish Christian Document in the Tiburtine Sibyl," in *Paganisme, Judaisme, Christianisme: Influences et afrontements dans le monde antique* (Paris: Editions de Boccard, 1978), pp. 153–83.

44. Augustine, *De Civ. Dei* 18.23. See Dronke, *Hermes and the Sibyls: Continuations and Creations* (Cambridge: Cambridge University Press, 1990), pp. 9–11.

45. References are to Jerome, *Against Jovinian*, in *Nicene and Post-Nicene Fathers*, vol. 6, pp. 364–416.

46. Parke, *Sibyls*, p. 10.

47. Vergil, *Aeneid*, ed. R. D. Williams (London: Macmillan, 1972), n. 465.

48. Ovid's *Ars Amatoria* 1: 629–30, 2: 731–32; the most celebrated medieval example is perhaps William IX's "Companho, faray un vers." See *Lyrics of the Troubadours and Trouveres*, ed. Frederick Goldin (New York: Anchor, 1973), pp. 20–22. For a modern parallel, consider the Bessie Smith song "Black Rider," or the Dixie Chicks' "Cowboy Take me Away."

49. Bernard McGinn, "Teste David cum Sibylla: The significance of the Sibylline Tradition in the Middle Ages," *Women of the Medieval World* (Oxford: Blackwell, 1985), p. 18.

50. Abelard, *De Ordine Sanctimonialium* (Letter VII to Heloise). *La Vie et les Epistres Pierre Abelaert et sa Fame Heloise* v. I, ed. Eric Hicks (Paris: Champion-Slatkine, 1991), p. 139. Unlike Augustine, Abelard does not condemn suicide in the defense of virginity but takes an Ambrosian approach, praising the determination of those who "turn their hands against themselves."

51. Hildegard must have known *of* Abelard; his great showdown with Bernard of Clairvaux at the Council of Sens took place in 1140, the year before Hildegard began write the *Scivias*; perhaps it was even the condemnation of Abelard that led her to write seeking the support of the famous and enormously influential Bernard in 1146 (Letter I). Once she had demonstrated her loyalty to the Church and gained approval for her writing, Hildegard would have been highly unlikely to compromise this by exploring the works of a heretic theologian who was also guilty on his own testimony of seducing a virgin, a sin she considered unforgivable.

52. Cited by Dronke, *Medieval Sibyls*, p. 583; the translation is his, as is the conjectured line 3.

53. Dronke, *Hermes and the Sibyls*, p. 11. Some versions of the Sibyl's song were performed as part of the Christmas ritual right through the nineteenth century in the Iberian Peninsula. See Paul Aebischer, "Le 'Cant de la Sibil.la' de la nuit de Noel a Majorque" and "Le 'Cant de la Sibil.la' en la cathédrale d'Alghero la veillée de Noël," in *Neuf études sur le théâtre médiéval* (Geneva: Droz, 1972).

54. Dronke, *Hermes and the Sibyls*, p. 11. The Latin text of the homily is reproduced in Karl Young, *The Drama of the Medieval Church* vol. 2 (Oxford: Clarendon, 1933), pp. 125–31.

55. Young, *Drama*, p. 145 (Laon) and p. 165 (Rouen).

56. Dronke is steadfast and convincing in arguing for an early date of composition and for full performance. See "Hildegard of Bingen as Poetess and Dramatist," in *Poetic Individuality in the Middle Ages: New Departures in Poetry 1000–1150* (Oxford: Oxford University Press, 1970), pp. 150–92; "Problemata Hildegardiana," pp. 97–131; and *Nine Medieval Latin Plays* (Cambridge: Cambridge University Press, 1994), pp. 152–55.

57. Pamela Sheingorn, "The Virtues of Hildegard's *Ordo Virtutum*; Or, It was a Woman's World," in *The Ordo Virtutum of Hildegard of Bingen: Critical Studies*, ed. Audrey Ekdahl Davidson (Kalamazoo, MI: Medieval Institute Publications, 1992) calls this "a road not taken in subsequent thought" (p. 58) although I would argue that it is a road independently rediscovered by at least one later mystical writer, *Marguerite Porete*, author of *The Mirror of Simple Souls*.

58. Audrey Ekdahl Davidson, "Music and Performance: Hildegard of Bingen's *Ordo Virtutum*" in *Critical Studies*, p. 14.

Chapter 5   Pelagius, Rupert, and the Problem of Male Virginity in Hrotsvitha and Hildegard

1. William Ian Miller, *The Mystery of Courage* (Cambridge, MA: Harvard University Press, 2000), pp. 233–34.

2. John Bugge, *Virginitas: An Essay in the History of a Medieval Ideal* (The Hague: Martinus Nijhoff, 1975), p. 4. For a pointed and very pertinent review of Bugge, see Joseph S. Wittig in *Speculum* 52.4 (1977): 938–41. Wittig points to Bugge's refusal to distinguish between chastity and virginity, and concludes that Bugge's book "fails to come to grips with the richness and complexity of the ideal of virginity in medieval thought" (p. 941).

3. Albertus Magnus, *De Bono* 3.3.6, ed. H. Kühle et al., *Opera Omnia* 28 (Munster: Aschendorff, 1951).

4. Thomas Aquinas, *Summa Theologiae*, ed. Collège Dominicain d'Ottawa (Ottawa: Harpell, 1941), II–II, 152, 1, praet. 3/2159b.

5. Aquinas, *Summa* II–II, 152, 1, praet. 4/2159b.

6. Aquinas, *Summa* II–II,152, 5, 1, res. / 2165b.

7. Gratian, *Decretum* C 32.5.1, *Corpus Iuris Cononici, Pars Prior, Decretum Gratiani*, ed. A. Friedberg (Leipzig: n.p., 1879).

8. Pierre J. Payer, *The Bridling of Desire: Views of Sex in the Later Middle Ages* (Toronto: University of Toronto Press, 1993), pp. 178–79, 258n90.

9. Kathleen Kelly, *Performing Virginity*, p. 93.

10. Jerome, *Life of Malchus, Patrologia Latina* 23, 55–62.

11. The story of John's visit to Córdoba is told in *Vita Johannis abbatis Gorziensis*, ed. George H. Pertz MGHS 4 (Hanover: 1841), pp. 335–77. See also Edward P. Colbert, *The Martyrs of Cordoba 850–59: A Study of the Sources* (Washington, DC: Catholic University of America, 1962), pp. 382–86, and Jessica A. Cope, *The Martyrs of Cordoba: Community and Family Conflict in an Age of Mass Conversion* (Lincoln, NE: University of Nebraska Press, 1995), pp. 66–69.

12. References to *Pelagius* are to Homeyer's edition, by line number.

13. For the liturgy, see *Acta Sanctorum Junii* 7 191b–197c; Simonet argues for a composition date in the 930s but it is difficult to see why. Francisco Javier Simonet, *Historia de los Mozárabes de España* (Amsterdam: Oriental Press, 1967), p. 592.

14. On dating, see Homeyer, pp. 123–25; Manuel C. Díaz y Díaz, "La pasión de S. Pelayo y su diffusion," *Anuario de estudios medievales* 6 (1969), pp. 106–10; and Marius Ferotin, *Le Liber Mozarabicus Sacramentorum et les manuscripts mozarabes*, rev. A. Ward and C. Johnson (Rome: Centro Liturgico Vicenziano, 1995), pp. 567–73; the manuscript of Raguel's *Passio* (BM add. 30845) is from Silos and dates to the late tenth or early eleventh century.

15. Mark D. Jordan's reading of this passage in *The Invention of Sodomy in Christian Theology* (Chicago: University of Chicago Press, 1997), pp. 11–18, is admirable; he emphasizes Pelagius's recognition of this ambiguous caress as an expression of same-sex desire, noting that the story becomes "through Pelagius' eyes, the story of a passionate triangle in which all the parties are male. He does not deny same-sex love so much as he vindicates it by choosing Christ as his lover" (p. 16). It is worth noting that standing forth naked, the same behavior that Jordan identifies as a rejection of "effeminacy," operated in the Thecla narrative to convey a rejection of *heterosexual* masculine desire.

16. For 'Abd al-Rahman's rise to power and reign, see Joseph F. O'Callahan, *A History of Medieval Spain* (Ithaca: Cornell University Press, 1975), pp. 117–20; Hugh Kennedy, *Muslim Spain and Portugal: A Political History of Al-Andalus* (London: Longman, 1996), pp. 82–97; Marcelle Thiébaux, "Hagiographer, Playwright, Epic Historian," *The Writings of Medieval Women: An Anthology* (2nd ed., New York: Garland, 1994), pp. 171–84.

17. Mahmoud Makki, "The Political History of Al-Andalus," in *The Legacy of Muslim Spain*, ed. Salma Khadra Jayyusi (Leiden: E. J. Brill, 1994), p. 38.

18. Makki, "Political History," p. 38.

19. John Boswell, *Christianity, Social Tolerance and Homosexuality: Gay People in Western Europe from the Beginning of the Christian Era to the Fourteenth Century* (Chicago: University of Chicago Press, 1980), p. 199. Boswell goes on to claim less convincingly that "Hroswitha does not suggest that homosexual acts are either praiseworthy or especially descpicable. She refers to

the Muslim ruler who is depicted in extremely derogatory terms as 'corrupted by the vice of the sodomites'. . .beyond this there is no indication that what he desires from Pelagius is sinful in itself" (p. 199). Boswell is invested in imagining a world in which "it was not 'unnatural' for men to relate sexually with men but simply 'unseemly' for Christian men to relate in any personal way with pagan men" (p. 200). This overlooks Hrotsvitha's description of the caliph as "perverse and profane in his life as well as in his religious practice" (*Pelagius* 33), which establishes a naturalized sexual perversity distinct from religious difference. Pelagius may be willing to overlook his captor's sexual preference, but the narrator is not.

20. Abdelwahab Bouhdiba, *Sexuality in Islam*, trans. Alan Sheridan (London: Saqi, 1998), p. 31.

21. On Umayyad erotic poetry in Spain, see Boswell, *Christianity and Social Tolerance*, pp. 194–99; M. Jesús Rubiera Mata, *Literatura Hispanoárabe* (Madrid: MAPFRE, 1992), pp. 57–64; Norman Roth, "A Research Note on Sexuality and Muslim Civilization," in *Handbook of Medieval Sexuality*, ed. Vern L. Bullough and James A. Brundage (New York: Garland, 1996), pp. 319–28 and " 'Fawn of My Delights': Boy Love in Hebrew and Arabic Verse," in *Sex in the Middle Ages: A Book of Essays*, ed. Joyce E. Salisbury (New York: Garland, 1991), pp. 157–72.

22. Ibn Shuhayd, "An Approach to Love," trans. James A. Bellamy and Patricia Owen Steiner, *The Banners of the Champions: An Anthology of Medieval Arabic Poetry from Andalusia and Beyond* (Madison, WI: Hispanic Seminary of Medieval Studies, 1989), p. 188.

23. Jordan, *Sodomy*, p. 10.

24. Kelly argues categorically that "the difference between the treatment of the male virgin and the female virgin is that between rape and seduction, between *assaulted* virginity and *assayed* virginity" (*Performing Virginity*, p. 95). This seems to me an overstatement; not only are there instances of attempted seduction rather than rape in stories concerning female virgins like Juliana, but the reaction of Hrotsvitha's Pelagius suggests that he, at least, perceives the caliph's kiss as an assault.

25. Reinhardt Dozy, ed., *Le Calendrier de Cordou*, trans. and rev. Charles Pellat (Leiden: Brill, 1961).

26. On the cult of Pelagius in Spain, see Javier Fernandes Conde et al., *Historia de la Iglesia en España de los siglos VIII al XIV*, vol. I (Madrid: Biblioteca de Autores Cristianos, 1982), p. 167.

27. Albar, *Indiculus Luminosus*, pp. 23–24, in Juan Gil, *Corpus Scriptorum Muzarabicorum* I (Madrid: Instituto Antonio de Nebrija, 1973). See Cope, *Martyrs of Cordoba*, pp. 47–51.

28. Cope, *Martyrs of Cordoba*, p. 43.

29. Cope, *Martyrs of Cordoba*, pp. 41–45.

30. On Hrotsvitha's reconfiguration of the allocation of responsibility for rape, see Gravdal, *Ravishing Maidens*, pp. 29–31.

31. Jerome, *Adv. Jov.* 366.

32. Vernacular equivalents of the word generally indicate unmarried, intact women. For a discussion of the Middle High German words *kint* and *maget*, "child" and "maiden," see James A. Schulz, *The Knowledge of Childhood in the Geman Middle Ages 1100–1350* (Philadelphia: University of Pennsylvania Press, 1995), pp. 23–31. These are the words and connotations with which Hildegard would have been familiar from her own childhood and social milieu.

33. Newman, *Symphonia*, p. 288.

34. The edition by Führkötter and Carlevaris places these lines at the beginning of the next chapter; I have followed Hart and Bishop, who restore them to the end of the previous chapter, where they clearly belong.

35. See Newman's discussion, *Symphonia*, p. 297.

36. References, abbreviated as *Rupert*, are to *Hildegardis Vita Rupertis, Patrologia Latina* 197, cols. 1085–90.

37. Cadden, *Meanings of Sex Difference*, p. 82.

38. Bede, *Historia Ecclesiae* XXVII.ix; compare Hildegard, *Scivias* I.ii.20. On the Gregorian letter, see C. Leyser, "Masculinity in Flux: Nocturnal Emissions and the Limits of Celibacy in the Early Middle Ages," in *Masculinity in Medieval Europe*, ed. D. M. Hadley (New York: Longman, 1999), pp. 103–20.

39. Constantine, *De coitu*, ch. 5, *Chaucer Review* 4 (1970); Thomas Aquinas, *Summa Theologica* 2a2ae, q 154 art 5 resp 43:224; Hildegard, *Causae et Curae*, ed. Paul Kaiser (Leipzig, 1903), p. 82. Jean Gerson's fourteenth-century treatise *On Pollution* is nearly hysterical in its detail; see Gerson, *Oeuvres Complètes*, ed. Palemon Glorieux (Paris: Desclée, 1961). On nocturnal emissions, see Cadden, *Meanings of Sex Difference*, pp. 141–42; Dyan Elliot, *Fallen Bodies: Pollution, Sexuality and Demonology in the Middle Ages* (Philadelphia: University of Pennsylvania Press, 1999), pp. 14–34. Elliot argues that the increased anxiety concerning nocturnal emissions is a form of transferrence of anxiety concerning transubstantiation, which was a subject of increased theological speculation in the fourteenth and fifteenth centuries as devotion to the *corpus christi* became more widespread. Classical writers were more willing than medieval writers to entertain the possibility of female nocturnal emissions; see Rousselle, *Porneia*, pp. 27–32.

40. Rémy de Gourmont, *Le Latin Mystique*, p. 12.

41. De Gourmont, *Le Latin Mystique*, p. 99.

42. On the discovery of the manuscript, see Edwin H. Zeydel, "The Reception of Hrotsvitha by the German Humanists after 1493," *Journal of English and Germanic Philology* 44 (1945), 239–49.

43. De Gourmont did not invent the accusation of forgery, which had been extensively argued by Aschback in 1868. The discovery of eleventh- and twelfth-century manuscripts of Hrotsvitha's work conclusively proved her authorship (Zeydel, "Reception," p. 249n56). De Gourmont himself softened his accusations in the 1912 edition of his book, presumably having familiarized himself with the various refutations of the Celtis theory, such as R. Köpke, *Hrotsvit von Gandersheim, Ottonische Studien* 2 (Berlin: 1869), pp. 237–41.

44. De Gourmont, *Latin Mystique*, p. 48.
45. De Gourmont, *Latin Mystique*, pp. 43–44.
46. Wilde's *Salome* was performed in Paris in 1894; the Wilde trials took place during the spring of 1895 and were closely watched on both sides of the channel; de Gourmont published *Le Latin Mystique* in 1895.
47. On Hildegard's systems of scientific classification, see Kenneth F. Kitchell and Irven M. Resnick, "Hildegard as a Medieval 'Zoologist': The Animals of the *Physica*," in McInerney, *Hildegard of Bingen: A Book of Essays*, pp. 25–52.

Chapter 6   Catherine and Marguerite: Vernacular Virgins and the *Golden Legend*

1. References are to *The Sequence of Saint Eulalia* (ca. 880–82) in Wendy Ayres-Bennett, *A History of the French Language Through Texts* (London: Routledge, 1996), p. 31, translation and commentary, pp. 32–39.
2. Jocelyn Wogan-Browne, " 'Clerc u lai, muïne u dame': Women and Anglo-Norman Hagiography in the Twelfth and Thirteenth Centuries," in *Women and Literature in Britain, 1150–1500*, ed. Carol M. Meale (Cambridge: Cambridge University Press, 1993), pp. 62–63.
3. On medieval women as book owners, see Susan Groag Bell, "Medieval Women Book Owners: Arbiters of Lay Piety and Ambassadors of Culture," in *Sisters and Workers in the Middle Ages*, ed. Judith M. Bennett et al. (Chicago: University of Chicago Press, 1976; rpt. 1989), pp. 135–61; Carol M. Meale, " '. . .alle the bokes that I haue of latyn, englisch, and frensch': Laywomen and Their Books in Late Medieval England," in *Women and Literature*, pp. 128–58.
4. Hans Jantzen, *High Gothic: The Classic Cathedrals of Chartres, Reims and Amiens*, trans. J. Palmer (Princeton, NJ: Princeton University Press, 1984), p. 160.
5. See Jocelyn Wogan-Browne and Glyn S. Burgess, *Virgin Lives and Holy Deaths: Two Exemplary Biographies for Anglo-Norman Women* (London: Everyman, 1996), pp. xxi–xxiii for a brief history of the cult of Saint Catherine. Since there is no record of the monastery of Saint Catherine on Sinai before the time of the Third Crusade (1189), it has been suggested that the translation of relics actually went from West to East and not the other way around. The authenticity of the relics at Rouen is at best dubious; see R. Fawtier, "Les Reliques Rouennaises de Sainte Catherine d'Alexandrie," *Analecta Bollandia* 41 (1923): 357–68. The Catholic church demoted Catherine in 1969 on the grounds of lack of historicity.
6. Brigitte Cazelles, *The Lady as Saint: A Collection of French Hagiographic Romances of the Thirteenth Century* (Philadelphia: University of Pennsylvania Press, 1991).
7. Wace, *Roman de Rou*, ed. A. J. Holden, 3 vols. (Paris: Societé des Anciens Textes Français, 1970–73), v.3, ll. 179–80. This not be taken as indicating that Wace was a member of the court, but that he was a *clerc lisant* within a monastic institution.

8. On Wace's career as a historian, see Peter Damian-Grint, *The New Historians of the Twelfth Century Renaissance* (Rochester, NY: Boydell, 1999), pp. 53–58.

9. Donald Attwater, *The Penguin Dictionary of Saints* (Harmondsworth: Penguin, 1965; rpt. 1976), p. 228.

10. Hrabanus Maurus's account can be found in *Rabani Mauri Martyrologium*, ed. John McCullough, *Corpus Christianorum Continuatio Medievalis* 44 (Turnhout: Brepols, 1979), pp. 67–68.

11. Hans-Erich Keller, *La vie de Sainte Marguerite* (Tubingen: Niemeyer, 1990), p. 10.

12. Phyllis Johnson and Brigitte Cazelles, *Le Vain Siecle Guerpir: A Literary Approach to Sainthood through Old French Hagiography of the Twelfth Century* (Chapel Hill, NC: University of North Carolina Press, 1979), pp. 130–31.

13. Wace's source appears to be the "Caligula" version of the *passio* (found in Cotton MS. Caligula.A.VIII) rather than the better known "Mombritius" version; it dates from the tenth or (more likely) eleventh century. For the text see Elizabeth A. Francis, "A Version of the 'Passio S. Margaritae,'" *PMLA* 42 (1927): 87–105.

14. Keller's diplomatic text draws on three manuscripts, Tours bibliothèque municipale 927 (M), Paris bibliothèque de l'Arsenal 3516 (A), and Troyes bibliothèque municipale 1905 (T). References (as Marguerite, followed by line number) are to A, the most complete text, supplemented with T when necessary.

15. On Wace's additions to his source, see Elizabeth Francis, ed., *La Vie de Sainte Marguerite*, p. viii.

16. Shulamith Shahar, *The Fourth Estate: A History of Women in the Middle Ages*, trans. Chaya Galai (London: Methuen, 1983), pp. 240–41.

17. Vergil's poems represent pastoral love as homosexual; the object of desire is always a beautiful shepherd boy. In the Middle Ages, the scenario becomes resolutely heterosexual, and violent. See Gravdal, *Ravishing Maidens*, pp. 104–14 for a discussion of the way that the *pastourelle* legitimizes rape by representing the generic shepherdess as enjoying forced sex.

18. In her discussion of thirteenth-century hagiographical romances, Cazelles notes what she defines as a central paradox of the genre: "In the biographical portion of the narrative, beauty and nobility combine to induce [the virgin's] transformation into an object of desire. The physical and social distinctions that characterise all the heroines commemorated in hagiographic romance serve to stress their vulnerability, since these very qualities attract the attention of the surrounding community, thereby contradicting their desire to avoid unchaste gazes. These saintly maidens seek, in principal, to remain invisible; yet the logic of the narrative goes counter to this aspiration, and their ordeal can be best described as a process of forced visibility." *The Lady as Saint*, p. 50. My disagreements with Cazelles are significant; I do not believe that the statement she makes here holds true for all hagiographical narratives, nor that the lives necessarily and exclusively embody

a "male perception of female sanctity" (p. 37). As a description of the process at work in this particular text, however, Cazelles's comment is apt.

19. Aquinas, *Summa Contra Gentiles* III:2:101–10.

20. Ovid, *Metamorphoses*, ed. W. S. Anderson (Leipzig: Teubner, 1977), 7, 192–200. These resonances exist in all versions of the Margaret story, more or less emphatically in different instances; I have discussed the Middle English Life of Saint Margaret, which presents a much more verbally accomplished and aggressive saint, in "Rhetoric and Power in the Passion of the Virgin Martyr," *Menacing Virgins: Representing Virginity in the Middle Ages and Renaissance*, ed. Kathleen Kelly and Marina Leslie (Newark: University of Delaware Press, 1999), pp. 50–70.

21. "Indeed, just as power is at the center of the accusations made against the strong women martyrs (Catherine of Alexandria, Juliana, and Margaret of Antioch) celebrated in this Anthology, power is also the central argument that justified the prosecution and condemnation of women accused of sorcery during the late Middle Ages." Cazelles, *The Lady As Saint*, p. 56.

22. Artemis was patroness of childbirth in spite of her virginity because she had helped her mother, Leto, deliver her twin, Apollo, shortly after her own birth. A life of Saint Margaret is appended to a thirteenth-century medical treatise apparently aimed at women (it includes remedies for various discomforts of pregnancy, cystitis, insufficient milk production, and snoring husbands). P. Meyer, "Notice du MS. Sloane 1611 Du Musée Britannique," *Romania* 40 (1911): 536–58. This version of the story, which is in French that Meyer characterizes as "shocking" (539) nonetheless represents a rather more energetic Margaret than Wace's heroine.

23. Vergil, *Bucolics* 8, l. 71. Pliny, *Natural History* 28, iv, 19.

24. On Roman magic, see Anne-Marie Tupet, *La Magie dans la Poesie Latine* (Paris: Les Belles Lettres, 1976).

25. Francis, "Passio," p. 101. *Crever* is still used in modern French to describe the blowout of a car or bicycle tire. Exploding snakes may be a near-Eastern motif that was easily adopted into the Greek Marina tradition. In the Babylonian Creation story, Marduk causes Tiamat, also a dragonish being, to explode; like Margaret's antagonist, she is divided into two parts: "When the mouth gaped open to suck him down he drove Imhullu [the wind] in, so that the mouth would not shut but wind raged through her belly; her carcass blown up, tumescent, she gaped—and now he shot the arrow that split the belly, that pierced the gut and cut the womb. Now that the Lord had conquered Tiamat he ended her life, he flung her down and straddled the carcass. . .he split it apart like a cockle shell. . ." *Poems of Heaven and Hell from Ancient Mesopotamia*, trans. N. K. Sanders (Harmondsworth: Penguin, 1971), pp. 90–92. The story of the philosopher Pythagoras is rather more loosely related to this theme, but irresistible nonetheless: bitten by a poisonous snake, he bit it back and it died.

26. Gravdal, *Ravishing Maidens*, p. 37.

27. According to Claude Lecouteux, "il faut absolument connaître le juste nom si l'on veut être obéi de l'entité invoqué." *Charmes, Conjurations et Bénédictions: Lexique et Formules* (Paris: Champion, 1996), pp. 7–8.
28. Francis, "Passio," p. 101.
29. Keller, *Sainte Marguerite*, p. 45.
30. On Angevin family politics see June Hall Martin McCash, "Marie de Champagne and Eleanor of Aquitaine: A Relationship Reexamined," *Speculum* 54.4 (1979); Ralph V. Turner, "Eleanor of Aquitaine and Her Children: An Inquiry into Medieval Family Attachment," *Journal of Medieval History* 14 (1988): 321–35, and "The Children of Anglo-Norman Royalty and Their Upbringing," *Medieval Prosopography* 11 (1990): 17–44. On the marriage of Henry the Young King to Marguerite of France, see Marion Meade, *Eleanor of Aquitaine: A Biography* (New York: Hawthorne/Dutton, 1977), pp. 191–95. All the most scurrilous contemporary gossip about Henry II and Eleanor can be found in Gerald of Wales's *De Instructione Principis*, ch. 27.
31. On dates of composition, see Keller, *Sainte Marguerite*, pp. 37–46. Keller inclines toward the early end of this range. On the didactic impulse in Wace, see Jean Blacker, *The Faces of Time: Portrayal of the Past in Old French and Latin Historical Narrative of the Anglo Norman Regnum* (Austin: University of Texas Press, 1994), pp. 178–79.
32. References are to Clemence of Barking, *The Life of Saint Catherine*, ed. William MacBain, Anglo-Norman Text Society 18 (Oxford: Blackwell, 1964).
33. Eileen Power, writing in 1922 in *Medieval English Nunneries c. 1275 to 1535* (Cambridge: Cambridge University Press, 1922) deplored the fact that "in England there is no record of any house which can compare with Gandersheim, Hohenburg or Helfta. . .The sole works ascribed to monastic authoresses are a *Life of St Catherine*, written in Norman French by Clemence, a nun of Barking, in the late twelfth century, and the *Boke of St Albans*. . ." (p. 239). The recent work of Jocelyn Wogan Browne and others suggests that there may have been more women writers working in Anglo-Norman England than Power suspected.
34. Wogan-Browne, "Wreaths of Thyme: the Female Translator in Anglo-Norman Hagiography," *The Medieval Translator* 4, ed. Roger Ellis and Ruth Evans (Binghamton, NY: Medieval and Renaissance Text Society, 1994), p. 59n7.
35. This was a mixed blessing, as the downfall of Abbess Alice demonstrates; Alice was charged with "notorious familiarity and cohabitation with Hugh your officer, who is an offence and a scandal to all religion." John of Salisbury, *Letters* 1.111, cited in Sharon K. Elkins, *Holy Women of Twelfth-Century England* (Chapel Hill, NC: University of North Carolina Press, 1988), p. 148. Elkins points out that, whatever misconduct there was may not have been sexual; Hugh may have been helping the abbess "defend her abbey's rights in the conflict over tithes"; in any case, after Alice, the king held the abbacy of Barking from 1166 until he bestowed it on Mary à Becket.

36. Wogan-Browne, "Clerc u lai, muïne u dame," p. 67; Duncan Robertson, "Writing in the Textual Community: Clemence of Barking's Life of St. Catherine," *French Forum* 21:1 (1996): 6.

37. Robertson, "Textual Community," p. 6.

38. Edited in *Seinte Katherine*, ed. S. D'Ardenne and E. J. Dobson, Early English Text Society (suppl. series) 7 (Oxford: Early English Text Society, 1981).

39. See Gábor Klaniczay, "Legends as Life-Strategies for Aspirant Saints in the Later Middle Ages," in *The Uses of Supernatural Power: The Transformation of Popular Religion in Medieval and Early-Modern Europe*, trans. Susan Singerman, ed. Karen Margolis (Princeton: Princeton Unversity Press, 1990), pp. 95–110. The issue of apostolic poverty was particularly charged in the early to mid-twelfth century, where radical examples of alms giving could be seen as *defacto* heretical behavior. See Herbert Grundmann, *Religious Movements in the Middle Ages*, trans. Steven Rowan (Notre Dame, IN: University of Notre Dame Press, 1995), pp. 7–30. The residents of Barking, an enormously wealthy institution, may have observed with interest Henry II's preoccupation with Fontevrault, founded by Robert d'Arbrissel, a once-radical pracitioner of apostolic poverty.

40. The first level of the liberal arts curriculum consisted of the *trivium* of grammar, rhetoric, and logic; it is not clear whether Catherine proceded to the *quadrivium*, mathematics, geometry, music and astronomy, but I wouldn't put it past her.

41. The paraphrase is that of Ermanno Bencivenga, *Logic and Other Nonsense: The Case of Anselm and His God* (Princeton: Princeton University Press, 1993), p. 24.

42. For a succinct definition of the aims and methods of twelfth-century dialectic, see Catherine Brown, *Contrary Things: Exegesis, Dialectic, and the Poetics of Didacticism* (Stanford, CA: Stanford University Press, 1998), pp. 36–41.

43. Peter Abelard, *Historia Calamitatum, The Letters of Abelard and Heloise*, ed. Betty Radice (London: Penguin, 1974), p. 58.

44. The word appears to be a *hapax*; see Wogan-Brown and Burgess, *Virgin Lives*, pp. 65–66n21.

45. Like several other words used by Clemence, *recreante* is a very unusual feminine form, not recognized by the *Anglo Norman Dictionary*. Normally, the word belongs to the register of formal combat; to call another man *recreant* is to challenge him; to recognize oneself as *recreant* is to admit defeat. The usage persists in Middle English at least as late as Malory.

46. For an extended analysis of Clemence's wordplay in this passage, see Wogan-Browne and Burgess, *Virgin Lives*, p. xlvii.

47. Cazelles and Johnson, *Le Vain Siecle*, p. 132. It is rather troubling that Cazelles and Johnson seem to associate humanity with pathos; for them, Margaret is a more satisfying hagiographic heroine precisely because she is weaker and more vulnerable than Catherine, whom they characterize as "inhuman" (pp. 132–33).

48. Wogan-Browne and Burgess, *Virgin Lives*, p.74n58.

49. M. Dominica Legge, *Anglo-Norman Literature and Its Background* (Oxford: Clarendon Press, 1963), pp. 67–69; William MacBain, "Five Old French Renderings of the *Passio Sancte Katerine Virginis*," *Medieval Translators and Their Craft*, ed. J. Beer (Kalamazoo, MI: Medieval Institute Publications, 1989) invites the comparison to Marie (p. 63); Robertson, "Textual Community," pp. 18–25 provides an extended analysis of the relationship between Clemence and Thomas.

50. Robertson, "Textual Community," p. 18; see also Catherine Batt, "Clemence of Barking's Transformations of *Courtoisie* in *La Vie de Sainte Catherine d'Alexandrie*," *New Comparison* 12 (1996): 102–23.

51. See E. Walberg, *La Tradition Hagiographique de Saint Thomas Becket* (Paris: Droz, 1929), pp. 75–92 for an account of the manuscript tradition and the circumstances of composition of Guernes *Life*. Cazelles and Johnson, *Le Vain Siecle*, pp. 296–304 summarize Guernes's text.

52. The history of the dispute between Becket and his king is too complicated to review here; for a lively account of the events leading up to the murder, see William Urry, *Thomas Becket: His Last Days* (London: Sutton, 1999). W. L. Warren's massive biography, *Henry II* (Berkeley: University of California Press, 1974) strives as hard as possible to give a balanced picture of Henry and downplays the death of Becket as much as possible. Warren points out that virtually all contemporary historians were writing about Henry after he had already been cast in the role of tyrant and assassin of a saint (pp. 215–16).

53. Urry, *Thomas Becket: His Last Days*, p. 3.

54. Willaim Caxton, preface, *The Golden Legend or Lives of the Saints as Englished by William Caxton* (London: Dent, 1900), v. 1, p. 2.

55. F. S. Ellis, ed., *The Golden Legend or Lives of the Saints as Englished by William Caxton*, 7 vols. (London: J. M. Dent, 1931), p. vii. Because of the extraordinary richness of the manuscript tradition, there has not been a critical edition of the text since that of Graesse in 1845, which was revised in 1850 and reprinted without alteration in 1890 and 1965: *Jacobi a Voragine, Legenda aurea vulgo historica lombardica dicta*, ed. Th. Graesse (Leipzig, 1850; rpt. Osnabruck: Zeller, 1965). I have consulted the following translations: Jacobus de Voragine, *The Golden Legend: Readings on the Saints*, trans. William Granger Ryan, 2 vols. (Princeton: Princeton University Press, 1993) and Jacques de Voragine, *La Légende Dorée*, trans. J.-B. M. Roze, 2 vols. (Paris: Garnier-Flammarion, 1967). Citations, abbreviated as *Legend* and followed by page number, are to Roze's translation.

56. On the structural and organizational principles of the text, see Alain Boureau, *La Légende Dorée: Le Système Narratif de Jacques de Voragine* (Paris: Cerf, 1984), especially pp. 240–49 and the charts pp. 36–38.

57. As does the absence of saints from the lower classes or mendicant orders. On the conservatism of the *Legend*, see Sherry L. Reames, *The Legenda Aurea: A Reexamination of Its Paradoxical History* (Madison, WI: University of Wisconsin Press, 1985), especially chapter 10, "On the *Legenda* as a Medieval

Best-Seller," pp. 197–209. Boureau notes that Jacobus includes only 6% of the saints canonized between 993 and 1255 in his collection and appears "more interested in the classic modes of sainthood than in new forms of devotion and sanctity." *La Légende Dorée*, p. 39 (my translation).

58. On "woman as riot," see Bloch, *Medieval Misogyny*, pp. 17–22.
59. Reames, *The Golden Legend*, p. 108.
60. See his sermons on Catherine and Agnes, cited in Reames, p. 260n28.
61. Reames, *Golden Legend*, p. 108.

Epilogue   Joan of Arc

1. See e.g. Nadia Margolis, "The 'Joan Phenomenon' and the French Right," *Fresh verdicts on Joan of Arc*, ed. Bonnie Wheeler and Charles T. Wood (New York: Garland, 1996), pp. 265–88; Kevin J. Harty, "Jeanne au cinema," *Fresh Verdicts on Joan of Arc*, pp. 237–64 and Françoise Melzer, *For Fear of the Fire: Joan of Arc and the Limits of Subjectivity* (Chicago: University of Chicago Press, 2001), pp.19–21. Recent manifestations of Joan on American television include the *Witchblade* cable series (dir. David Carson et al., starring Yancy Butler), which premiered during the summer of 2001, and "Bone of Arc," an episode in the PBS *Wishbone* series starring a Jack Russell terrier. In California, a woman named Frances Marie Klug has been receiving revelations from Joan herself (among other saints) since 1982; these are posted on a regularly updated website: http://www.stjosephhillsofhope.org/home.htm.
2. On Joan's military abilities see Kelly DeVries, *Joan of Arc: A Military Leader* (Stroud, Gloucestershire: Sutton, 1999).
3. Jules-Etienne-Joseph Quicherat edited the transcripts of both trials, as well as an exhaustive collection of other documents related to Joan, in the 1840s: *Procès de condemnation et de réhabilitation de Jeanne d'Arc, dite la Pucelle* (Paris: Jules Renouard 1841–49; rpt. New York: Johnson Reprint Corp., 1965). References to the trial documents are to Quicherat's 5 volumes.
4. Karen Sullivan, *The Interrogation of Joan of Arc* (Minneapolis: University of Minnesota, 1999), p. xv.
5. Marina Warner, *Joan of Arc: The Image of Female Heroism* (Berkeley: University of California Press, 1981; rpt. 2000), p. 22.
6. His testimony—he "palpated her abdomen and she was very narrow" (Quicherat 3.50)—reminds us that many medival tests of virginity had nothing to do with assessing the condition of the hymen. The testimony of Marguerite La Touroulde, with whom Joan stayed in Poitiers, echoes this broader sense of what it meant to be virgin; Marguerite went to the baths several times with Joan, observed her naked, and stated that she was a virgin "as far as she could tell." On the variety of tests for virginity, see Kelly, *Performing Virginity*, especially chapter 1.
7. Twentieth-century readers of Joan have often felt it necessary to deny the virginity that even her enemies were forced to admit; Andrea Dworkin, for

whom Joan is both feminist heroine and victim, insists "It is inconceivable that she was not raped during the period she was in female clothing if the men, or a man, an English lord, determined that she should be raped. . .any woman who can be badly beaten can be raped. . .Once raped, she was nothing, no one, so low, 'the common level of women,' precisely what the inquisition wanted. After her heroic escape from being female, she was made twice female: raped and burned." *Intercourse* (New York: Free Press, 1987; rpt. 1997), pp. 104–05. In a different vein entirely, Manuel Gomez, who wrote a book, which he claims is based upon a newly discovered version of the confession of Gilles de Rais, makes Joan both a hermaphrodite and a lesbian, physically incapable of vaginal intercourse, but who engaged repeatedly in anal sex with the Maréchal de Rais. Manuel Gomez, *Jeanne d'Arc, Légende et Vérité* (Paris: Cheminements, 2000). Such interpretations, like the various efforts to make Joan a royal bastard tell us more about the authors than their subject.

8. On the reliance of Joan's interrogators on Aquinas, see Sullivan, *Interrogation*, pp. 36–38.

9. Warner, *Joan of Arc*, p. 24. Deborah Fraioli suggests an alternative possibility: "Joan's French coaches, counselors and mentors very carefully kept the saints hidden from view, and rightly so." *Joan of Arc, the Early Debate* (Woodbridge, Suffolk: Boydell, 2000), p. 197. The churchmen who interviewed Joan at Poitiers may have foreseen the traps that were laid for her by their colleagues at Rouen.

10. Quicherat, 5.114–21. On de Boulainvilliers's letter, see Charles Wayland Lightbody, *The Judgments of Joan: Joan of Arc: A Study in Cultural History* (Cambridge, MA: Harvard University Press, 1961), pp. 56–57.

11. Sullivan, *Interrogation*, p. 30.

12. Wheeler, "Joan of Arc's Sword in the Stone," in *Fresh Verdicts on Joan of Arc*, p. xi.

13. Wheeler, "Joan of Arc's Sword," p. xiii.

14. As Wheeler notes, "had Joan's trial judges pursued their original queries about the sword, they might well have provoked or enhanced associations dangerous to their own cause." "Joan of Arc's Sword," p. xv.

15. Warner, *Joan of Arc*, pp. 78–79.

16. On the prophecies surrounding Joan, see Warner, *Joan of Arc*, pp. 24–26.

17. Christine de Pisan, *Ditié de Jehanne d'Arc* 32 in Quicherat, 5.12–13. On the *Ditie*, see Fraioli, *Early Debate*, pp. 103–25 and Anne D. Lutkus and Julia M. Walker, "PR pas PC: Christine de Pizan's pro-Joan Propaganda," in *Fresh Verdicts*, pp. 145–60. Lutkus and Walker argue that Christine's poem was not composed, as it claims to be, in July 1429, but at the end of the summer, in support of Joan's decision to try and take Paris; the poem would thus be a deliberately self-fulfilling prophecy.

18. Quicherat, 1.446, n. 1. On the signing of the cedula, see Régine Pernoud and Véronique Clin, *Joan of Arc: Her Story*, trans. Jeremy duQuesnay Adams, ed. Bonnie Wheeler (New York: St. Martin's Press, 1998), p. 233.

19. Pernoud and Clin, *Joan: Her Story*, p. 136.

20. Melzer, *For Fear of the Fire*, p. 200.

21. Quicherat, 5.96–98. As Quicherat points out, the Letter to the English exists
     in several versions, but they are all compatible except for minor details. Joan
     herself admitted dictating it, although she told her interrogators that she had
     not used the term *chef de guerre* (war chief) or *corps pour corps* (body for
     body). These phrases do, however, exist in most surviving copies.

INDEX

DATE DUE

DEC 1 4 2004			
GAYLORD			PRINTED IN U.S.A.